Modern Railways International Review

Below: TOFC traffic is mixed with orthodox wagonload freight in this Union Pacific train heading west near Green River, Wyo: fronting the quintet of diesel locomotives is a pair of EMD Type SD40-2 3,000hp Co-Cos. *Union Pacific Railroad Photo*

Modern Railways International Review

G. Freeman Allen

LONDON
IAN ALLAN LTD

First published 1981

ISBN 0 7110 1123 0

Published by Ian Allan Ltd, Shepperton, Surrey; and printed by Ian Allan Printing Ltd at their works at Coombelands in Runnymede, England

Contents

Cover: A British Rail HST unit approaches Sunderland on 27 March 1981. *P. J. Robinson*

Left: The OBB's latest thyristor-controlled Class 1044 Bo-Bo deploys a peak output of 7,250hp; one pauses at Innsbruck in September 1979 with a Linz-Bregenz express of the OBB's 'Schlieren'-type Inter-City stock. *John C. Baker*

Introduction

In most of the world's industrialised countries — but, sadly, not as yet in the country where this book is being first published — concern over the future availability and price of oil has generated an eagerness to regenerate rail transport not experienced since the immediate aftermath of the last war. In some countries, such as West Germany, the proportion of the gross national product that is being invested in railways of all kinds, passenger and freight, long-haul and metropolitan, full-scale and Light Rail, must by now be at its highest level for a quarter of a century.

With this upsurge of public backing for a new age of the train there is a detectable growth of lay interest in the way countries and railways other than their own are organising and equipping to make trains and their operation more economical and market-effective. Generally speaking, however, the amateur finds it harder than the professional to keep adequately in touch with the way railways abroad are financed and run.

There are one or two countries where railway periodicals on newsstand sale do a laudable job of international as well as domestic coverage. But the great majority pay foreign affairs only sporadic or selective attention. Some virtually ignore the existence of railways beyond their own frontiers — except, of course, where some of the traction remains steam.

Book publishing generally follows the same pattern. Here annual reviews have left a yawning gulf between the popular anthology and the trade reference book, invaluable for its wealth of up-to-date statistic but rather an impenetrable wall of trees for the layman trying to work out how the forest is being fertilised, nursed and shaped.

That gap this book attempts to fill. Within the pages at its disposal it makes not the slightest pretension to comprehensive coverage of every facet of current rail progress. I have selected certain areas of rail activity and technology and tried — with no more recourse to technical detail than is unavoidable for basic understanding — to provide a broad-brush picture of world development. And I have selected one or two countries for an overall account of their railways' response to today's demands — that is to say, how they are reshaping and marketing their services as well as how they are modernising their hardware — as further yardsticks against which to measure performance in one's own country.

Inevitably the production time for this book has meant that some of the points raised have been or will be overtaken by events. *Modern Railways International Review* is intended to provide background information to the news as it happens. As developments occur, they will be reported monthly in *Modern Railways* magazine.

Blockley, Glos.
November 1980.

G. Freeman Allen

Right: The British contender for world markets in economical high-speed technology — one of British Rail's first three automatic tilt-body APT-P 25kV ac train-sets leans to a reverse curve near Beattock summit, between Carlisle and Glasgow. The APT-P's ability to curve up to 40% faster than conventional rolling stock without passenger discomfort is cutting journey time for the 401 mile London-Glasgow journey to $4\frac{1}{4}$hr, inclusive of one intermediate stop.

The 'Corail' Era of French Inter-City

The massive new fleet of 'Corail' coaches spearheaded French Railways' drive of the 1970s to 'democratise' its inter-city market. Along with the new hardware went the development of energetic marketing, which since early 1979 has had the scope for market pricing. Culmination of this change will be the debut of regular-interval, 160mph Paris-Lyon service by standard TGV train-sets in the early 1980s.

The past few years' 'democratisation' of French Railways' (SNCF) inter-city passenger service reaches its ultimate in the next few years with the progressive commissioning of the 160mph Paris-Sudest TGV line — the southern 169 miles, from a junction with historic PLM Paris-Dijon-Lyon main line at St Florentin to the outskirts of Lyon, in October 1981; the remainder from St Florentin to the start of the new route on the outskirts of Paris at Combs-la-Ville two years later. From the autumn of 1981 18 trains each way daily will be pathed over the completed stretch of the new railway, among them a pair of through Paris-Geneva trains at the peak business hours in each direction. The latter will leave the new line south of Macon on one of its high-speed junctions with the existing SNCF network, then continue to Switzerland via Bourg and Bellegarde, cutting the Paris-Geneva transit time eastbound to $4\frac{1}{4}$hr, a gain of $1\frac{1}{2}$hr on the best schedule between the two cities on offer in 1980. As for the domestic TGV service, the best Paris-Lyon non-stop time in this first phase will be 2hr 45min, just over an hour quicker than the fastest previously available on the ex-PLM main line, by the 'Lyonnais' and requiring a 101.8mph average.

The final TGV timetable will translate the patterned short haul working of systems like BR's Southern Central and Sout Eastern Divisions or the Netherlands Railways to an inter-cit distance comparable to London-Newcastle. From Paris Gare d Lyon to Lyon via the TGV will be 264 miles and the standard non-stop timing will be an even 2hr, for an end-to-end average o 132mph. Between 06.00 and 21.00 Paris-Lyon service will be a strict hourly intervals, supplemented by peak period extras anc trains tracing part only of the new line en route to and from Switzerland or eastern French centres, to hoist the daily throughput to around 25 trains each way.

All of course, will be furnished by standard TGV train-sets saloon from end to end, and with a standard catering provision Just about the only adulteration of a long-haul Metro image will be the imposition on some services of a sometimes hefty supplementary fare (of which more shortly).

Until now the only SNCF exercise in regular-interval inter-city working with fixed-format equipment has been with the initial ETG gas turbine multiple-units on the Paris-Caen-Cherbourg route. Elsewhere, although within a decade or so of the last war the SNCF had begun to fill some of the traditional mid-morning and mid-afternoon gaps in French inter-city timetables, the trains congregated in morning, midday and evening froups that gave a marked priority of path and speed to supplementary-fare and often first-class only *rapides*, all with full restaurant car service. So favoured was the first-class market that middle-class France was starting to brand train travel as primarily a premium-fare mode.

Below: A TGV train-set at its top 160mph speed on the specially prepared test section of Alsace main line between Strasbourg and Selestat. In the foreground is a special installation of the 135mph turnout incorporated in junctions of the TGV line proper. *Y. Broncard*

Right: Interior of second-class TGV saloon; the seats in each half face in opposite directions.

Below right: A thyristor-controlled 5,900hp Class BB7200 winds a train of 'Corail' stock around the Lac du Bourget, near Aix-les-Bains. *Y. Broncard*

SNCF

But at the end of the 1960s the SNCF's graph of passenger-mileage, until then forging upward at a consistent 3½% per annum, faltered and flattened out. While the second-class market was becoming more and more wedded to the car, the first-class clientele was being eroded by improved and intensified European air services. That drain accelerated as wide-body jets enhanced airline capacity and comfort.

Worried market research convinced the SNCF that it must change market tack. The second-class motorist and not the first-class air traveller was the biggest and most accessible prize. To maximise the second-class market potential, though, the SNCF second class product and its presentation had to be transformed.

The first and crucial outcome of the new policy was the 'Corail' coach design for domestic inter-city service. BR had already decided to standardise air-conditioning in second-class inter-city coach construction. In its 'Corail' fleet the SNCF was the first system on the European mainland to adopt the same course — taking, incidentally, a diametrically opposed line to West Germany's DB, which at the time regarded the air-conditioning of all its first-class stock as a commercial priority. At the end of the 1970s, though, the DB bowed to French wisdom and, with much of its first-class fleet still conventionally ventilated, belatedly commissioned new air-conditioned second-class saloons for its new hourly-interval Inter-City network.

The 'Corail' designers' brief was to maximise payload/tare weight ratio but to achieve this with a totally new approach to passenger comfort and travel ambience. The first parameter dictated a saloon layout, within which 88 second-class seats were contrived, for a body length of 86.6ft, by resort to an airliner arrangement with folding tables in seat backs. But the 'Corail' seat itself is arguably the most comfortable on offer in European second-class, even if leg-room is rather cramped by comparison with the space under the fixed tables separating facing seats in a BR MkIII car, which seats 72 in a 75ft body.

Where 'Corail' stock to my mind is unsurpassed is in the flair and thoughtful detail of its decor, furnishing and — not least — passenger aids (every railway, ought to copy, for example, the neat panel of pictogram-illustrated hints to passengers on how to recline their seats, switch on reading lights, see whether the lavatory is occupied, know what catering is on offer, and so on, which the SNCF sensibly fixes to every seat-back table). Decor is especially beguiling in the 'Corail' first-saloons, with their deep red seat covering, box-pleated curtains, smoked-glass dividers between smoking and non-smoking sections, and grey or black ceilings — even if, after dark, the concealed lighting's soft spread on the rich red upholstery and black ceiling of the smoking saloon hints at one of those Continental city bars *'interdit aux agés moins de 18 ans'*. All SNCF industrial design is externally commissioned from specialist firms mostly by the SNCF but sometimes by the equipment builders. The TGV train-sets are a notable case of interior decor left to the constructors to sub-contract.

'Corail' — the name is a contraction of 'Confort' and 'Rail' — now equips in complete train-sets the great majority of the SNCF's locomotive-hauled inter-city services, as a glance at any main station train-sheet (which identifies all the 'Corail'-fitted trains) soon shows. The massive 'Corail' fleet of day coaches is no longer to be all-saloon, however. Early batches of 'Corail' included a compartment design in standard body-shell for international operation and hence with three-a-side seating (these are classified VU75, the domestic 'Corail' stock VTU75). When market research showed that 25% of the internal French clientele had a rooted aversion to the open configuration, the SNCF accepted the need to infiltrate the VTU75 sets with roughly that proportion of compartment vehicles — but not at the cost of payload/tare ratio.

By the end of the 1970s the SNCF rolling stock engineers managed to come up with an 88-seater compartment second coach draft. It is promised not to sacrifice a square millimetre of seat area by comparison with an open second (the first of the build is due in 1981 and had not appeared when this was written). The designers have achieved this by moving the bogies inward from the body ends. That permits 40cm more of body width without risk of clearance infringement on curves and thus makes room for four-a-side seating in each of 11 compartments. In a thoughtful touch the SNCF is taking these 'Corail' compartment seats tip-up, essentially so that in a less than fully-loaded coach families can make some extra floor space for their children to move about.

In the fading 1970s the SNCF also adopted the 'Corail' body-shell for its first air-conditioned couchette cars, both first and second class. These have been a powerful aid to the SNCF's energetic latter-day promotion of overnight travel, which is proving the railway strongly competitive with road for journeys of 8-10hr duration — not least now that an SNCF couchette supplement buys the softness of sheets as well as air-conditioning.

Both first- and second-class couchette carryings were climbing significantly in 1980, but the first-class 'Corail' couchette seems to have specially captivated the market. 'It's the only new vehicle', SNCF Deputy Commercial Director of Passenger Services M Poinsignon told me in Paris recently, 'which I've ever known not draw a single letter of criticism. Only letters of congratulation, in fact.'

Not that the decades-old argument whether first-class couchettes are commercially logical on a railway selling second-class sleeper berths is dead or even dormant. The SNCF at least concedes its 'anti' faction the point of not operating first-class couchettes in a sleeping-car train, but it has yet to update an age-encrusted tariff structure that for no obvious present-day marketing reason makes a second-class sleeper berth the cheaper buy to about 750km journey distance, then veers the advantage to the first-class couchette. So from Paris to Nice, for example, it pays to go sleeper.

Symbolic of the rising popularity of overnight travel in the middle ranges of the SNCF passenger market are the 1979-80 reshaping of a historic service and the introduction of two new ones. The legendary 'Train Bleu', once the four-star, all sleeping-car preserve of Riviera-bound Parisian society, is now two trains, each a mix of sleepers and second-class couchettes, that divide the task of serving the string of Cote d'Azur resorts. In September 1979 this new breed of mixed, all-berth overnight trains was prefigured by the 'Palombe Bleu', a newcomer from Paris to Irun, Tarbes and the Basque country with — uniquely for that itinerary — no public call until Morcenx, south of Bordeaux and 431 miles from Paris. Next, in the spring of 1980, emerged the 'Rhône-Océan'. This is the first all-berth overnight train on one of the SNCF's transversal routes, the increasingly significant cross-country path from Lyon to Tours and Nantes, where the SNCF has conjured up 50% more passenger business since the mid-1970s.

'Corail' moved into the 125mph club in the autumn of 1980. For four years the SNCF balked at the cost of adding multi-class trains to the two TEEs, the 'Aquitaine' and 'Etendard', which make 125mph between Paris and Bordeaux. Pathing complexities were compounded by such extra expenses as locomotive double-manning and by the load limitation essential to keep the 8000hp CC6500 Co-Co's appetite for current within the capacity of the lineside feeders, all to be set against the prospect of lower revenue per train-mile with a major proportion of the passengers paying second-class fares. But imminent

Left: Air-conditioned second-class comparisons, (top) SNCF 'Corail'; (bottom) the DB's recent product for its Inter-City network.

completion of a throughout Paris-Bordeaux *autoroute* forced the SNCF's hand. A balancing pair of limited-load Paris-Bordeaux 'Corail' trains made their 125mph debut in October 1980, with a second pair to come in the following May.

Train catering has undergone radical change in the 'Corail' era — and not without some traumas. 'C'est ma croix', M. Poinsignon sighed to me, jestingly attributing to it most of the white hairs in his beard.

Ten years ago, with the catering bill climbing steeply by the year, the SNCF decided to end the Wagon-Lits company's monopoly and three other concerns now have a share of SNCF catering. Two others have been used but discarded, either for failure to control prices or deficient product quality. Their fall from grace was probably the result of learning the hard way the full cost and complexity of putting on a viable train catering service. Their experience, moreover, seems to have stilled most other entrepreneurs' inclination to try the job. When the SNCF sought to empanel two fresh companies to run TGV catering, only one concern was prepared to tender; and their bid was unacceptable.

The 1979-80 recession steepened a fall in French demand for train meals that had been marked for some time. The SNCF has reacted more ruthlessly in restaurant car economy than BR or the DB. Full waiter service of meals on the SNCF is now confined to TEEs, where it has been quite substantially up-priced to offset dwindling demand. In the autumn of 1980 the full five-course lunch (five-course including cheese, that is) on the Paris-Milan 'Cisalpin', for instance, carried a basic tag of Ffr 97, or about £8.70. One might note, though, that this traveller at the same time found a good three-course meal in Paris hard to buy for much less: but then meal prices in Paris were on average at least 25% higher than the equivalent in the provinces.

The SNCF's substantial fleet of redundant modern and air-conditioned restaurant cars is being converted either into second-class saloons with 'Corail'-pattern seating, or into th 'Bar-Dancing' and 'Bar-Disco' cars with the full array of strob lighting gimmickry which are increasingly sought by the tou operators chartering special trains. In the summer of 1980 on of the saloon transmutations was experimentally given a nove extra — a children's playroom, to which about a quarter of th body-length was handed over at one end of the car.

That innovation was typical of SNCF's present-day readines to act on market research. The motivation in this instance was a study showing that half of all French trips of more than 100km length were family affairs including at least one child. Less than 2% of this travel was by air, 90% of it by car. Few of the motoring families polled were happy about going by road, however, because of the safety risks and the certainty that the children would be fidgetting at their restraint within a small seat well before the trip was over. The SNCF's experimental conversion, operated in a Paris-Le Croisic express during the 1980 summer, was a market sampler and hence not elaborately furnished in the playroom, but customer response was enthusiastic enough for the car to be taken into the workshops in the autumn for more refinement, including equipment of the playroom with a video playback. On the same theme the SNCF has experimentally equipped two 'Corail' coaches with Scandinavian-type compartments fitted out for nursing mothers.

To revert to train catering, the SNCF does aim to make it viable in its own right. But under the 1979 contract concluded with the Government passenger management is set a target contribution to total costs from its inter-city operation, so that the red ink has to be strictly curbed. That means seeking the

Below: Inside a 'Corail-Bar'.

Below right: 'Corail' first-class seating.

most economical service consistent with the satisfaction of an acceptable majority of passengers.

The original 'Corail' catering plan envisaged service of airliner-type tray meals from galleys in both first and second class, but second-class demand soon proved minimal. This market sector clearly preferred to buy pizzas, *croques-monsieur* (toasted cheese sandwich) and the like from a 'Corail-Bar' car. So the tray-meal service, usually offering a choice of hot or cold dishes, is now purveyed only in the first-class cars of 'Corail' trains not including a 'Gril-Express' self-service cafeteria. A 'Corail-Bar' is the basic catering car of the 'Corail' era, but some high load-factor trains feature both bar and 'Gril-Express'. Like the TRUBs and TRUKs of BR's East Coast HSTs, they are juxtaposed in the train formation for staff economy, to the annoyance of some SNCF marketing men who would prefer them well separated for passenger convenience.

The second-class clientele voices few complaints over the 'Gril-Express', but they are excoriated by most first-class passengers. The SNCF believes this antipathy could be muted by re-design, currently under review. No doubt about it, the starkly plastic ambience of a 'Gril-Express' dining area is bleakly uninviting compared with the elegant decor of a 'Corail' first. Too much stress, it seems, was laid on functional economy — ease of cleaning, and so on — in the original 'Gril-Express' design specification, which was also muddled by a requirement to make tables and chairs easily movable so that the vehicles would be easily adaptable as dancing saloons for charter trains, which in practice has been rarely demanded. Wanted now is a more colourful and relaxing interior style, with separate smoking and non-smoking areas, most importantly more comfortable seating, and surfaces easier to keep free of the debris and stains of successive customers.

In the TGV train-set the only catering car is a bar serving the same wares as a 'Corail-Bar'. For second-class travellers this will be supplemented by trolley service of cold dishes and snacks, but first-class travellers will have a galley-furnished service of superior tray meals, probably priced at around Ffr70 (roughly £6) a tray, with the proper accoutrements of correct wineglasses, linen cloth and linen napkin as well as an appropriate *hauteur de cuisine*. The resuscitation of frozen dishes for a hot tray meal service of this kind, M. Poinsignon emphasised to me, has now been considerably refined. For instance, dishes are no longer reheated as individual packages of meat and vegetables, with the result that the former's taste is drowned by water from the latter: now the two are heated separately, five portions at a time, and the individual plates made up in the galley.

Given all the measures to broaden competitive appeal so far outlined why, I asked M. Poinsignon, does the SNCF still stand out against its biggest neighbours through its disinclination to adopt a regular-interval inter-city timetable (the coming TGV service apart, of course)? Because, he said, unlike the UK, West Germany, the Netherlands or Switzerland, with their major population centres mostly in close proximity to each other, France's people were dispersed in a few widely separated zones of concentrated population and commerce, between which lay numerous small towns. The distances covered by the radial main lines from Paris to the remoter cities made it very difficult to marry up a regular-interval main-line service with patterned connections on the lateral lines in the provinces — and moreover transversal main lines such as Lyon-Tours-Nantes were now gaining commercial significance very rapidly.

Granted, refusal to follow the neighbours in patterned timetabling had made the pathing of international services and connections a more taxing job for the SNCF's train service planners. But the disadvantages were offset by the facility with which the SNCF inter-city train speed band could be kept high and narrow if *rapides* were 'flighted' in periodic groups through other traffic. Anyway, the one pre-TGV essay in regular-interval timetabling, on the Paris-Caen-Cherbourg line, had not performed as expected. Intended to spread the load as well as enhance convenience, it had certainly pulled in some extra off-peak traffic, but at the same time peak loadings had climbed higher still.

More important, competitively, than patterned timetabling, in M. Poisignon's view, was more attractive packaging of rail travel and improvement of what has lately become a keyword of SNCF marketing — *'L'acceuil'*, or the reception of the passenger. In the SNCF context, this covers a gamut of concerns, from station refurbishing and staff courtesy and solicitude to coordination with other public transport, parking provision at stations and facility for car or even cycle hire on arrival.

In the past few years the SNCF's architects have been doing fine work in the rejuvenation of historic stations, leaving their usually cherishable fabric untouched but skilfully and harmoniously refurbishing the interior as a welcoming and functionally modern access to a thoroughly modern form of transport. It helps, of course, that in France a local authority contribution to station reconstruction is commonplace. To quote one of many recent examples, Bayonne put up a quarter of the £1.5millions cost of refurbishing its station.

At the start of the 1980s the biggest SNCF station projects were undoubtedly the creation of new underground suburban stations at the Nord and Lyon terminals of Paris, partly to obtain urgently-needed extra peak capacity on the surface, partly as a step towards fulfilment of the Paris 'Interconnection', the mid-town underground knitting together of the Paris RER and the SNCF's Paris suburban system, which is discussed in more detail elsewhere in this book. One should not overlook the value of the future 'Interconnection' working to many cross-country SNCF inter-city travellers as well as to Parisians. Today, for instance, a trip from Lille to Lyons is likely to take at

Above: For connecting short-haul services of a standard to match today's long-haul trains — the TGV especially — the SNCF has created a new electric-multiple unit, the Z2, with 100mph capability. Its red and blue livery is thought likely to be standardised for SNCF short-haul emus. *SNCF, CAV*

Right: Second-class saloon of a Z2. The first examples took up public service between Bordeaux and Archachon in the autumn of 1980, observing a 35min schedule for the 36.7miles. Others were to follow on the lines from Bordeaux to Angoulême and Toulouse. *SNCF, CAV*

ast 6½hr, including the Paris transfer from Nord to Lyon rmini by Metro or taxi. With direct and frequent SNCF train rvice between the two Paris stations and TGV service on to yon it will probably need less than 5hr, with the bonus of a uch more comfortable and convenient transfer between the aris termini.

Some other instances of the SNCF's latter-day readiness to nnovate in search of fresh markets demand mention. There is e enterprising application of creative tourism to a regular-ervice train in the 'Cévénol', which takes the scenic route to Iarseilles via Clermont-Ferrand, the Cévennes mountain line nd Alès. On the 'Cévénol' passengers are not only primed with terature on the region they traverse, but presented with live ntertainments or lectures en route, and offered both a saloon ith electronic game diversions and a TV screen show of SNCF lms and buffet dispensing Auvergnat specialities. Worth note, oo, is the recent experimental and apparently promising xtension of the Motorail concept to a service for accompanied notor-cycles.

SNCF passenger fares were raised twice in 1979, by 7.5% in ebruary and 5.5% in September following the new agreement vith the Government, but that created headroom for the market ricing scope now allowed the SNCF — scope which anyway vas marginal when French Governments were holding down asic fare scales in the earlier 1970s. The 1979 contract also ermits the SNCF to hoist the supplements it charges to control he loading of its prime *rapides* and to tackle its serious inter-city peak problem. The latter is most acute at weekends, when nalf France seems infected by *wanderlust* and the Friday vening exodus from the Paris termini can triple the volume of receding weekdays. Consequently the SNCF plans to levy a ubstantially higher supplement for travel by peak Friday vening and Monday morning TGVs than the probable 10% irst-class and 30% second-class surcharge on basic fares for use of peak morning and evening TGVs on other weekdays.

The main thrust of the SNCF's present-day market pricing is hrough cards stimulating plural travel outside the peaks. To dentify the critical periods the SNCF has borrowed the simple red, white and blue' codification devised by Canadian National n the 1960s. 'Red' covers the few mass-travel days of the year — Christmas, the peak winter sports period, Easter, etc; but some public holidays are 'white', which otherwise is chiefly each weekend from Friday 15.00 to Saturday noon, and Sunday 15.00 to Monday noon; the rest of most weeks is 'blue'.

A *'billet séjour'* secures the single traveller making a return or circular trip totalling at least 1,000km, staying at least five days at destination and setting out and returning in 'blue' time a 25% discount on the basic fare. With a *'Carte couple'*, available free and valid for five years, a man and woman (not necessarily man and wife) can get a 50% reduction on one of their tickets for any journey, single or return, begun in 'blue' time. Also issued free and good for five years is the *'Carte famille'*, which is for use by a minimum of three travellers in a party, of whom all but the first get 50% off the normal fare for any journey started in 'white' as well as 'blue' time. Finally *'Vermeil 50'* is the card for the elderly — men over 65 and women over 60 — which, costing Ffr41 (£4.10) and lasting a year, saves the holder 50% of the price of any journey, but only if it is started in 'blue' time. The Paris suburban system, one should add, is excluded from the coverage of all these discounted fares.

One more important development is burnishing the French image of train travel. That is the devolution from Central Government to the country's Regional administrations of power to plan more of their own public transport systems within a given envelope of State financial support, and within a Government-approved forward plan to contract with the SNCF for improved local services at the cost, if necessary, of investing their own money in new rolling-stock. The most spectacular outcome so far has been in the Nord-Pas-de-Calais Region, where the authority has staked a large part of its public passenger transport future on the railway, to the extent of acquiring no fewer than 195 new diesel multiple-unit cars. These are distinguished — as are those bought by other administrations — by the Region's own yellow and grey livery. At least half-a-dozen other administrations have now concluded or are negotiating agreements for improved local service with the SNCF.

Below: The new X2100 diesel railcar, besides re-equipping the SNCF's fleet, has been bought with minor modifications by several of the Regional administrations subsidising improved rail services in their area, including that of the Nord-Pas-de-Calais.

Spain's New Age of the Train

Below: Spain was almost the first European country to react to the 1973 threat of oil starvation by ordering a major rail electrification programme that has already doubled the track mileage under wire. Now, following the 1979 conclusion of a new contract with the Spanish Government whereunder RENFE has been freed of the cost of maintaining deficitary social services, encouraged to transfer a good deal of rural traffic to road and enabled financially to compete with market-based tariffs, the railways are set in the 1980s to electrify a further 1,500 track-miles. Some of this programme covers double-tracking of trunk routes to permit a major intensification and acceleration of RENFE's passenger services, which is to include inauguration of new inter-regional trains as well as betterment on the radial routes from Madrid. A 30% increase of long-haul passenger train capacity is envisaged, in which a new development of the Talgo train figures prominently. This is one of the Talgo III trainsets produced in the mid-1960s for RENFE inter-city services, hauled by one of the low-slung 2,400 or 3,000hp Krauss-Maffei diesel-hydraulic B-Bs specially designed for Talgo haulage. Since the spread of electrification it has become necessary to build four-wheel generator vans for addition to Talgo sets when they are hauled by electric locomotives not equipped to power Talgo auxiliaries (a development which has also created a striking colour contrast when a scarlet-and-silver Talgo rake is matched with the orange-lined bright green of a Mitsubishi-built Class 269 electric).

Above left: The new Talgo development — garbed in a new dark blue-and-white livery (and note the modern RENFE logo below the waistline) — is an automatic tilt-body version, slightly longer than the Talgo III, which is said to cost no more than a car with the original Talgo running gear. Tested at up to 143.8mph, they are designed for regular 125mph operation, but RENFE — which has ordered 132 day and 56 sleeping cars — is initially limiting them to 112.5mph. A version with adjustable-gauge axles will allow the summer 1981 introduction of a Paris-Madrid all-sleeper train connecting the capitals in about 3hr less time than the 'Puerta del Sol', the through cars of which have had to undergo a bogie change at the Franco-Spanish frontier.

This page: The cafeteria, a first-class and a second-class saloon of one of the new Talgo tilt-body train-sets.

Above: Since the late 1970s RENFE has had under evaluation a sister of the Italian 'Pendolino' tilt-body electric multiple-unit, constructed by the Spanish builders CAF to the Fiat design. The trials have been chequered, but in 1980 the 'Tren Basculante' — as the RENFE version is known — was in regular Madrid-Albacete public service, covering the 173.4miles in 163min. Besides investing in tilt-body equipment RENFE is spending heavily on trunk route realignment; on the Madrid-Andalusia route, for instance, besides double-tracking to Cordoba and electrifying on to Malaga it is straightening the passage of the Sierra Morena mountains at high cost in tunnelling to establish more route-mileage with 100mph potential. Not dead either is the dream of fulfilling the UIC Master Plan's requirement for a brand-new 455-mile, standard-gauge 150mph line from Madrid through Zaragoza and Barcelona to a junction with the SNCF at Port Bou.

Left: RENFE's rolling stock is fast becoming the most externally vivid in Western Europe. Delivered in 1980, the first of a new series of Spanish-built Class 444 three-car electric multiple-units with air-suspension bogies for Inter-city routes such as Madrid-Valencia, is a bright red overall with raked flashes of broad gold on the bodysides. The latest version of the Mitsubishi electric Bo-Bo locomotive design, Class 269-200, built in Spain under licence, has been turned out with a boldly jagged yellow lining on a dark blue base; some other locomotive types have been repainted Talgo red and silver, and suburban multiple-units display several different livery styles.

Right: A feature of RENFE's current long-term plan, prepared under the 1979 agreement with the Government, is the comprehensive rebuilding of city main stations as convenient, modernised interchanges with other transport modes. These are views of the first station to be treated, Madrid Chamartin. Similar rebuilding is nearing completion at Barcelona Santo.

CERCANIAS

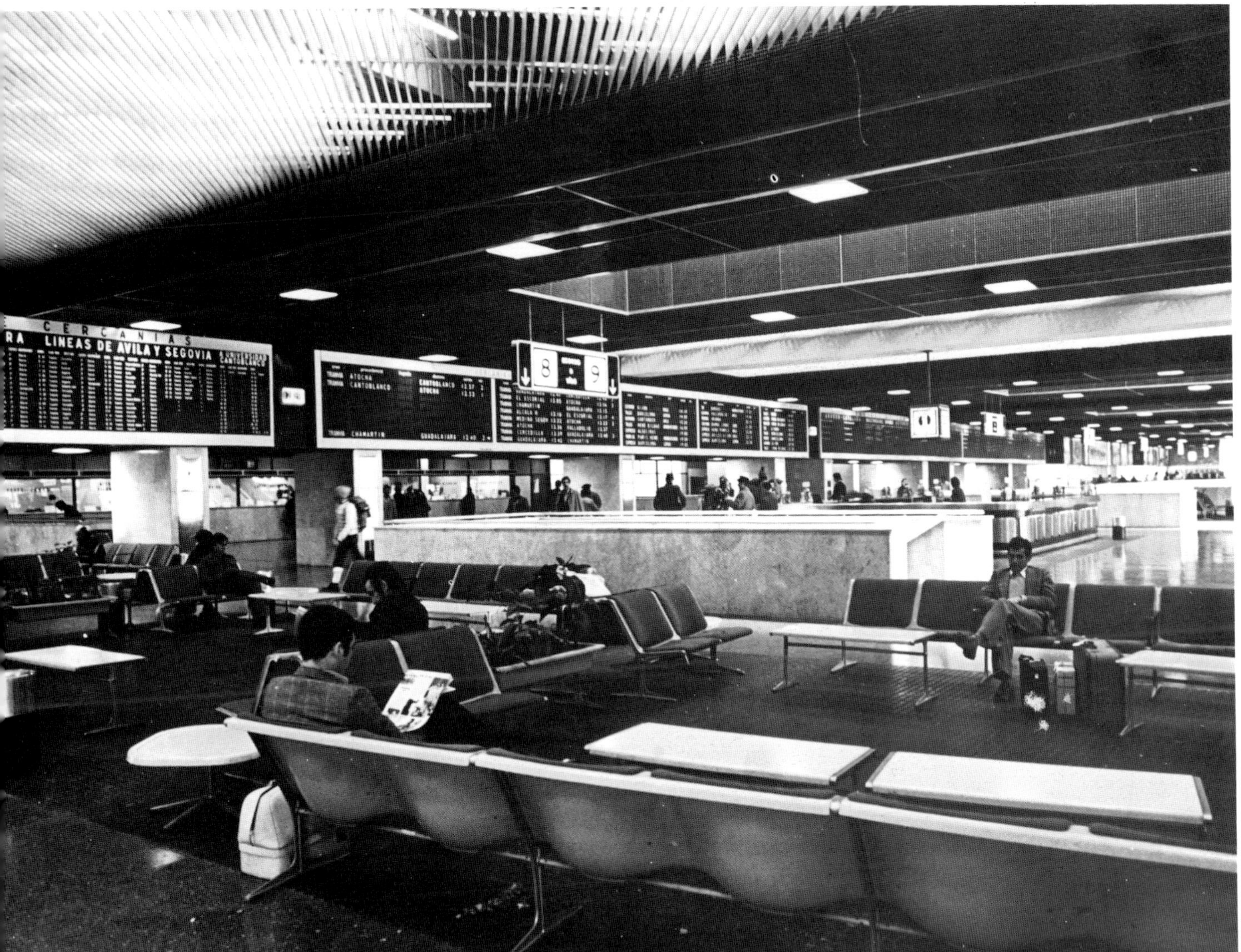
CERCANIAS
LINEAS DE AVILA Y SEGOVIA

Right: Exterior and interior of the latest Series 5000 train-set of the Madrid Metro. Assembled by CAF-Wesa in Spain, these two-car units are mounted on Sumiride air-suspension bogies by MTE of France, use Knorr air brakes, Krupp-Bochum resilient wheels and are powered by Jeumont 280hp motors. Each 63ton set seats 80 and is said to have standing room for 360 more. After a lull in new construction for financial reasons the Metro opened new extensions in 1980 to increase its network to 46.6miles and more were underway.

Below: Steadily expanding, too, is the Barcelona Metro, of which the four standard-gauge lines in 1980 totalled 30 route-miles and served 72 stations — an increase of 167% in distance covered since 1966; in the same period the system's car fleet has almost trebled. Further extensions and the construction of a totally new line are planned to bring the route-mileage up to 75, with 157 stations. This is a station on Line 5, with a train of 1000 series stock built in the early 1970s.

'Inter-City 125' — the First Two Years of BR's East Coast Route

The popular success of BR's HSTs on the main routes from Kings Cross to the North has highlighted anew the problems of working with fixed-format train-sets in a market with daily peaks and troughs of demand — problems aggravated by the Government's refusal of adequate train-sets to fulfil the original timetable plan.

The majority of world railways with ambitions of higher inter-city speed seems to be opting for fixed-format train-sets. West Germany's DB is the conspicuous exception, convinced that the penalties of inflexible seating capacity outweigh the benefits of dispersing traction plant weight throughout the train. In the USA Amtrak and the Federal Railroad Administration seem as yet unsure which horse to back for the rehabilitated Boston-New York-Washington corridor; on the one hand they are investing in AEM-7 locomotives based on ASEA's Rc4 design, on the other expensively refurbishing some of the 'Metroliner' emus and sampling Canada's tilt-body LRC in the northern sector of the Northeast Corridor.

Where fixed-format, high-speed train-sets are applied to a new railway conceived for their exclusive use, like Japan's Shinkansen or France's Paris-Lyon TGV to come, no transitional difficulties best either operators or passenger managers. But where they are grafted on to an existing railway its managers face not only the tough job of efficient timetabling within an extended speed band, but also some ticklish commercial dilemmas. Must the fixed-format train-set offer the same style of travel as the system's locomotive-hauled services to be sure of public acceptance? Will the customers revolt at measures to control demand either for seats or amenities so as to maximise use of the fixed capacity?

Where these problems are compounded by tightening clamps on investment, as they have been on British Rail's East Coast Route, the managers' task is daunting. What has been achieved — and learned — in the evolution of 'Inter-City 125' with BR's twin 2,250hp diesel locomotive-powered HST train-sets on routes from Kings Cross to the West Riding, the North-East and Scotland may thus be textbook reading for systems making a similar switch to fixed-format push-pull or multiple-unit formation in the future.

First, why did the ER back a fixed-format development? There was no tenable option. When the ER was denied the electrification it had been promised in the 1955 Modernisation Plan, because realism soon had to acknowledge that conversion of both East and West Coast Routes in short order was beyond practical resources, the Region's management had determined to follow its aborted electric timetable as closely as possible with diesel traction.

Below: An East Coast HST makes for London, leaning to the curve of Durham Viaduct with the city's cathedral in the background. *BR*

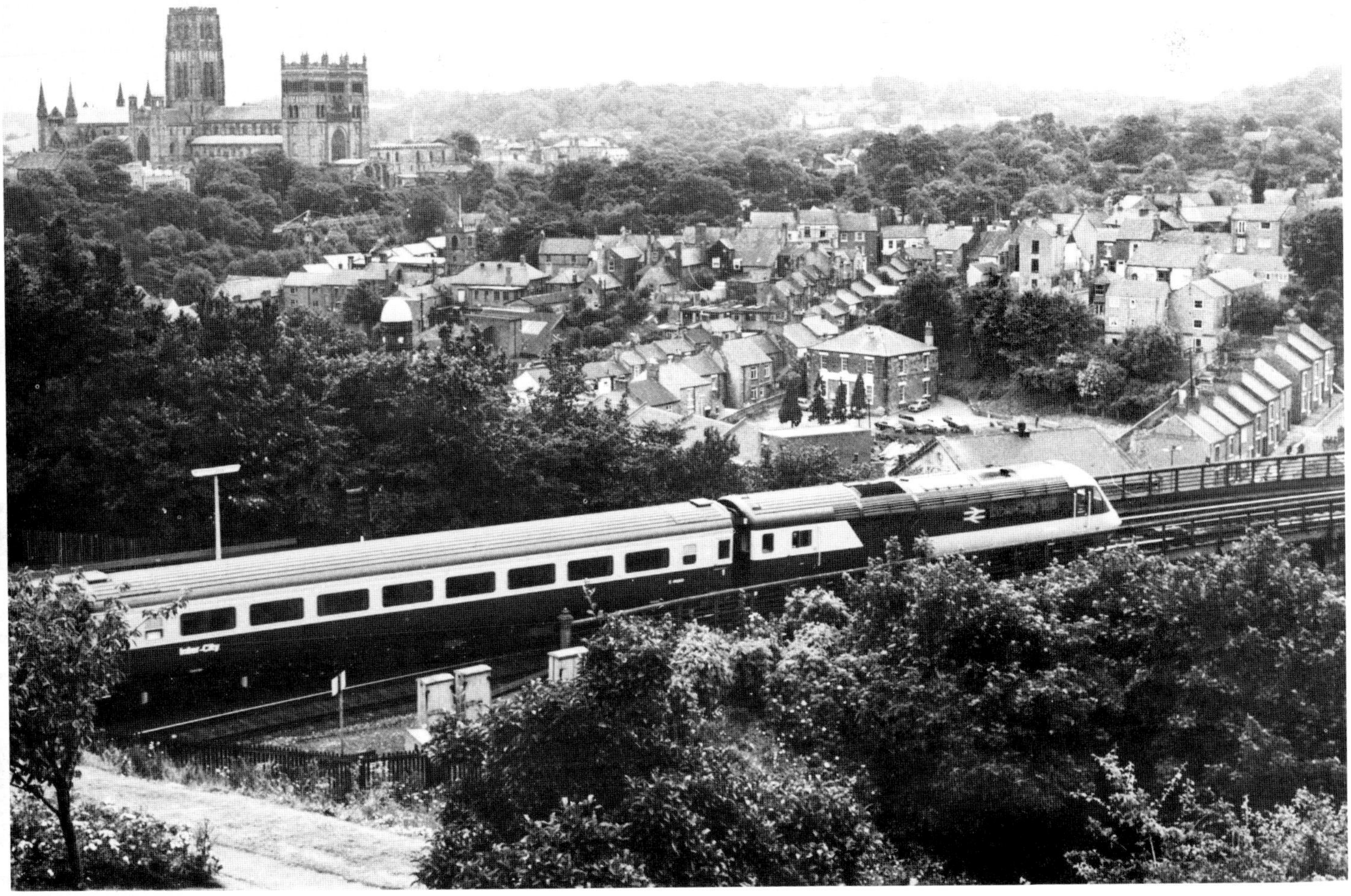

Ultimately, to attain the peak transit times of the 3,300hp Class 55 diesel locomotive era, it had had to resort to strictly controlled loading — the familiarly-known ' "Deltic"-plus-eight' workings. But these were the end of the feasible road with front-end single-unit power. The commercial pressures for still shorter journey times were not capable of satisfaction with any imaginable 4,500-5,000hp diesel locomotive design that would have given the civil engineers untroubled nights.

From its formation under Beeching in 1963 the British Railways Board had made standardisation the cornerstone of its rolling-stock policy. Thus the revolutionary titlt-body Advanced Passenger Train was to be the standard Inter-City equipment of the 1980s. And when the APT proved so difficult a research and development nut to crack that a further stage of conventional engineering had to be accepted, the HST too was proclaimed the standard tool for the interim. Its adoption for the prime routes would steadily 'cascade' locomotive-hauled trains of BR's Mk II coaches to less prestigious lines and progressively retire Mk I coaches of 1950s origin.

The Government seemed perfectly amenable to the theory when it approved the first HST order, which was sufficient to transform the Western Region's entire Paddington-Bristol/South Wales service. So no dissent was expected from the ensuing request for 42 sets to cover not only the Kings Cross-West Riding/Newcastle/Edinburgh services but also the ER's Inter-City trains between London and Hull and Cleethorpes, plus the Kings Cross-York service that was to serve such intermediate stations as Huntingdon, Newark and Selby and gather them into the high-speed operation by interconnection with the HSTs at York. North of Peterborough, in other words, the ER would be still closer to the electrification ideal of a predictable common performance by every train, with the whole basic East Coast main line service covered by fixed-format HSTs.

But with the country's economy wilting in the wake of the oil crisis, inflation rampant and BR's overall prospects none too comforting, the Department of Transport insisted that the East Coast order be cut from 42 to 32 sets. At that juncture the civil servants were not concerned with the deployment of the sets, or the detail of revenue projection for each service. They argued only that the rate of return on investment in the smaller fleet would be greater.

BR immediately set about preparing a fresh submission for 'The Last Ten', as the exercise was popularly code-named, but eventually put its finger to the Whitehall wind and decided that to put the case formally was pointless. Instead, while the passenger managers glumly revised their revenue projections downward, the operators and planners renewed their grim experience with the problems of timetable pathing for trains of varied weight, capacity and running characteristics within a fairly wide speed band. The Hull, Cleethorpes and York services would all have to be re-cast for locomotive haulage.

There is no room here to dissect the full, revised East Coast 'Inter-City 125' timetable, which anyway has been rehearsed in the finest of detail in *Modern Railways*. Enough to say that some tight grouping of trains at the approach to key stations was inevitable through the compulsion to run trains calling at up to eight stations in the 188.2miles between Kings Cross and York behind 95-100mph diesel locomotives, and at the same

Below: The Kings Cross-Hull service was denied HSTs in the inaugural East Coast 'Inter-City 125' timetable: here Class 55 'Deltic' No 55.008 *The Green Howards* does its best to narrow the speed band, passing Welwyn Garden City, 20¼miles out of London, in even time — if the station clock is to be believed — with the 12.05 Kings Cross-Hull on 13 May 1980. *Ken Harris*

me to create enough room for 125mph HSTs to cover the same distance with only one or two calls en route at overall average speeds of up to 92mph. This essential 'flighting', enforced by the mixed timetable, generated recurrent operating difficulties, especially at Kings Cross, a terminus none too generously supplied with platforms.

The regular-interval cycle of HSTs and locomotive-hauled trains consistently had three trains due into the London terminus hard on each other's heels — and prompt admission of the HSTs was a priority because the double-ended high-speed trains' terminal turnround times were minimal to satisfy the pressures for their utilisation to the absolute maximum of feasibility.

Prime worry were the so-called 'semi-fasts', the 'Deltic'-hauled Kings Cross-York trains serving the eight intermediate stations, which epitomised the harassments of attempting to run an intensive passenger service with mixed equipment. Even with 3,300hp up front these trains could only just be timed into York with a comfortable clearance ahead of an HST leaving London 55min later.

The 'Inter-City 125' timetable was still quite young when availability of the ageing Class 55s lapsed. As usual when power is short, it was the second half of the day when London generally ran out of available 'Deltics'. Frequently forced to make do with 2,650hp Class 47 power was the 16.05 Kings Cross-York, consistently one of the best-loaded 'semi-fasts' and one despatched straight in front of the peak evening stream of HSTs. Time and again the 17.00 Kings Cross-Edinburgh had to dawdle from Doncaster to York on the tail of the underpowered 16.05, compelling the ER eventually to insert a Doncaster stop in the 17.00's schedule (admittedly, the move was partly justified by commercial demand too).

Without the 'Deltics' — and they are most unlikely to last longer than 1982 — the York 'semi-fasts' would have to be permanently decelerated to Class 47 capability. That would entail a substantial timetable redraft. Either each northbound 'semi-fast' would have to start just ahead of an HST 'flight' and be overtaken by it on a four-track stretch, or the connections with the HST network for its intermediate station passengers would have to be made at Doncaster instead of York; or some of the 'semi-fast' calls would have to be loaded on to the HSTs. The ultimate course might be a mixture of both the latter options. The Kings Cross-Cleethorpes trains, one should perhaps add, were timed for Class 47 haulage from the start.

Another predictable consequence of the mix of equipment and speed was that the customers shunned the slower locomotive-hauled trains if there was a chance to travel 'Inter-City 125' for even part of their journey. For a long time the 12.20 Kings Cross-York, locomotive-hauled, ran with plenty of seats to spare, because York travellers preferred even to stand on the 13.00 HST, which arrived in the cathedral city just 5min later. Bank Holiday extras, locomotive-hauled (and admittedly with no refreshment service), were almost totally ineffective in reducing the overcrowding of Anglo-Scottish HSTs. To keep the speed band as narrow as possible they had anyway to be severely restricted in formation.

Earlier exchanges with the Department of Transport had made it clear that its analysts were either oblivious to or unimpressed by the forecast of these problems. Despite warning that the imminent life expiry of the 'Deltics' could precipitate some deceleration of the 'Inter-City 125' HSTs, for reasons already outlined, they regarded the idea of Kings Cross-York 'semi-fast' operation by HST as an incomprehensible extravagance. They could grasp only the revenue promise of re-equipping the principal inter-city services with HSTs.

So when the ER, fortified by a swift 11% increase of East passenger journeys but worried by the often severe pressure of custom on key London-Newcastle-Edinburgh services, decided to launch a fresh claim for HSTs, it deliberately excluded the Kings Cross-York and Kings Cross-Cleethorpes services from the submission. Seven extra sets were sought, some to convert the Kings Cross-Hull service and add Tees-side to the 'Inter-City 125' network, others to establish additional workings that would ease the Anglo-Scottish route overcrowding.

The prospective work rosters for the latter would have a margin to insert an up morning and down evening 'Inter-City 125' service between Kings Cross and Sheffield via Retford. That would do something to mollify the business community of Sheffield, who were the ER's direct commercial concern though essentially reliant for Inter-City Service on the London Midland route from St Pancras. Their only hope of a high-speed service that way was through electrification and APTs some time in the late 1980s.

Although both the York trains — which did steadily pull in business after an uncertain start — and the Cleethorpes services were making a contribution to indirect costs when the second formal submission for HSTs was presented, the ER recognised that inflation had worsened the case for their conversion to HST operation. The first 32 sets had run up a total bill of £52million; but now the tag on each new set was over £2million. On top of that the HSTs demanded specialised maintenance facilities; their maintenance costs were higher than those of an equivalent locomotive-hauled formation; and for 125mph running their cabs had to be double-manned under agreements with the unions.

All this was taken into account in the market analyses and projections which the ER this time elaborated for each of the seven extra units it did formally claim. But that form of presentation evidently prompted the Department to argue the submission train by train. Consequently when the civil servants finally consented only to four additional sets (at first they tried to cut the order down to only two), they were arguably usurping an area of railway management's judgement. Instead of accepting, rejecting or reducing the claim on broad economic grounds, they seemed to be dictating the individual services which they felt deserved HST or locomotive-hauled operation. The concept of the HST as a new generation of standard Inter-City train-set was a dead letter.

Specifically questioned was the need of the extra units requested to supersede the remaining, disregarded locomotive-hauled trains between London, the North and Scotland and thus relieve the crush on the mid-morning Anglo-Scottish departures each way. Yet the severity of the overcrowding on these HSTs, expecially in summer, was implicit in the ER's judgement that the case for extra units on this service was strong enough to put formally, unlike the argument for conversion of the London-York stopping trains.

The Department, however, responded that the irritation might well be soothed if fare offers were less generous. This despite the fact that the ER was already hedging use of discounted fares on its HSTs with more restrictions than other Regions applied to their 'Inter-City' services. Only the Senior Citizen railcard was admissible without let or hindrance on any 'Inter-City 125' train; every other type of reduced fare was barred from certain peak services to spread the loading.

Denial of the extra Anglo-Scottish sets automatically deprived Sheffield of its daily HST business service to and from Kings Cross. The four additional units that were conceded for the Hull and Tees-side routes would all be active on their own ground in the morning and evening peaks. Sheffield was left with a farily forlorn hope that one or perhaps two sets for the Anglo-Scottish requirement might be found from a reconsideration of the whole HST fleet's deployment that the BRB was now forced to undertake, with the pace of future electrification and APT series production still uncertain and the HST assembly line due to end at 95 sets instead of the 170 or so that had been confidently predicted in the mid-1970s as operational by 1980. The HST was no longer standard equipment, but in the depressing argot of the 1980s 'a scarce resource'.

25
30
0000

In the 1980 summer a Western Region misfortune handed the ER a temporary solution to the Anglo-Scottish capacity difficulty. Six of the WR's second batch of HSTs were sidetracked for lack of serviceable power cars because of nagging malfunction of the latter's traction motors (supplied for this tranche of 14 units by GEC Traction, as opposed to the Brush motors fitted to the preceding nine-car Class 253 and ten-car Class 254 HSTs, in accordance with latter-day BRB policy of not concentrating specialised equipment orders on one manufacturer). The ER could therefore borrow some of the temporarily spare second-class trailers to enlarge HST sets covering such key Anglo-Scottish workings as the 08.00, 10.00 and 16.00 Kings Cross-Edinbrugh and the 10.15, 14.15 and 16.15 back by one car. Theoretically the extra vehicle cost 4min in additional running time, but no decelerations were publically advertised because the recovery margins built into the schedules could cope with the imposition provided trains were not clobbered by operational checks.

One must be wary of leaving any impression that the introduction of fixed-format HSTs reduced East Coast seating capacity. For a start, the seating space in the eight trailers of a Class 254 HST was actually greater than that of any locomotive-hauled formation it supplanted, with the solitary exception of the 'Aberdonian'. But that additional room per train was substantially multiplied, because the full 'Inter-City 125' timetable prescribed 40% more daily train mileage than the 1977 schedules with locomotive-hauled sets.

This extra performance was achieved with only 5% more train-sets than in 1977, moreover, thanks to the very intensive diagramming of the HSTs around the shortest possible terminal turnrounds. Since the start, in fact, slightly more daily train-mileage has been extracted from the fleet of Class 254 HSTs, though in 1980 the timetable was still planned around daily working of only 25 of the 32 sets on eight two-day and nine one-day work rosters.

The ER was hopeful of increasing this availability factor in time, but the maintenance requirement had been more exacting than expected. The imperative need to schedule adequate night-time hours in depots for servicing of the units in use has so far frustrated ambitions in some quarters to exploit HSTs for nocturnal, non-sleeper passenger work. The ad hoc expedient of adding a ninth trailer to some sets, incidentally, aggravated the servicing problems, since the HST depots were laid out for eight trailer formations and the extra length incurred some depot shunting during the maintenance routine.

For a period in 1979 the ER agonised that the full 'Inter-City 125' timetable, with its 18 daily trains each way between Kings Cross and Newcastle averaging more than 83mph overall, 13 to and from Leeds averaging more than 81mph overall, and sectional sprints timed up to a peak of 106.3mph over the $47\frac{3}{4}$miles between Stevenage and Peterborough start to stop, was over-ambitious. But the service had had an unlucky launch.

Most of the UK had a bitter 1978-9 winter which repeatedly disrupted railway operation. Then, in March, came the tragic cave-in of Penmanshiel tunnel, between Berwick and Edinburgh, during its reconstruction to accommodate Freightliners bearing 8ft 6in containers, which prevented any of the scheduled Kings Cross-Edinburgh 'Inter-City 125' services until a bypass had been laid by the following August. All these dislocations left the operating staff with something of a hangover which was a root

Left: The 95mph Class 47s also had to mingle with HSTs on East Coast express services because of the cut in the HST requirements: in this shot, taken before the start of 'Inter-City 125', No 47.493 pulls out of Peterborough with the 15.00 Kings Cross-Newcastle in July 1977.
L. A. Nixon

cause of the all-too-frequent lapses from punctuality in the 1979 summer and autumn. By the following year, with the HSTs chalking 87-90% of their arrivals on time or within 10min of it day after day, confidence in the plan was completely restored.

Overcrowding and indifferent punctuality apart, the 'Inter-City 125' service also came under passenger fire in its opening months for catering deficiencies. Like so much other sophisticated apparatus translated from successful use on the ground to a moving train environment, the electronic equipment of the kitchens and buffet cars revealed unsuspected frailties that too often left trains serving only drinks and cold snacks. Difficult, too, was the recruitment of adequate staff to man all the advertised catering services.

These snags could be overcome. Less easy to resolve was the issue of catering service scale on each train.

In contrast to French Railways management, who had firmly decided that the fixed, limited-capacity format of their high-speed Paris-Lyon TGV train-sets and the standard 2hr Paris-Lyon transit dictated airliner-style meal service from galleys with the support of train-centre buffet-bar, the BRB insisted that traditional dining service be perpetuated in the 'Inter-City 125' era. An arguable decision from a marketing standpoint, no doubt, but one bound to aggravate the difficulties of economically adapting fixed train formats to fluctuating demand both for accommodation and catering.

Recession and inflation had already cut back full table meal demand to such an extent that the BRB revised its HST catering car policy on the eve of 'Inter-City 125's' debut on the WR. The outcome was a division of the East Coast HST fleet between 20 sets in the orginally conceived format, with a separate kitchen-restaurant car (TRUK) adjoining the first-class trailers and a buffet-bar car (TRSB) marshalled amid the second-class trailers; and 12 sets with just the afterthought, all-purpose buffet-kitchen-restaurant car (TRUB) between the first- and second-class sections of a set. The TRUK-TRSB variant had 37 fewer second-class seats than the TRUB, but the capability to serve 120 meals at a sitting, as against the limit of 65 breakfasts or 41 lunches/dinners feasible from a TRUB kitchen.

These were distinctions that might have been useful a quarter-century earlier, when formations were tailored to the market characteristics of specific routes, periods of the day or the traditional style of some titled train with scant concern for stock utilisation. But they set present-day planners some almost intractable problems of roster shaping to satisfy variations of demand without prejudicing maximal employment of each set.

Since the start of 'Inter-City 125' the demand for table meals has become progressively more unbalanced. The market for breakfast stays high — so high, in fact, that it was and remains primarily the cause of a brouhaha over the 24, first-class-style 2+1 seats installed at one end of the TRUK vehicle specifically for second-class meal customers. At the launch of the East Coast 'Inter-City 125' operation these 24 seats were so consistently needed to satisfy assured first-class meal custom that the ER concluded it was both economic and marketing stupidity to leave them spare for very speculative second-class trade. So, over-riding anguished protest from Travellers Fare, the BRB's catering subsidiary, the ER announced that on a few HST services second-class passengers were barred from waiter service of meals.

Public as well as internal pressures soon forced the Region to rescind the embargo. Since then, of course, not a few wily business travellers have grasped that, provided any of the 'loose' 24 seats on a TRUK-TRSB set are free and their journey is within, say, 2hrs' duration, they can travel in first-class style on second-class tickets for the extra price of taking a meal.

Although demand for dinner has remained quite substantial — but well below the level for breakfast — that for lunch has slumped, partly as a consequence of the drop in foreign tourism. Consequently the economics of staffing for full meal service in equipment that is intensively rostered to cover return trips spanning breakfast and lunch, or lunch and dinner, have become seriously unbalanced. The ER no longer sees any justification for the TRUK-TRSB combination on rosters without a reasonably assured high demand for full meals. Market-pricing of lunch might mitigate present losses, but it could never be more than a palliative. Another marginal relief has been secured

n the TRUK-TRSB sets by remarshalling them so that the two atering cars are neighbours, which has permitted a significant :aff saving.

Having decided to persist with the full gamut of traditional 'ain catering in the HSTs, instead of boldly going for a system nore economically suited to the framework of an intensive peration with inflexible train-sets, BR would find a drastic hange of catering pattern more difficult now that 'Inter-City 25' is well established — not only because the TRUKs and 'RSBs exist but because the market has become accustomed to he full range of present HST catering (which, moreover, has een stressed in 'Inter-City 125' promotion). Market research on he eve of the East Coast's 'Inter-City 125' launch underlined hat this route's passenger market was the most vulnerable on 3R to any modification of catering facilities.

Can French Railways' key Paris-Lyon market though, be that nuch less sensitive? This critic was once sceptical of French udgement in discarding full meal service on its TGVs. But with indsight, no more. In the long-haul Metro age — for that, urely, is the character the economics of high rail speed impose nore forcibly on 200-300mile inter-city operation from year to 'ear — trainboard meal preparation must become an untenable nachronism.

Meanwhile, the TRUB variant of the HST has been made less :asy to operate because of the HST trolley fiasco. Travellers-Fare devised a sophisticated new trolley (which greatly mpressed at least one mainland European railway) to perambulate a fine array of hot and cold drinks as well as cold snacks throughout the train. As in West German trains where the catering is provided by one of DSG's captivating 'Quick-Pick' cafeterias, the aim was to encourage purchase of lighter snacks at seats from the trolley so as to avoid more substantial food purchasers having to queue behind a string of mere cola or coffee buyers in the buffet-bar. But decades of world airline and mainland European experience with food trolleys notwithstanding, BR yielded to objections that the trolleys' restriction of gangway movement constituted a hazard to passengers (more so, one had to infer, than car entrance doors incapable of locking from a central position — something that no railway on the European mainland would now tolerate on 125mph vehicles). So the trolleys have been immobilised as fixed 'micro-buffets' in the rased lavatories of non-HST vehicles; and patronage of HST buffet-bars all too frequently entails wearisome queuing.

None of this, however, inhibited a steady climb of passenger business after the East Coast debut of 'Inter-City 125'. In face of that, and with scant hope of any further increase of HST resources, the critical job of Norman Blackstock, the ER's 'Inter-City 125' Services Group Manager, has become what he calls 'capacity management' to maximise seat-mile revenue.

A prerequisite for that, of course, is prompt analysis of seat occupation data. BR is now virtually the only Western European railway without a central seat and berth reservation computer facility. The governments of the day deprecated BR's 1960s clamour for one as an unacceptable extravagance, but the East Coast 'Inter-City 125' service's problems have won it time and data storage space in the computerised reservation system BR's shipping subsidiary, Sealink, will have operative by late 1981 or early 1982.

Not that this will resolve all current difficulties. In fact, if seat reservation is then made compulsory on several peak-period HSTs — which is a possibility — it might stimulate even more speculative reservation. Even now 'no shows' on a heavily-used train like the 17.00 Kings Cross-Edinburgh may run as high as 25% of all reservations, because executives returning north have booked on three or four trains to be sure of an immediate seat whenever their business in London is over. With the computer operative, the ER might possibly make seat reservation impossible without simultaneous purchase of a rail ticket.

One development is pretty certain. With the East Coast Inter-City business now worth over £100million annually and sure of more, the chances of finding a seat on any train on demand must steadily decrease. When reservation in advance becomes simpler and perhaps obligatory to a degree, availability of a place on the first train of one's choice is bound to become less and less assured.

Left: The morning Anglo-Scottish HSTs have suffered seriously from overcrowding: this is the 10.00 'Flying Scotsman' from Kings Cross, skirting the Northumbrian cliffs north of Newcastle. *P. J. Robinson*

Right: On many popular HST services the models who posed for this publicity still of an HST buffet-bar would find themselves elbowed away from the counter by an impatient queue. *BR*

In the meantime the ER management has been impressing on guards the critical importance of taking consecutive passenger counts at the starting point and also after some key stations en route during each HST journey. At HQ the need to spend money for more rapid processing of this data has been recognised.

Both capacity management and financial considerations colour the ER's attitude to the upsurging demand for 'Inter-City 125' service from intermediate towns that have lost some commercial status through BR's concern for high speed to the most lucrative goals of the West Riding, the North-east and Scotland. To some extent this pressure derives from empty space people of Grantham, Newark and Retford, detected on the East Coast HSTs in the 1979 summer when Anglo-Scottish traffic was crippled by the Penmanshiel Tunnel collapse. Compared with 1979, though, Anglo-Scottish travel via 'Inter-City 125' was 50% higher in the 1980 summer.

The three complainant towns would automatically get HST attention when the additional HSTs converted three Hull-London and two Tees-side-London workings each way to 'Inter-City 125' in the 1980-1 winter, since they had been served by some of the locomotive-hauled Hull-London trains. But as things are Lincoln, Grantham, Newark, Retford and the rest have no hope of regular-interval HST service — still less so since the Department of Transport has decided to set the BRB a target contribution to indirect costs for its Inter-City operation. That obliges passenger management to set net revenue maximisation from proven markets high above the testing of prospective ones. Moreover, the Department of Transport has yet to accept an attested fact of all BR experience since the GE Line's pioneering London-Ipswich-Norwich regular-interval service of the 1950s — or perhaps since Sir Herbert Walker's main-line electrification enterprise on the Southern in the 1930s: that frequency of service is as indispensable as speed in developing Inter-City business.

The dictates of capacity management and revenue maximisation also preclude the old preference for a standard pattern of intermediate stops in each direction. True, at the end of the day the ER managed to include a stop at Stevenage, the outer London railhead, in the intineraries of both pairs of the new Tees-side-Kings Cross HSTs inaugurated in the 1980-1 winter. The Stevenage call by the up morning member of this quartet is the first in 'Inter-City 125' history at that time of day. It was tabled to cater for a significant flow of ICI employees between two of the company's plants at the start of the business day and for a time it looked as though there would be no balancing down evening stop, partly because the ICI men's hour of return was much less predictable, partly because of the timing complexity of halting an HST in outer London in the midst of suburban rush-hour and northward evening flow of Inter-City trains. But at the end of the day the Stevenage stop was standardised in the morning and evening Tees-side-London schedules each way. But the down morning train has a Peterborough stop which is not duplicated in the opposite direction.

En passant, the average businessman's clear choice of one departure to set out, but the range of possible time for his return to base, is a perennial marketing complication for BR's men. The high ratio of 'no shows' for reserved seats on afternoon and evening departures from Kings Cross stresses the point. Wherever economically and practically possible the ER tries to give this market a wider choice of return train: hence, for example, the imbalance of four up morning and five down afternoon HSTs between Bradford and Kings Cross.

To revert to issues of capacity management and revenue maximisation, these explain the incidence of 'calls to pick up only' and 'calls to set down only' limitations in the East Coast 'Inter-City 125' timetable. Business may justify a facility from Kings Cross to Newark by a West Riding-bound HST, for instance, but the Newark call will be 'to set down only' to avoid incurring a commitment to some nebulous demand for a Newark-Leeds HST link.

By mid-1980 the ER had already absorbed valuable lessons from two years of operating costly, fixed-format 125mph train-sets. It had also learned, through its enforced real pricing of every HST route, that in 'Inter-City 125' BR has an impressively saleable product. Though in standard money terms it is quite substantially the most expensive form of day rail travel in Western Europe — even when the opportunities to buy discounted fares are taken into account in the UK and elsewhere — its steady accumulation of business showed little sign of slackening until it could no longer elude the extraordinary pressures of the worse national economic slump since the 1930s.

Left: A perplexing problem for the East Coast service planners is to devise rosters that will not have the TRUK-TRSB catering capacity essential to cope with the heavy breakfast demand on a train like the morning up 'Bradford Executive' (here emerging from Peascliffe Tunnel, Grantham in July 1979) grossly under-utilised in the middle of the day. *Geoffrey D. Griffiths*

The 1980s Look in Couchettes

Above: The European air-conditioned couchette of the 1980s is a striking advance with the hard, PVC-covered berths of the 1950s. This is one of a batch of 20 lately built within the Eurofima body-shell by Schlieren for the Swiss Federal.

Below: A compartment of the Schlieren coach made up for day and night use. Mounted on Fiat Yo362 bogies, the 10-compartment car has two lavatories and washrooms plus an attendant's room with hotplate and refrigerator, and has 100mph capability.

Above: A special configuration of couchette car was styled by DSG, the West German Restaurant and Sleeping Car Co, and built by Waggon Union for the 'TUI Ferien Express' acquired in 1980 by the West German tourist agency combine, Touristik Union International, for its rail-based package tours in Western Europe.

Below: Styled for family occupation, each full-size compartment of the 'TUI Ferien Express' has four full-size berths in the usual lateral arrangement with a fifth for a small child fitted horizontally on one side-wall above window height. By day, as seen here, a child's seat can be made up. Out of view here is the lockable chest of drawers provided in each compartment. Also available are half-width compartments designed for two adults and one child.

New Dawn for the US Passenger Train — or Dusk?

'Trains are the transportation of the future, not the past', said President Carter in the 1980 spring, signing a Bill laying out $75million more on the North-East Corridor project. And the growing eagerness of individual States for a new generation of high-speed passenger trains suggested that in this at least US public opinion was beginning to swing behind him. But has President Reagan signed Amtrak's death warrant?

The about-face in political and public attitudes to the North American passenger train was one of the more unexpected features of the closing 1970s. In 1978 Washington seemed set to rein in quite drastically Amtrak's efforts to rebuild a saleable long-haul operation from the decrepit assets which the passenger carrier was handed to start operation in 1971. But within a year many of the service cuts demanded by the Carter administration had been quashed; more importantly Amtrak's operating subsidy had been sharply increased and its annual investment allowance almost doubled. That was not a generous enough recantation for some individual State Governors. By 1980 some were seriously thinking of raising funds to finance their own intercity services.

When Congress wore down the Nixon administration's antipathy and created Amtrak, the Federal passenger train-operating corporation was not expected to be self-supporting. Nor, though, was Amtrak expected to call for dollars on such a steeply rising scale as it did during the 1970s.

On the one hand Amtrak needed a steadily increased operating subsidy to offset the combined effects of inflation, especially soaring oil prices, and of a mounting bill for the upkeep of worn-out, malfunction-prone equipment (plus the disastrous effects of the USA's two phenomenal winters, 1976-7 and 1978-9). On the other the corporation was desperately in need of accelerated investment to replace its high percentage of obsolete vehicles and thus cut operating costs. Short-changed on both counts, its future looked bleak.

The political issue was whether the USA really needed a passenger carrier which claimed such a small percentage of the country's travel; and which, running by the later 1970s at a loss three-and-a-half times the deficit of its inaugural year, was costing the nation an average of $40 for each American it transported. In its first decade, through one channel or another, Amtrak had absorbed almost $6½billion.

Some railroads were just as keen as long-haul bus operators to see Amtrak go, especially those happily contemplating big increases in bulk coal movement as a result of the energy crisis. Attitudes were typified by the Southern Pacific President's public response early in 1980 to pressure for a new Eugene-Portland passenger operation over his tracks. 'Southern Pacific', he warned, 'isn't enthusiastic about our single-track freight railroad being pressed into service for additional passenger trains, especially since bus services could readily be provided at

Below: One of the Amtrak trains which did not escape the 1979 axe — a train that was born of political log-rolling, the 'Hilltopper' from Washington DC through Virginia and across the Appalachian Mountains into Kentucky: soon after leaving Washington a 3,000hp FP40H B-B rolls the train's two Amcoaches into Alexandria, Va. Chicago's Regional Transit Authority (CTA) operates a 3,200hp version of this locomotive. *Amtrak*

Above: Track machinery, US style: Amtrak was the first customer for this mammoth (devised by the Canron Rail Group of South Carolina), which is employed in NECIP track rebuilding. Some 221ft long and grossing over 100tonnes, the machine removes the old track complete, renews the ballast, lays new sleepers (it can work with either concrete or timber), then mounts new continuous welded rail in place, the complete operation proceeding at an average pace of 1,200ft/h. The machine propels cars fitted with motorised portal gantries that pass the new sleepers down for placing. *Amtrak*

much less expense on the highway that runs right alongside our track'. Santa Fe, too, was strongly resisting the drive of California's Department of Transportation for the daily addition of two return trips to the 128-mile Los Angeles-San Diego service.

Many railroad executives took the view that the passenger train had lost its place and priority on their trunk routes to their crack container/piggyback freights for good. What also irked them was that — some star operators like Union Pacific, Southern Pacific and Santa Fe apart — the railroads were generating a miserably small return of around 2% on their assets. Considering how strapped for investment resources that left them, where was the justice in granting Amtrak, whose passenger trains ran only 10% of the annual train-miles recorded by the railroads' freight trains, as much as a third of the investment the private railroads could finance? And of mulcting the taxpayers for the money, what's more.

In late 1978 the Carter administration decided that a good deal of Amtrak's operation had become an expendable luxury. Early in 1979 it laid before Congress a prescription for drastic surgery. Some 43% of Amtrak's route network should be cut away, reducing the total to 15,700 route-miles. Therewith and through simultaneous reductions of some retained services Amtrak's annual train-miles should be pared by a third (though the economies advocated, it was claimed, would affect only 20% of Amtrak's customers); fares should be adjusted so that every passenger paid at least half his movement costs, instead of an average 37%; and provision of sleeping cars, parlour cars and full meal service should be less prodigal.

The economy programme came on the Congressional agenda just as the Iranian revolution curtailed US petrol availability, gas-hungry motorists were queuing ill-temperdly and many Americans were awakening to the alternative of passenger trains. In June 1979 Amtrak booked almost 25% more passengers than in the same month of 1978. In California, most highly motorised of all States, the San Diego-Los Angeles trains registered more passengers per month than Santa Fe had when it was operating them in the all-time US rail passenger travel peak period of World War II. Amtrak reservation lines were choked with callers and a number of trans were sold out two weeks and more in advance of running.

For a time Congress seemed unmoved. Then it stalled execution. And finally Amtrak's friends in both House and Senate won a sheaf of reprieves by astute politicking.

In the spring a Washington reporter had quoted the opinion of the House of Representatives' Democratic Party leader as typical of many Congressmen at that time. This politician was prepared to accept his State's share of Amtrak cuts for the good of the national budget's balance. But, he warned the journalist, 'if one political train goes back in, I'll sure as hell get mine.'

Amtrak's moles played on this self-interest. Sagely they did not campaign for rejection of the whole package, but went to bat on behalf of one or two individual services. Successful on these, they pressed for retention of one or two more. Before long one legislator after another grew paranoic that his constituents were missing out on the reprieves, and those with seniority muscle had little difficulty in coercing a majority to vote their pet trains back on to the map. One influential committee chairman in the Senate didn't need a word of debate to get his requirement compliantly accepted. At the end of the day a House amendment to forget the whole closure plan and freeze the existing route structure intact narrowly failed, 214 to 197. A similar proposal, excluding only one notoriously 'political' train, the Washington-Roanoke-Catlettsburg 'Hilltopper', got as close to Senate approval as a tied vote.

So in the autumn of 1979 the 'Hilltopper' went. So did the Chicago-Miami 'Floridian', the Chicago-Houston 'Lone Star', the New York-Kansas 'National Limited' and the Chicago-Seattle 'North Coast Hiawatha'. But instead of 43%, Amtrak's route-map was trimmed by no more than 17% — and to offset that curtailment it was to start up a brand-new service, the 'Desert Wind' between Ogden and Los Angeles. Several important routes which the Department of Transportation had marked for the axe were saved, such as Washington-New

Left: Amtrak style in new station architecture in Florida: the entrance hall of Miami. *Amtrak*

Below: A '403(b)' service: sponsored by the state of Pennsylvania, the Philadelphia-Pittsburgh 'Pennsylvanian' reintroduced day service over the Conrail main line for the first time since Amtrak's youth in the spring of 1980. Formed of Amcoaches and an Amcafe, the train rounds the Pennsylvania's famed Horseshoe Curve past a preserved sample of the route's onetime steam passenger protagonist, a Pennsylvania RR K4s Pacific. *Amtrak*

Above: Amtrak has been spending $43.6million on reconstruction of the former Pennsylvania RR passenger car servicing depot at Chicago and on re-equipment of the 48-acre site with the most modern cleaning and maintenance apparatus. When the scheme is finished in 1981 the depot will take care of all but the heaviest overhauls of about a third of Amtrak's cars and an adjoining traction depot will look after about 40% of the Amtrak locomotive stud. *Amtrak*

Orleans, Chicago-Los Angeles via the Santa Fe and those crossing to Vancouver and Montreal in Canada.

So long as Amtrak sustained the traffic increases of mid-1979, the slimmed-down network looked secure, because Congress had agreed new criteria of minimum ridership and maximum subsidy for each service's survival. Most pleasing of all, Congress substantially increased Amtrak's overall operating subsidy, guaranteeing the figure for the next two years, and upped its capital investment from $130million to $230million a year, a level that was assured for three years.

Congress built another unexpected financial provision into its 1979 legislation. The founding Amtrak Acts had included a clause — 403 (b) — offering a tapering Federal grant to any States prepared to put up their own money towards additional trains not deemed a case for full Federal subsidy. Illinois, Michigan, Minnesota, Missouri, New York, Pennsylvania and California had all taken advantage of this in the first decade of Amtrak.

In 1979 Congress implicitly invited the States to make good some of the national cutbacks. It set up a special $20million fund for support of '403 (b)' trains in 1980, rising to $29million in 1981, and arranged for Washington to absorb more of the start-up bill. In 1979 only $7.5million went in Federal support of '403 (b)' trains from the fund covering Amtrak operations. Federal money was now on offer for 80% of the first year's costs of a '403 (b)' service, 65% of the second year's and 50% thereafter.

Very large sums of Federal money have been flowing into the Northeast Corridor Improvement Programme (NECIP), the refettling of the trunk route from Boston through New York to Philadelphia, Baltimore and Washington for accelerated intercity service. Everywhere else Amtrak runs its trains over railroad-owned and operated tracks, but in this corridor it is master of the infrastructure except for tracts owned by regional transport authorities such as the NYMTA. It got the property on knockdown terms in the wake of the Penn-Central collapse of 1970, when Congress took the view that because the route was so busy with passenger trains — notably the high-speed 'Metroliner' emus inaugurated under President Johnson's High Speed Ground Transportation project — the otherwise standard roles should be reversed. Amtrak should in this case be the landlord, and the new Federally-supported corporation set up to reshape the area's bankrupt freight system (Conrail) the tenant operator of the freight trains.

The NECIP was launched on a budget of $1.75billion and slated for completion by 1981. Miscalculation, muddled direction through the involvement of too many agencies and resultant infighting between them, and inflation have made nonsense of both estimates. Completion is now improbable before 1983 at the earliest and the budget has had to be inflated to $2.5billion. Even so, one major item of the original concept has had to be sacrificed. The route is still to be newly electrified at 25kV 60Hz ac from the extremity of the existing electrification at New Haven, north of New York, to Boston. But matching conversion of the ex-Pennsylvania 12kV 25Hz ac catenary between New York and Washington is out unless and until traffic demand outstrips the current supply capacity of the existing electrification system.

This is not necessarily a body-blow. The railway scene at the southern end of the corridor is bafflingly complicated, not only by the overlapping of Amtrak and Conrail operations but by the

Amtrak's Superliners
Above: First train to be re-equipped with the trouble-wracked 'Superliners' was the 'Empire Builder', here heading out of Chicago behind an FP40H on its 2,281-mile run to Seattle. Completion of the order was delayed by legal wrangles, when, in the spring of 1980, car-builders Pullman-Standard (who have now abandoned rail passenger car construction) claimed that no contract to build the final 35 of the 284-car fleet was ever signed, so that it was not obliged to build them. The company sued for start-up work and also for extra cost incurred through Amtrak's design changes during construction of the remainder. The vexed 35 cars included the projected 25 'Sightseer' cafe-lounges, with full upper-level armchair observation saloon.
(See also pp36-37.)

ntrusion of short-haul trains sponsored by more than one Regional Transportation Authority. Over the 103 miles between Philadelphia and Harrisburg, for instance, Conrail men crew South-East Pennsylvania Transportation Authority (SEPTA)-owned trains over Amtrak rails. Arrangements are just as ntricate between Philadelphia and Trenton. Re-electrification in this territory is arguably best left until everyone involved has a clear-cut idea of the future shape of its operation and network — and, of course, until Amtrak has got some experience of 60Hz technology between New Haven and Boston.

The Boston-New York-Washington belt is the most densely-trafficked belt in the USA. With the marginal exception of trains on the popular vacation path from the eastern seaboard to Florida it is the only route on which Amtrak's trains consistently meet their running costs. Nevertheless, other States grumble at the disproportionate amount of Federal money being lavished on the NECIP.

For instance, Adriana Gianturco, the dynamic lady who heads California's newly rail-orientated Department of Transportation (Caltrans), protests that around 20million people, almost four times as many as the NECIP affects, live in her State's southern coastal corridor, the 500-odd miles from Sacramento and the San Francisco Bay Area to Los Angeles and San Diego. She wants to see it served by a rail route upgraded for 110mph on straight track and reckons the project just as deserving of a Federal aid programme. Why should California's tax dollars be poured on an every-increasing scale into the North-East Corridor on the other side of the country?

State feeling of this sort prompted two influential Congressmen to follow up the 1979 reprieve of Amtrak with a drive for funds to reinvigorate rail passenger service in other US population corridors. At Congressional request Amtrak and the DoT's Federal Railroad Administration listed 11 corridors where they reckoned traffic might potentially repay investment — principally in the Mid-West and on the West-Coast — and Congressmen filled out the list with seven of their own predelictions.

Amtrak and the FRA picked their corridors for development on the bases of aptness for upgrading for passenger speeds of 79mph (the limit permissible under Interstate Commerce Commission statutes without availability of continuous cab signalling) or 110mph maximum, and operating capacity for three, six or 12 pairs of passenger trains daily, also with an eye to local availability and price of petrol. At the time of their research the impression was that petrol scarcity was more influential in persuading people to take the train than the rising price of fuel.

The Congressional hearings concluded that in any development, frequency of service should be the priority objective, not three-figure speed and the high capital cost that would incur. Experience showed that an extra three to six trains on a given route were likely to conjure up 70% more rail users, but 12 each way daily would probably generate a 110% increase. At the latter level of service, if it were attainable in each of the 13 corridors recommended by the Government agencies, the nation might save just over 50million gallons of oil a year. In

Left: Day-coach saloon: the car also includes four unisex 'rest rooms' and a ladies' retiring room.

Below: Economy bedroom, in which the two seats form a lower sleeping berth and an upper berth is folded into the wall above the window. The room contains a cupboard and storage space for two suitcases.

Bottom: Extending the full width of the car is the family bedroom, able to accommodate three adults and two children; by night the seats make up to a double bed and one full-length and two children's berths are unfolded from the transversal and side walls.

79mph maximum trains the travellers would move at a consumption rate of 110 passenger-miles/gal — not quite as efficiently as in a bus, though, as the road transport industry was claiming 129 passenger-miles/gal on average — compared with a figure of 35 in private cars.

The final criterion was the capital cost of fettling up track and signalling for a more intensive passenger service. When that factor was injected, corridors threaded by already well-manicured and signalled tracks like those of the Union Pacific gained points. At the end of the discussion the most promising corridors were reckoned to be: Los Angeles-San Diego; Los Angeles-Las Vegas; New York-Albany-Buffalo; and Philadelphia-Atlantic City.

A Bill to make $55million available for feasibility studies of enhanced passenger service in these corridors winged easily through the House of Representatives early in 1980. The Senate was not nearly so convinced of the case. Nor was the Carter administration, and at one time it looked as though the provision would be limited to a beggarly $5million. But the House and Senate eventually compromised at $38million and President Carter signed the Bill for that amount at the end of May 1980.

This and the DoTs grudging support for Amtrak was not good enough for some State Governments in the USA. They were fretting not only over the remorseless rise of petrol prices and the threatening exhaustion of oil supplies, but also over the effects of the Carter administration's de-regulation of American airlines. Some towns and cities which had relied on air transport for long-distance access were likely to lose it because they were at best marginally profitable places for scheduled service.

California's impatience has already been touched upon. Here the Los Angeles-San Diego operation mentioned earlier heads the list of '403 (b)' triumphs so far. At its 1976 launch Amtrak ran three trains daily in this 128-mile corridor, but since then the service has been doubled under the '403 (b)' provisions and in 1979 it moved more than a million passengers. By the summer of 1979 more than 80% of the operating costs of these additional '403 (b)' trains was already being met out of revenue — and one of the three pairs was actually in the black. Hence Caltrans' natural eagerness to intensify the service still more.

Easier said than done. In the first place, Amtrak is not yet so flush with traction and passenger stock or anywhere near it, that

Left and below: Upper-deck rooms include de luxe bedrooms with private toilets. Some of these adjoin and are separated by a partition which can be opened up to create a suite.

t can extemporise additional trains at will. But more mportantly, Caltrans' pressure for a seventh and even an eighth air of San Diego-Los Angeles trains made a crunch issue of rack capacity, because the Santa Fe route followed by the ervice is mostly single track. 'It's finally gotten to the point vhere our operating people say we cannot tolerate any dditional passenger trains', a Santa Fe Vice-President was eported as protesting in the US trade journal *Railway Age*. 'The ind of service they're talking about isn't compatible with an xisting railroad operation.' Already it was alleged, Santa Fe vas forced to do a good deal of its track maintenance on this oute at night under floodlights. However, Santa Fe did ventually yield to California State pressure and a seventh San Diego-Los Angeles service started in the 1980 autumn.

With some railroads Amtrak has been sporadically at oggerheads over track space for its trains ever since its creation. In 1977, for instance, differences with Missouri Pacific erupted n an Amtrak threat to sue over the persistent halting of the passenger carrier's 'Inter-American' in a lonely Texas loop, ostensibly to allow passage to a Mopac freight in the opposite direction. But, alleged Amtrak, the freight was a phantom train that never showed up before the 'Inter-American' was eventually let back on to the single-track main line. Early in 1980 the US Department of Justice did actually file suit against the Southern Pacific on Amtrak's behalf, alleging that SP was deliberately sidetracking Amtrak's New Orleans-Los Angeles 'Sunset Limited' in favour of its own freights — a practice allowable only in an operating emergency under the founding Amtrak legislation. As a result, it was claimed, the 'Sunset Limited' failed to make a single on-time run for six months.

In the spring of 1980 the New Jersey Congressmen chairing the House of Representatives' Transportation Sub-Committee, James Florio, introduced a Bill that would impose drastic financial penalties on railroads failing to operate Amtrak's trains punctually, starting from a 75% on time floor in 1981 and tightening to a 85% requirement by 1985. In the same legislation Florio sought to authorise the Federal Railroad Administration of the DoT to compel railroads to maintain track to the standards prevailing at Amtrak's birth, and also to force railroads to accept additional Amtrak passenger trains unless they had a cogent case for refusing on grounds of capacity fully

Left and below: Superliners have an 18-table, 72-seat saloon on the upper deck and an air-conditioned, all-electric kitchen on the lower, with dumb-waiter service between the two levels. *Amtrak*

Right: One of Amtrak's 'Turboliners', based on French Railways' RTG design, skirts the Hudson River en route to New York. *Amtrak*

occupied by freight trains (another Congressman was seeking to have the railroads obliged to take on extra Amtrak workings whatever the existing occupation of their tracks).

Meanwhile, however, the SP court case had jolted a number of railroads into reviewing their treatment of Amtrak trains. By then, though, some of the recalcitrants were softening anyway, realising that passenger trains sailing under '403 (b)' colours could hand them some track and signalling modernisation at public expense. It is thanks to State support, for instance, that the USA at the start of the 1980s regained its first 100mph trackage since abortive launch of the New York-Washington 'Metroliner' emus at that speed.

In 1974 New York State persuaded its electors to approve a $250million bond issue for rail improvement. Of that some $43million has gone on relaying and resignalling stretches of the 437-miles from New York via Albany to Buffalo, with the aim by 1984 of cutting the transit time for the whole journey from the present best of just under 8hr to 6hr and trebling passenger business. At the end of 1979 the first 28-mile stretch west of Albany was fit for Turboliners, the Rohr-built versions of the French RGP gtmu design which supply almost all the daytime service on this route, to hit 110mph for the first time in their Amtrak careers. With another $500million bond issue just voted New York intends to pursue this upgrading steadily where track alignment is conducive and the route is not badly plagued by level crossings.

In 1980 six states — California, Illinois, Oregon, Pennsylvania, Massachussetts and Virginia — were queuing for fresh '403 (b)' trains, 24 in all, and Michigan had already filed an application for 1981. But some States had much more spectacular development in mind.

A historic quirk of Ohio's constitution debars it from bidding for '403 (b)' train service, but for several years past the State has been scheming its own high-speed rail passenger system. By the start of the 1980s Ohio had already laid out $1million on preliminary research and planning, including buying-in consultancy from Japanese National Railways. The Ohio State Representative who was instrumental in creating the Ohio Rail Transportation Authority in 1975 is convinced that an intercity network linking eight of Ohio's major conurbations could be adequately financed — and that includes Ohio's own research centre — out of a modest sales tax; and also that once in operation the network would pay its way. In the spring of 1980 Ohio took the next step of voting $1.3million to plan its own high-speed test track, to construct which it will probably spend a further $63million in 1981.

Elsewhere the Texas Railroad Commission has had talks with the Japanese (so has Illinois) and is mulling over the possibility of high-speed passenger service between Dallas, Houston and San Antonio. Florida is investigating a plan to interlink its major cities and airports by electric trains. And Michigan, Pennsylvania and Illinois have joined Ohio in a high speed rail information-sharing compact.

So widespread is State interest, in fact, that for their annual conference of 1980, held in Denver, Colo., the National Governors Association invited the railwaymen and railway industries of Britain, France, Germany and Japan to set up their technological stalls and discuss their wares with interested State Governors. The Japanese and the British, one should add, already have consultancy jobs with the Federal Railroad Administration on the NECIP.

It is probably superfluous to emphasise that at this stage the State activity was more significant of changed political attitudes to the intercity passenger train than of imminent physical development. Even Amtrak's most passionate supporters were sanguine of solid moves to create European-style intercity services in the really promising US corridors before the mid-1980s.

Meanwhile, Amtrak was looking better than at any time since its foundation. In 1979 it recorded 21.5million passengers, 14% more than in 1978. And because on average each of them travelled further and were made to pay more per mile by successive fare increases, the corporation met 41.5% of its costs out of revenue, as against only 38.5% the previous year. For a gamut of reasons ranging from antiquated vehicles to its dependence on the operating goodwill of its host railroads and their staffs its performance was still patchy, however; that was reflected in a retrogression of its on-time record from the 91% level claimed in 1978 to 82%.

The equipment problem, though it was still costing Amtrak too many failures and in some areas lost business for lack of cars, was getting less acute. The first of the 284 new bi-level 'Superliners', so long delayed by labour troubles at their makers, Pullman-Standard, and some technical snags, emerged late in 1978. The following autumn they premiered their transcontinental role on the Chicago-Seattle 'Empire Builder' (a train stepped up from thrice-weekly to daily operation in the summer of 1980). During 1980 the new cars transfigured successively the 'Pioneer', the 'Southwest Limited', the 'Coast Starlight', the 'Sunset Limited' and the 'San Francisco Zephyr'; they also formed the newborn 'Desert Wind'.

The 'Superliners' and the single-level 'Amfleet' cars Amtrak had Budd build in the 'Metroliner' body-shell for shorter-haul, daytime services are fitted for electrical train-heating. The domes, diners, sleepers and parlours which Amtrak took over from railroads in 1971 were, of course, steam-heated — which was more and more an operational irritant as Amtrak modernised its diesel fleet with units fitted for head-end supply of electrical train auxiliaries.

Many routes in the eastern USA could not accept the dome cars of the pre-Amtrak streamliners and are barred to the new Superliners. Unable for years to finance new custom-built cars for their really long-haul trains, Amtrak had to embark on conversion of the inherited cars to electric power. In the late 1970s this programme was accelerated. One outcome, in the 1979-80 winter, was a long-overdue reinvigoration of two historic New York-Chicago services, the 'Lake Shore Limited' which keeps an ember of 'Twentieth Century Limited' memory glowing on the old New York Central route, and the one time Pennsylvannia flag train, the 'Broadway Limited'. Thanks to substantial Conrail progress in rebuilding the neglected tracks it inherited, moreover, both were confidently accelerated in the spring of 1980, though the quicker schedules were still hours away from the New York Central and Pennsylvania best.

In the spring of 1980 Amtrak finally had the resources to order 150 more single-level cars for its eastern and southern routes. Yet again Budd was to be the builder, because Amtrak had decided that to get the quickest possible delivery the Amfleet design would be used yet again, though with interior layout and auxiliaries refashioned for long-haul operation.

Escalating oil prices have nullified the energy consumption advantages of the French-pattern Turboliners, which cover some Mid-West routes such as the Chicago-Milwaukee corridor as well as the New York State services mentioned earlier. However, the French have shown how to mitigate the fuel cost penalty by replacing each set's Turmo IIIF 1,100hp turbines with a single 1,160hp Turmo X11s turbine; that cuts oil consumption by almost a third for a negligible addition to journey times. Consequently the Turboliners have a continuing Amtrak role. But not the ill-starred, ambitiously innovatory United Aircraft Turbotrains, which were laid aside, hopefully for sale, in 1979.

Decelerated since their inauguration, the New York-Washington electrified route's hourly Metroliner emus remain the USA's fastest trains, averaging just under or over 90mph on four daily timings over the 68.4miles between Baltimore and Wilmington. But after putting about half the 61-car Metroliner fleet through the substantial modifications assessed as necessary to eradicate the last of their original weaknesses and extend their usefulness well into the age of a refurbished Corridor infrastructure, Amtrak balked at the cost of around $1million a vehicle for the reconstruction.

The main reason was the now apparent ability of locomotive-

Above: One of the refurbished 'Metroliner' electric multiple-units in its latest Amtrak livery; the expensively modified cars are distinguished from the original by the unsightly new equipment-housing bulges added to their roofs. *Amtrak*

Above right: 'Mighty Mouse' — the immediate US nickname, it seems, of the new 6,100hp Class AEM-7 electric to ASEA's class Swedish thyristor-controlled design which GM's Electromotive Division is building for Amtrak's North-East Corridor service. *Amtrak*

Right: One of the two Canadian-built, automatic body-tilting LRC train-sets which Amtrak has on two-year lease, and which may answer the need for higher speed on the New York-Boston sector of the North-East Corridor. *Amtrak*

hauled lightweight trains to equal Metroliner capability within the constraints of the Corridor track and signalling. That had come about through Amtrak's choice of a multi-voltage version of the Swedish thrysistor-controlled Rc4 Bo-Bo to supersede the last of the very elderly Pennsylvania GG1s and take over senior role from the disappointing E60CP locomotives Amtrak had bought earlier as potential GG1 replacements. The first 6,100hp AEM-7 — or 'Mighty Mouse' as Amtrak men had already dubbed the lightweight locomotive assembled by Budd (as a General Motors sub-contractor) to the Swedish firm ASEA's basic design — made its revenue-earning debut between New York and Washington in May 1980.

Some question marks are poised over choice of equipment for the less comfortably-aligned Corridor sector between New York and Boston. The target schedule of 3hr 40min set for the 231.8miles between the two cities after completion of the NECIP has never sounded impressive and in 1980 the signs suggested that Amtrak was minded to shorten it by recourse to automatic body-tilting. The immediate candidate for the job was likely to be the LRC created in Canada by Bombardier-MLW, but Amtrak also commissioned Budd to retrofit Amfleet cars with a tilt system of Budd's devising, and it was eyeing Japanese passive and Swedish active tilt mechanisms as well.

The pair of LRC train-sets on which Amtrak had taken out a two-year lease/purchase agreement (cost price of each power car-five trailer set was likely to be $4.5million) came off the Canadian production line in the spring of 1980, ahead of the strike-delayed order of 22 power cars and 50 trailers for Canada's own Via Rail. The first Amtrak LRC began trial in the North East Corridor between New Haven, Conn and Providence, RI, in July 1980. Amtrak originally bespoke the LRCs for its Vancouver-Seattle-Portland service, but now appears to see the automatic tilt-body concept as the answer to the crying need of higher speed between New York and Boston than the NECIP will make possible for orthodox vehicles.

In the autumn of 1980 Amtrak eased the two LRC sets gently into public service on New Haven-Boston and Boston-New York services, initially under a 90mph limit. But private tests conducted in August with the trailers using both the LRC power car and an AEM-7 electric locomotive as traction had Amtrak hopeful of running the LRCs publicly at up to 125mph by the following spring. On these 1980 trials the cars performed satisfactorily with a cant deficiency of 15in, taking a previously 50mph-restricted curve comfortably at 76mph. That reinforced belief that for conventionally-suspended vehicles the historic 3in cant deficiency limit applied to US passenger trains (it has been unchanged since 1914) could be relaxed to at least 5in for a useful saving of minutes in North-East Corridor journey times.

As 1981 dawned Amtrak needed all the goods news it could contrive. President Reagan's new men were advocating abandonment of all its long-haul routes as a lost transportation cause, even though Superliners had added 50% to the 'Empire Builder's' ridership and halved its per-passenger-mile loss. Congressmen, however, had to be convinced; and they had already had a taste of voters' outraged reaction to the previous Amtrak slimming plan. That kindled hope that Reagan's 1981 Budget proposal to end all operating subsidies by 1985 would not get by Congress unscathed. If it was accepted, then the future of Amtrak outside one or two inter-city corridors was bleaker than at any time in its brief history.

901
901
Amtrak
901
Amtrak

Amtrak

Family or Economy Size?

Above: As more US State administrations incline towards the sponsorship and subsidisation of selected short-haul passenger services as well as Inter-City operation a market opens up for a successor to the Budd RDC diesel railcars of the 1950s. Some 350 of these were built (a number of them for foreign railways) and those which survive are at the end of their life-span, if not beyond it. Budd itself has evolved a contender, the SPV-2000, which is an adaptation of its Metroliner body-shell mounted on Budd air-suspension bogies and claimed to be capable of arrangement as a 120mph Inter-City vehicle as well as a rural servant or high-density commuter car. The SPV-2000's first customer was Connecticut, which bought 13 for Amtrak's operation, principally between New Haven and Springfield.

Left: For this Connecticut service the SPV-2000 is equipped to almost the same standard as the Amfleet cars on Amtrak's Inter-City routes — reclining seats with chair-back tables, carpeted floors, and individual reading lights.

Right: A sharply contrasting vehicle vying with the orthodox Budd railcar design is the LEV — Leyland Experimental Vehicle — which mates the advanced two-axle suspension developed by British Rail's R&D organisation with a standard Leyland single-deck bus body and a six-cylinder, 220hp Leyland diesel engine. Early in 1980 the US Federal Railroad Administration had the prototype LEV 1 — shown diagrammatically — imported for some 1,500 miles of test running in the Boston area. It then ordered a prototype of its own, a 56-seater grossing only 19.8tonnes with a 15.3m-long body, which was built by D. Wickham of Ware and exported to the US in October 1980 and seen here. During exhaustive trials on BR, the LEV 1 prototype was satisfactorily tested at up to 80mph under its own power.

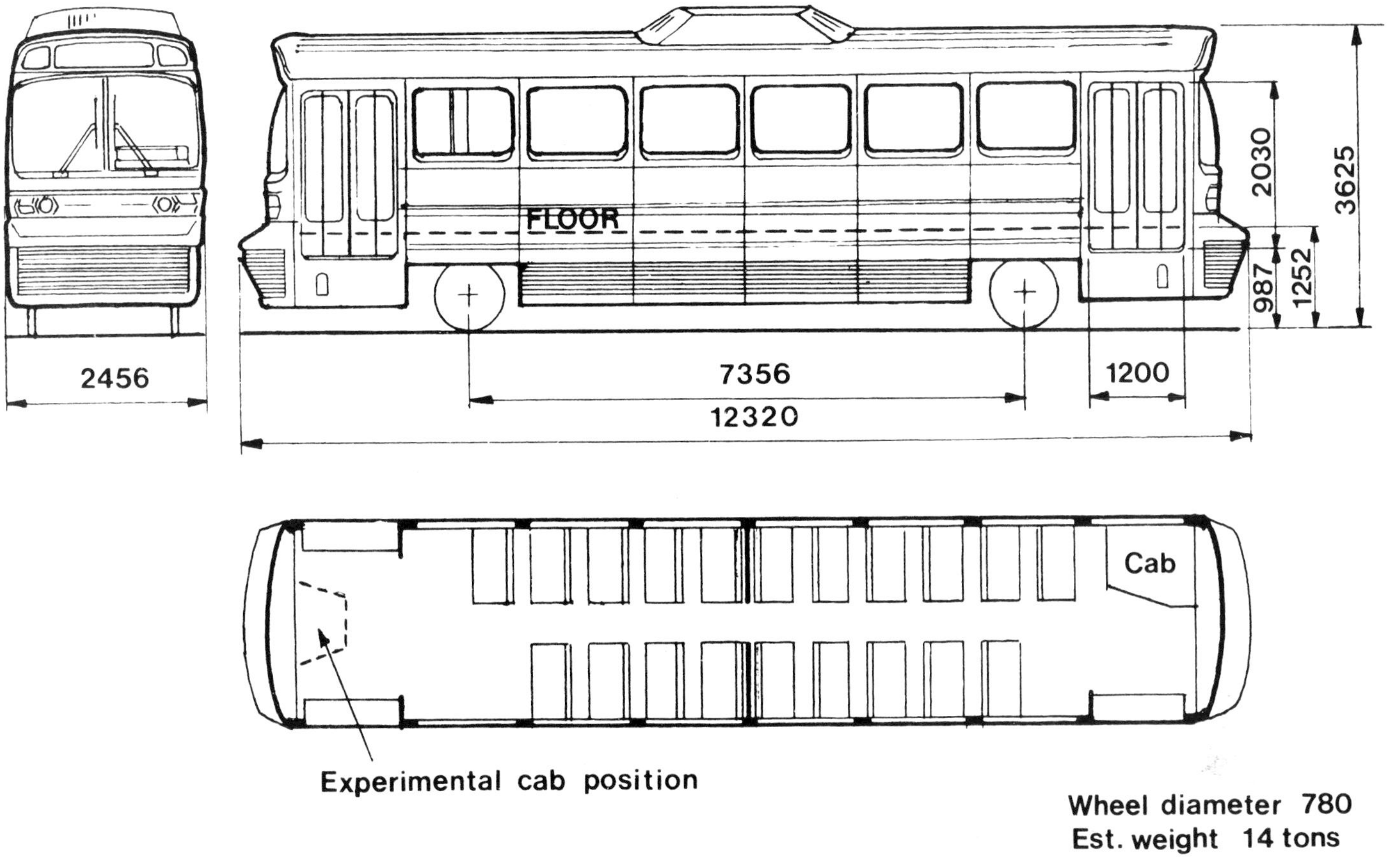
FLOOR
2030
3625
987
1252
2456
7356
1200
12320
Cab
Experimental cab position
Wheel diameter 780
Est. weight 14 tons

Zurich Adds a New Dimension to Europe's Rail-Air Links

With the world belatedly roused to the need of effective city station-airport rail links, the Swiss open their main airports to direct Inter-City rail travel from every part of the Swiss Federal's trunk system.

'Intermodal' has been a catchword of transportation planning since the 1950s. But for the passenger there have mostly been only two modes in it — road and rail.

For the first two post-war decades most European railwaymen were wary of having rail rub shoulders too intimately with air transport. That was the period when they doggedly clung to a belief that luxury trains could keep a grip on a respectable share of the premium transcontinental travel market. As for public authority planners, even if they foresaw the wide-body jet age, they did not grasp the size of the air travel surge it would generate.

Consequently a number of opportunities to mitigate urban road congestion by installing attractive, mass rail access to city airports were fumbled or missed altogether. The rail link with London's Heathrow was a blatant example.

The benefit of a main-line rail-link is now patent at London's other chief airport, Gatwick. That fortunately developed in the inter-war years alongside the Southern Railway route from London to the South Coast and the SR had the vision to build an adjoining station in 1935. Today half the rapidly expanding traffic of the airport travels to and from it by BR's 15min-interval electric multiple-unit service, which links Gatwick Airport station and the London Victoria terminus in a 36-39min transit time (the trains also ply throughout the night at hourly frequency).

In the late 1970s BR plugged Gatwick into its national network through a new Manchester-Crewe-Birmingham Brighton service via Gatwick Airport station, operated twice daily and aimed primarily at holidaymakers taking the package tour flights that dominate Gatwick's activity. And in the summer of 1980 BR inaugurated a cross-country diesel multiple-unit service between Gatwick Airport and Reading, opening up a much quicker access for air travellers emanating from South Wales and the West Country on BR's 'Inter-City 125' trains, with only a change of platform at Reading to be negotiated instead of a traipse across London from Paddington to Victoria station.

The growth potential of this airport traffic — largely stimulated, one must admit, by the British Airports Authority's anxiety to shift more of the London air traffic load from Heathrow, but to some extent a factor of Gatwick's convenient rail access — determined BR to allocate £4½millions of their cramped investment resources to streamlining the interchange arrangements between station and main air terminal in the late 1970s. In 1979 3million passengers used the Gatwick rail link, more than half the airport's total clientele.

Heathrow could have been just as smoothly and easily reached by rail, not just from London but from the provinces. In the mid-1960s BR worked up a scheme to widen the exit from West London down the Staines-Reading line so as to make track space for express emus that would branch off near Feltham on to a new line beneath the Heathrow runways that was to terminate below the air terminal complex. Passengers could have checked in at air offices in the London terminal and had their baggage containerised to Heathrow, where it would have been ferried straight from the rail platform to their flight.

But the Government of the day opted for the low-cost alternative — extension of London Transport's Piccadilly Line from Hounslow to a Heathrow terminal. So although Heathrow is some 15miles from London's West End as against Gatwick's 25miles, the rail journey to the former takes 6-9min longer, and in all-stations Tube trains with quite inadequate room for

ggage. Access to Heathrow from BR's Intercity network has be by special bus links, from Woking, Reading and Watford. he final penalty of the short-sighted 1960s economy is that, if a hannel Tunnel is built, the chance has been lost of creating an leal, all-purpose international station in West London where oth Heathrow and Channel Tunnel trains could exchange affic with BR APTs from and to the North of England and cotland.

What could and should have been at Heathrow has been emonstrated by the Swiss at Zurich. There, in the spring of 980, a rail link was opened which has stitched a substantial umber of key stations on the Swiss Federal main-line system traight into the international airline network.

Well before the 1950s the Swiss Federal had been ccumulating a portfolio of schemes for the remodelling and nodernisation of its system in the Zurich area. Expanding assenger traffic, short- as well as long-haul, was taxing the omplex of flat junctions outside the main station more and nore severely, and the aggravations were complicated by the eversals which the station's dead end enforced on practically all assenger traffic. On the vital east-west exit from the city to Baden, en route to Basle or to Berne and Geneva, extra track capacity was desperately needed to segregate disparate flows of raffic, plus one massive, highly mechanised yard to concentrate he area's wagonload marshalling.

The essential needs were embodied in a comprehensive plan of 1954. Much of this has already been executed, such as four-racking of the westward route out of the city as far as Dietikon; ay-out of the big Limmatal yard just beyond Dietikon; upgrading of subsidiary routes so as to keep Limmatal's freight out of the regular-interval passenger service's path; and construction of a new flying junction line that enables through freight to North-East Switzerland to traverse the city without reversal. But in 1980 some major projects were still unstarted — above all the *S-Bahn* project to eliminate the reversal of part of the city's busy commuter train service in the main station by burrowing a line from beside the terminus, the so-called Zurichberg Tunnel, through a new underground Museumstrasse station in the city centre straight to the busy commuter route which hugs the north shore of Lake Zurich to the latter's eastern tip at Rapperswil.

As the 1960s progressed the Swiss Federal recognised that the country's principal airports were gradually supplanting frontier rail stations as the main point of international entry and departure for certain sectors of the passenger market. So a Zurich Airport link was added to the 1954 plan.

Then market research revealed that 55% of the business travellers using Zurich Airport were making for or coming from more distant regions, as were 45% of its optional passengers. A significant proportion of these air travellers were from as far away as Austria, since Austrian Airlines has so far eschewed any intercontinental air service. That decided the SBB to knit the putative Zurich Airport rail service into its nationwide intercity timetable, the more so because of the potential size of the longer-distance travel to and from the airport; the busiest in Switzerland, it handled 8million passengers in 1979, so that around 4million were possible clients for rail journeys of quite remunerative distance. Passengers apart, there was additional promise in the airport's 16,000 workers.

Planning of the airport link began in the summer of 1969. Construction was launched without any certainty of public financial support. This did not crystallise until 1974, when the two chambers of the Swiss Parliament authorised a grant of some £25millions and a further £5millions was proferred by the Zurich Canton. The railway itself has footed the greater part of the ultimate bill, which including major layout remodelling and very sophisticated resignalling at Zurich Oerlikon and Effretikon, on either side of the new airport loop, will run out at around £125millions.

A single-track branch looping off the main line from Zurich to Winterthur and St Gallen passed within a mile or so of the airport terminal, but that was not close enough for the intermodal convenience in mind. Only the loop's start and finish were adapted as infrastructure for a new double-track route that dives beneath the airport, diverging from the original Kloten branch in a burrowing junction at Opfikon and rejoining its alignment 4miles further on in the neighbourhood of Bassersdorf.

Just over three-quarters of the entirely new infrastructure is in tunnel, where the track is laid on a concrete slab foundation to simplify maintenance. Besides the tunnelling, the contrivance of new flying junctions at Oerlikon to eliminate path conflict

Left: A pioneer rail-air link undergoing further development costing £4½million at the start of the 1980s is British Rail's between Gatwick Airport and London Victoria. Here one of BR Southern Region's 4VEG electric multiple-units specially branded 'Rapid City Link Gatwick-London' leaves a Gatwick Airport station shrouded in scaffolding in March 1980. It is likely that push-pull trains, formed of adapted Mk 2d coaches and powered by electro-diesel locomotive will be introduced on a 15min-interval non-stop Gatwick Airport-London service in 1984. *Les Bertram*

Right: An SBB Type Re4/4II pauses at Zurich Airport station on a push-pull train for Zurich Hbf. Note the multi-coloured artwork on the retaining walls which contrasts very effectively with the fluorescently-lit dark blue of the remainder of the underground structure.

between the various traffic streams heading north and north-eastward out of Zurich and the costly construction of the airport station itself, the scheme incurred a good deal of other prestressed concrete bridgework, a new station at Bassersdorf and a new electronic signal centre at Oerlikon.

The Oerlikon centre commands operations all the way from the outskirts of the city at Oberhausenried, on the double-track Wipkingen exit from the main station in the Winterthur direction which is the most densely-trafficked in Switzerland, to the extremity of the airport loop at Hürlisten, plus the single-line Kloten branch, the original Winterthur main line between Oerlikon and Hürlisten, and the entrances to the Schaffhausen line and Limmatal yard which converge in the Oerlikon area. All main running lines between Oerlikon and Effretikon have been reversibly signalled for operational flexibility.

Scheduled operation, however, is based on rule-of-the-road running, since normally route-setting is automatic, activated by the Digital Equipment Corporation PDP11/34 computers which are the kernel of the centre's technology. The centre's operators, seated at VDU-equipped desks with Integra keyboard panels in front of a panoramic illuminated diagram, intervene only if the working goes awry, if the computers are confronted by a train description they cannot trace in their working timetable data bank, of if an unscheduled operation has to be initiated within the control area. The Integra equipment can store operators' commands it is prevented from executing immediately by the state of an interlocking. All Solari-type train indicators on station platforms are activated by the Oerlikon centre's computers.

The four tracks of the Airport station are paired around two wide platforms, the surface of which is at the Swiss Federal's 48cm height above rail level recently adopted for regional express routes, not the traditional 30cm. The dominant colour scheme of this rail vault, the floor of which is 18m below the surface and 12m below the ground water table, is a noble dark blue, which ideally softens the lunar-white fluorescent lighting. But the side walls are white, with some striking overlays in scrolls of varied and vivid colour mixes; the designs of these enamelled sheets were commissioned from professional artists, who have achieved a brilliantly satisfying complement to the dark shade of the rest of the subterranean structure.

The platforms are monitored by 16 closed-circuit TV cameras with the aim — over-optimistic, experience suggests — of running them without inspectors (unusually in Continental practice, train conductors have the responsibility for waving their trains away). To help passengers find their train accommodation unaided the Swiss Federal has followed recent German Federal practice in the latter's reshaping of its Inter-City service. The Airport station platforms have been sectioned by key letters — A, B, C, etc — and the individual train formation displays on each platform show in which lettered stretch of the platform individual cars will come to rest (the information is also repeated over loudspeakers before each Inter-City train's arrival). In the first months of operation, however, the Swiss Federal was compelled by a volley of criticism from bemused passengers to introduce some supervisory staff both on the platform and on the next floor up, a cavernous concourse flanked by railway ticket and information offices and by a beguiling array of shops, snack-bar and restaurant.

Above that is the main plaza of the terminal complex on the threshold of the airline business area. The various levels are connected by a battery of lifts and escalators. Negotiation of the latter is no problem for baggage-encumbered travellers because the Swiss Federal has procured from a German firm a highly ingenious design of luggage trolley with a serrated underframe fitting that easily and firmly engages the steps of an escalator as they shape into a flight.

But some railborne passengers are not bothered by luggage.

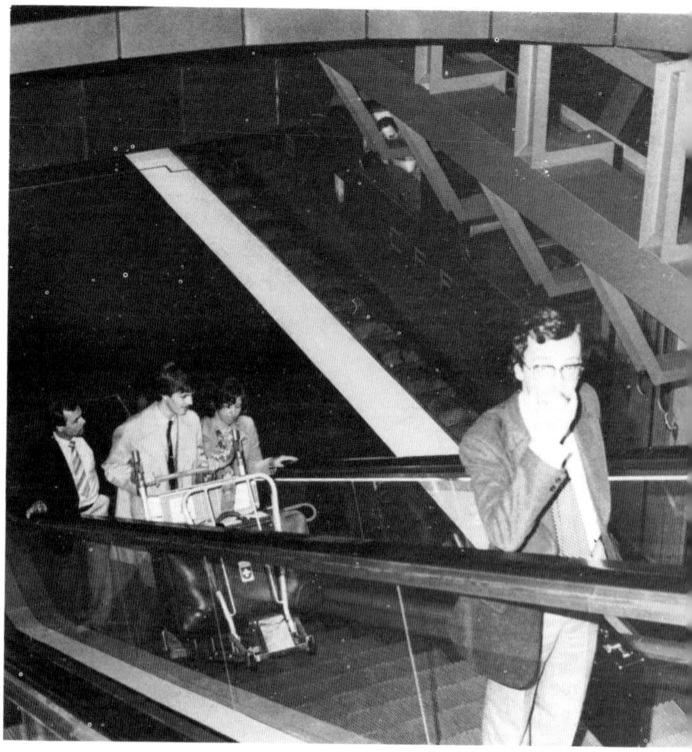

Swissair and the Swiss Federal have combined in a unique facility branded 'Fly-Luggage' whereby air travellers can register baggage direct from their rail starting-point to their airline destination. By 1981 'Fly-Luggage' was offered from over 60 stations in Swiss cities and holiday resorts, but the ultimate objective is availability from around 100 rail, lake steamer and postbus stations. The scheme is now extended to Geneva-Cointrin Airport.

Prerequisites for use of the 'Fly-Luggage' scheme are possession of an air ticket with a confirmed reservation and handover of the baggage at starting point with time enough for the railway to get it to Zurich Airport at least 90min ahead of the passenger's scheduled take-off. Cost of the facility is Sfr5 per piece of luggage, or about £1.35.

Trains serving the Airport are marshalled so that luggage vans always come to rest alongside a demarcated platform area. Here the baggage is transferred to robot powered trolleys, guided by sub-surface conductor wires, which take it up an inclined tunnel to a concentration centre on the floor above for transfer to the appropriate flights. In the first month of operation, when around 1,000 'Fly-Luggage' items were handled weekly, the 'lost luggage' complaints averaged less than 0.03%. Naturally, a comprehensive facility for incoming passengers is virtually impossible to arrange because of Customs constraints but on arrival at Zurich they can similarly register their luggage for independent rail transfer to their destination station in Switzerland.

This 'Fly-Luggage' scheme has added marketing value because of the Airport's direct service by SBB inter-city trains. The inaugural Airport line timetable of the 1980 summer had all the hourly interval SBB inter-city expresses between Geneva, Berne, Zurich and St Gallen each way re-routed over the new line to call at the Airport, plus the Zurich-Romanshorn trains. In addition two trains each way daily between Zurich and Chur, Interlaken/Brig and the Ticino were extended to and from the Airport, and three to and from Lucerne.

Thus the Airport was served by at least one or two inter-city trains every daytime hour, with the rest of the timetable guaranteeing a train every half-hour between 05.30 and 23.30 furnished by a shuttle service between Zurich Hbf and the new Bassersdorf station. Only extra peak-hour local trains and the Munich-Zurich 'Bavaria' IC train of the German Federal still sustain passenger operation on the original main-line exit to

eft: The Airport luggage trolleys are ıgeniously designed for easy use on the scalators linking the station platforms with he mezzanine and Terminal building floors bove. *SBB*

ight: The mezzanine floor, where SBB ticket nd enquiry facilities are surrounded by an ttractive array of shops and cafeterias.

elow: A sample of the massive civil ngineering works needed at the approaches o Zurich Airport to thread the new Airport line asily through a complex area of the SBB ystem. A new bridge carries the old Kloten ine, being traversed by an RBe4/4 motor oach and train, over the new Airport line, vhich is being taken by an Re4/4II and 'Inter-Ville' train of MkIII stock, at the crossing of the Glatt river on the rim of the Airport. *SBB*

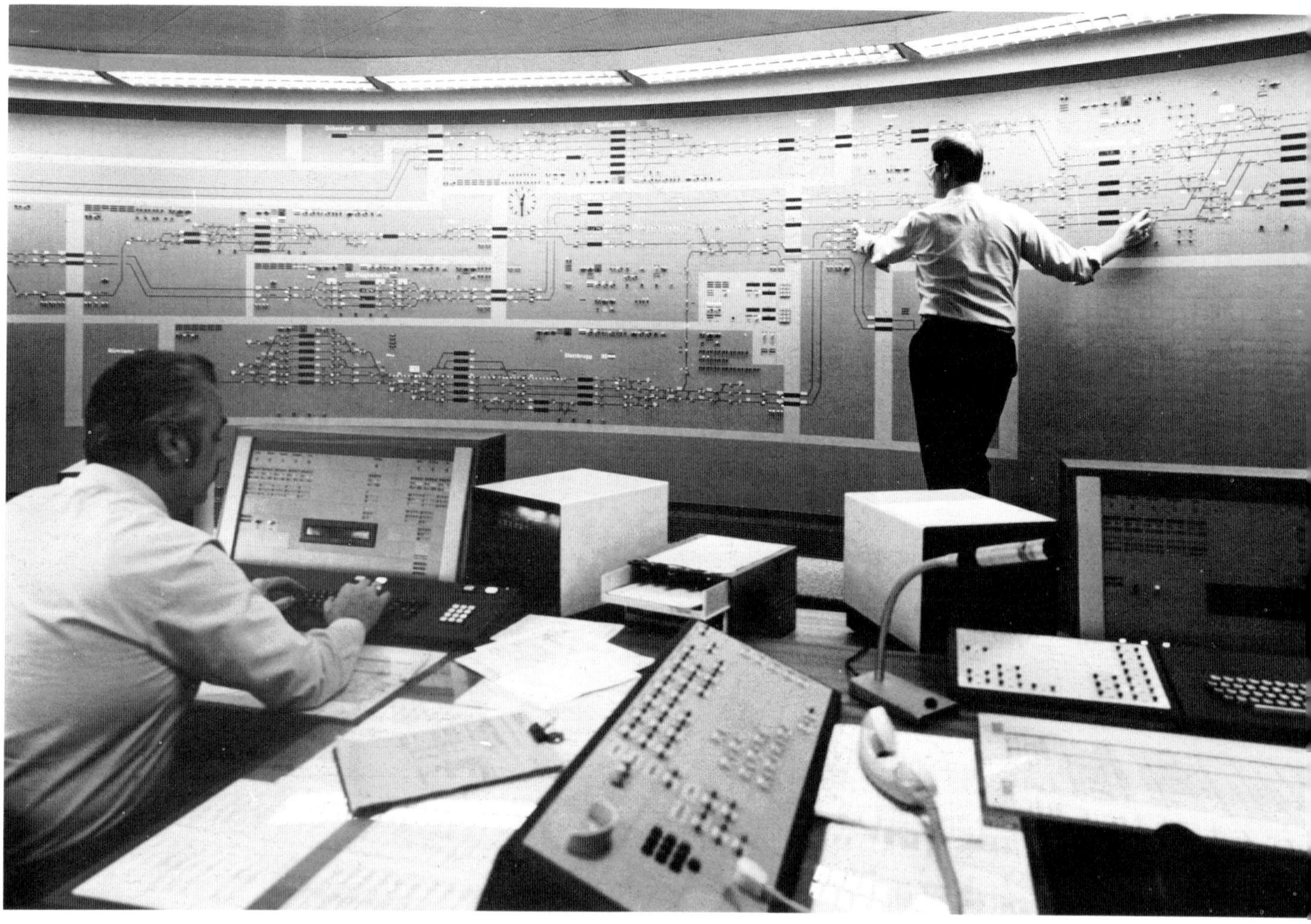

Above: The intricacy of the SBB's route system in the vicinity of Zurich Airport is patent from this view of the route diagram in the new Zurich Oerlikon signalling centre. In the foreground are two of the operators' consoles on which routes are keyboard-set. All running lines are reversibly signalled. *SBB*

Winterthur. Needless to say, Swissair's airport bus shuttle was terminated as soon as the Airport rail service opened (even in first class, the train journey between Airport and city is slightly cheaper).

In 1980 the Airport station handled around 50 trains each way daily. But in May 1982, when the SBB launches its intensified, system-wide regular-interval timetable that is forecast to inflate the whole railway's daily train mileage by 17%, considerably more long-haul trains will be channelled to the Airport. Practically all the Lucerne-Zurich trains, together with those which travel via Baden Brugg and Olten to Berne, will serve the Airport, which will then enjoy five trains hourly each way to and from Zurich Hbf, at intervals ranging from 3 to 22min.

This surcharge will aggravate the pressure points of the Zurich layout, which were wincing under the initial Airport timetable in the 1980 summer and inflicting enough unpunctuality on the local commuter service to worry the Zurich press. It irked Zurich commuters already niggling at the inadequate seating capacity of their peak-hour trains, to which the SBB says it has no track space for addition. That is partly because of the high incidence of reversals in Zurich Hbf.

The SBB has critical safety objections to push-pull working with its Re4/4II electric locomotives and conventionally braked Schlieren-type lightweight coaches. But it is not enamoured of a modern electric multiple unit formation of equivalent seating capacity because that is 70% more expensive in first cost — and what is more the SBB has had some painful reliability experience with its most recent Type RABDe8/16 emus that offsets the regality of their interior furnishing and purple-and-yellow external livery.

The short-term solution to this capacity problem is probably French Railway's highly successful Paris suburban double-deck equipment. In the 1980 summer the SBB borrowed a set for trial on the Zurich-Thalwil-Pfäffikon commuter service along Lake Zurich's south shore, and also on the Zurich Hbf-Airport-Bassersdorf shuttle — in the latter instance operated push-pull, but with locomotives front and rear. Despite its traumas with the RABDe8/16s, however, the smart scheduling permitted because of the acceleration possible with their power to all axles is said to incline the SBBs to multiple-unit operation when the final choice is made.

The time for decision may not now be so far distant, because in the summer of 1980 the omens looked good enough for the SBB to resurrect the S-Bahn proposal, with the proclaimed objective of operating a basic 30min interval service on all the city's radial short-haul routes as a result of the end-on connection of several of them via the Zurichberg Tunnel. In the inner area day long frequency would be greater since some of the routes converge over significant distances. Total cost is now put at about £160millions, most of which would be sought from Zurich and its suburban authorities; the SBB share would be some £25millions. Zurich was to decide the issue by popular referendum in September 1981.

The S-Bahn case is the more cogent because initial results have persuaded the SBB that the Airport link outlay will be remunerated earlier than cynics expected. Even in the first fortnight of the link's operation a specimen midweek day generated 7,100 rail travellers to and over 6,500 from the Airport; Saturday and Sunday carryings were about a third higher. By the first month's end the trains were carrying twice the passengers of the previous bus link and volume was 20%

Above: With an SBB Re4/4II locomotive at each end, a set of French Railways latest double-deck type — the VO2N, with two lavatories per coach to suit its intended employment on long Paris commuter routes such as to Sens and Château-Thierry — is listed push-pull on the Zurich suburban system in September 1980. *SBB*

above forecasts. At that rate the SBB could well be moving more than 5million of the Airport's anticipated 8.5million passengers.

Meanwhile, in November 1979 the Canton of Geneva advanced about £1½millions for preliminary work on a rail link to Geneva Airport, Switzerland's second busiest with a tally of 4.7million passengers in 1979. Federal support on the same scale as for the Zurich project was voted in June 1980, leaving the SBB as at Zurich to stand 60% of the total £51millions cost, and the SBB expected to start construction in 1982 and finish in 1987.

Like Zurich, Geneva's Airport station will be plugged into the national inter-city system. Cornavin, in the city centre, will remain Geneva's main station, but for most services it will become an intermediate stop. They will carry on to and reverse in a subterranean four-track Airport station of similar design to Zurich's. For just over 2.1miles the Geneva Airport link will adopt the existing, SNCF-operated main line from Geneva to Lyon via the border station of La Plaine; the present double-track will be re-strung with SBB-pattern catenary and resignalled in SBB style, and a third track will be laid in for SNCF trains, which will go their way clear of SBB traffic via a new flying junction. Beyond that the remaining 1.7miles to the Airport will be new route in tunnel, on a ruling 1 in 50 gradient.

The SBB forecasts an annual passenger traffic of at least 2million over the Geneva Airport link. Provision has been built into the 1982 national regular-interval timetable for hourly service between the Airport and all Switzerland's principal centres, with complementary local workings to build up a 15min interval service between Airport and Cornavin station. There a fourth and new through platform will be built to handle the additional traffic.

Switzerland's third main airport, Basle-Mulhouse, processed just under 1million passengers in 1979 and is not seen as an early candidate for a rail link. In any event its connection would be a complicated exercise, because the airfield is in French territory and its connection would not only require the SNCF to re-locate its Mulhouse-Strasbourg-Paris main line north of St Louis, but also to adapt it for SBB intercity service to and from the Airport station, as at Zurich and Geneva. The possibility of a Geneva Airport link abstracting traffic from Lyon airport seems real, but that of a Basle link threatening Strasbourg still more so were SNCF expresses to Basle re-routed via the Airport: this risk would surely colour French attitudes to the Basle concept. Nevertheless, the SBB would like preliminary planning to begin with the aim of reserving land for a Basle link against the day the airport's traffic growth justifies it.

In 1980 the only other European airport with regular, direct rail connections to centres beyond its adjoining city was Frankfurt/Main, in West Germany, It would be joined in 1981 by Amsterdam Schiphol, following completion of the new direct route from that airport's handsome new underground station to Leiden and The Hague, as described on page 81; unhappily, though, it will take much longer to link Schiphol with a conveniently-sited station the heart of Amsterdam itself.

Frankfurt is Western Europe's most heavily-trafficked airport after London Heathrow. In 1979 it handled 17.5million passengers, of which 9.4million were starting or ending their journeys in the Frankfurt area itself. In 1972, when the airport railway was looped off the main line from Frankfurt Hbf to Mainz, Koblenz and the north as a component of the Rhine-Main territory S-Bahn project's early stages, the respective traffic totals were only 11.6 and 6.2millions.

At the start the Airport trains, chiefly locomotive-powered push-pulls on the Mainz or Wiesbaden stopping runs from Frankfurt Hbf, took the exisiting exit from the city to the divergence of the new line just beyond Sportfeld station (which, incidentally, serves the nearby ground of Frankfurt's illustrious Eintracht football club). But besides its weight of traffic for the north of the country, this carries trains for Mannheim and the south-west as far as Sportfeld; and in that vicinity it is also joined by one of the tracery of orbital lines avoiding Frankfurt's dead-end main station. To stitch a regular-interval airport passenger service into the mix of long-haul passenger and freight traffic threading Sportfeld was impossible. Consequently the initial airport train service was irregular, with some gaps as irritating as an hour.

The first stages of the Rhine-Main S-Bahn scheme, which fed six of Frankfurt's northern and western commuter lines into a new double-track tunnel below Frankfurt Hbf to the city centre at a Hauptwache interchange with the U-Bahn network, were budgeted at around £320million of civil engineering costs in 1968 agreements which — in accordance with latter-day German urban transportation improvement statute — apportioned them 60% to the Federal Treasury and the rest to the affected Land (provincial) and city administrations. The German Federal's expense, as usual, was limited to planning overseeing the work and to furnishing the rolling stock. At least £230million more was provisionally earmarked to continue the mid-town S-Bahn tunnel so as to complete a connection with the DB lines on the city's southern side (the first phase of this extension, from Hauptwache to Konstablerwache, was well under way in 1980).

Despite this formidable financial commitment, the public authorities agreed in 1972 to an additional outlay of almost £20millions for the creation of a new and segregated double-track exit from the throat of Frankfurt Hbf to the start of the airport loop. Only 4.3 miles of new route were involved, but they incurred over 1,700ft of continuous bridgework in taxing locations to lift the new tracks over existing DB installations on the city bank of the Main and then over the river itself by an elegant single-span bridge, 539ft long, which alone absorbed £3millions of the cost. Signalling at Sportfeld was modernised and a new station built at Niederrad, the bleak outcrop of high-rise office blocks on the Main's further shore (which, one is told locally, was designed and completed with such dedicated commercial purpose that its hordes of office workers were moving in before someone remarked that provision of medical services in the neighbourhood had been overlooked).

The works were finished in the autumn of 1979 and in June 1980 a new timetable instituted a regular-interval service between airport and downtown Frankfurt, with a journey time of only 11min between the former and the city's main station. In the peak hours train frequency is every 10min, with half the service furnished by Frankfurt Hbf-Mainz-Wiesbaden workings on S-Bahn Route 14 and half by those on S-Bahn Route 15, a shuttle between the Airport and Hauptwache which ferries air travellers straight to the heart of Frankfurt's top-grade hotel enclave. The latter maintains its 20min frequency all day, subsiding to hourly only in the small hours, but off-peak the Mainz-Wiesbaden service is thinned out to 40min frequency. Altogether 93 trains each way serve the Frankfurt Airport station daily, with the S-Bahn workings now dominated by Class ET420 electric multiple-units.

Included in this total of airport trains are three services — morning, midday and mid-evening — from and to Darmstadt, Mannheim and Ludwigshafen, operated with stock boldly branded 'Airport Express' and liveried in the airport's two-tone blue house colours. The DB has gone a step further than the SBB's 'Fly-Luggage' scheme and essayed trainboard check-in of air travellers on these workings, using a baggage van rigged out internally as an airport counter, manned by airport staff and

radio-linked with the airport's reservation computers. In the summer of 1980 the word from Frankfurt was that the radio link had been found satisfactorily foolproof, but that the experiment was unlikely to have a lasting follow-through because of complexity of communicating with the multiplicity of carriers flying into and out of Frankfurt.

The DB has been urged to re-route some of its long-haul hourly Inter-City trains via Frankfurt Airport, but has so far objected that the deviation would overtax a daily operation already fraught enough because of its web of interconnections and its intensity. Without that benefit Airport rail traffic has grown strongly enough. Even before the 1980 inception of the regular-interval S-Bahn service the daily average of Airport station users had soared from 12,500 in 1972 to 20,000 by 1979's end, so that as much as three-quarters of all air travellers to or from Frankfurt itself were using the rail link. That represented more than a third of the Airport's passengers in total.

The majority of West Germany's other major airports are or will be served solely — but directly to their terminals — by S-Bahnen. Düsseldorf has a 30min shuttle to and from the city's main station, 12min and 6.2miles away, via a short branch off the Ruhr S-Bahn tracks paralleling the main line to Duisburg and Essen. Connections to and from both the latter cities are available hourly at Unterrath, the branch's junction station.

Munich Airport, at present accessible only by buses to and from nearby Riem station, will have a new S-Bahn line to its terminal by 1983. Stuttgart will be plugged straight into its S-Bahn system by 1985. That leaves Hamburg, where a direct connection with Fuhlsbüttel Airport was only at a preliminary planning stage in 1980; and Cologne-Bonn, where the same applied.

The terminal of Vienna's Schwechat Airport, almost 14miles from the city's centre, was in the late 1970s connected to the Schnellbahn, the Austrian Federal Railway's route through the

eft: A DB Class 420 electric multiple-unit in ne orange-and-silver livery of Frankfurt's -Bahn network in Frankfurt Airport station. *B*

op right: Three times each way daily the DB uns the 'Airport-Express' in specially-liveried ocomotive-hauled coaching stock between Darmstadt, Mannheim and Ludwigshafen and rankfurt Airport. *DB*

Centre right: An NS electric multiple-unit at ne of the Schiphol Airport station platforms.

elow: RENFE's Barcelona Airport station.

city centre which mingles a regular-interval local electric multiple-unit service with inter-yard freight in a complex operation. The airport line was created for most of the distance by adapting an existing branch. Except in the early morning the Schwechat service is no more than hourly and the trip to the interchange with the Schnellbahn at Vienna Mitte takes 32min.

As yet the only other Western European centres with direct rail links are Barcelona and Malaga, of which the former has a 15min interval service from the city's Central station, the latter a half-hourly frequency of trains from Malaga Guadalmedina and the RENFE station. And, of course, the first of the links to be established after the last war, that from Brussels Central and Nord stations to the Belgian capital's airport, which runs every 20-30min until mid-evening.

Of the cities whose airport terminals are in sight of a railhead but still a bus ride from it, the best-placed is surely Birmingham. When Britain's new National Exhibition Centre was laid out nearby, BR in 1976 erected a new Birmingham International station astride the London Midland electrified main line which courses between the exhibition halls and the airfield. There air travellers have immediate access to a half-hourly, 100mph Inter-City service to and from London Euston as well as local electric multiple-units to and from BR's provincial hub, Birmingham New Street, which radiates other Inter-City trains to the north, west and east of the country.

The city airport links which most surprisingly lack the ultimate convenience of direct access from rail station to air terminal complex are those of Paris — surprisingly — in view of the gigantic expenditure on other latter-day projects to enhance the usefulness of the French capital's rail services. Orly, to the south of the city, has to share rail facilities with the neighbouring Rungis market, laid out in the 1960s after the decision to supersede the legendary Les Halles produce market in central Paris. The cumbersomely-named Pont de Rungis-Aéroport d'Orly station, built in 1969 astride a section of the capital's

Above: The SNCF's terminus at Roissy, serving Paris' Charles de Gaulle Airport, with a Z6400 electric multiple-unit at the platform. *SNCF*

Grande Ceinture orbital line, stands on the rim of the market area (the site of which was partly dictated by the proximity of a rail route connecting with the main lines radiating from Paris), but a bus ride's distance from the air terminal. At present Paris Austerlitz is the starting point for the 15min-interval 'Orlyrail' electric multiple-unit service.

It is also a 5min bus ride from Roissy station to the terminal of the newer airport on Paris' north side, Charles de Gaulle. When an 8.3mile branch to Roissy was laid from the Gare du Nord-Soissons line in the mid-1970s, the Paris press was stupefied by the decision to terminate it well beyond the air terminal complex. The airport authority's argument was that it was being farsighted: the rail station ought to be equidistant from the then air terminal and a second which would be needed if Charles de Gaulle's traffic expanded as anticipated.

A compensation is that the Roissy line, opened in May 1976, was the first to be worked by the SNCF's punchy, well-furnished and handsomely blue-and-yellow-liveried Type Z6400 electric multiple-units. Each four-car set packs an aggregated 3,165hp output in its two power cars, so that it can sustain its 75mph top speed over the quite severe gradients of the airport branch. That helps to make the Charles de Gaulle airport link one of Europe's fastest, mile for mile: the 16.8 miles from Gare du Nord are covered in only 20min by limited-stop trains every 15min from 05.30 to close on midnight.

In the second half of the 1980s the two Paris airports will be connected by a through Orly-Roissy rail service offering a frequency as tight as 10min in the peak hours. This will be one of the first 'Interconnexion' services to follow the link-up of the SNCF's Nord and Sud-Est Region suburban networks by the immense tunnelling works between Gare du Nord and Gare de Lyon via elaborate subterranean junctions at the big Châtelet interchange station. To effect the inter-airport service the Orly trains will be re-routed via Massy-Palaiseau on to the Sceaux line, which, beneath Paris, has already been extended to the new Châtelet station.

he Double-Tracking of the Bern-Lötschberg-
Simplon

low: Except for its $9\frac{1}{4}$-mile long Lötschberg nnel the BLS main line, the key but dependent route from the Swiss Federal's rne-Interlaken line at Spiez through the rnese Alps to a junction with the SBB's one Valley main line at Brig, was built igle-track with passing loops, though its ilders made some infrastructure provision for second track which the company could not ford in this century's first decade. The rapid growth of international traffic after World War 2 prompted talk of doubling as early as the 1950s. Subsequent recessions left the idea in abeyance until 1970, although in the 1960s seven route-miles were doubled in the easier terrain between Spiez and Frutigen and some loops were extended. The scheme was revised in 1970, then lapsed through another recession, but in 1976 the Swiss Government finally undertook to advance some £180million for the first phases of widening. But as the money was not forthcoming until the spring of 1978 the BLS started work with its own money between Blausee-Mitholz and Kandergrund early in 1977. In this pre-doubling view a BLS 6,780hp Re4/4 Bo-Bo heads one of the blue-and-cream, air-conditioned sets which the BLS operates on Brig-Basle and Interlaken-Basle inter-city services. *BLS*

Left: In the spring of 1980 a slender new ferro-concrete viaduct starts to take shape for the second track alongside the original, 265m Kander Viaduct. A separate bridge for the new track had to be erected some distance from the original to avoid damaging the latter's structure.

Left: In the majority of the route's 32 tunnels — a figure that excludes the Lötschberg Tunnel itself — the arch was built to a radius suitable for later double-tracking, but not completely excavated, as here. *BLS*

Below: An Re4/4 winds a passenger train downhill between Kandergrund and Blausee-Mitholz, where the BLS completed double-tracking by the start of December 1979; note the concrete pinning of the rock at the rim of the enlarged bore. In this area the Kander Valley narrows and steepens so abruptly that to restrict the ruling gradient to 1 in 37 the BLS builders had to spiral the line in two successive semi-circles, one in tunnel to gain height quickly. That helps the railway to climb 1,275ft in five miles' distance.

Right: After threading the Lötschberg Tunnel and the ensuing Lötschental and Lonza Gorge, the BLS turns into the Rhone Valley some 1,500ft up its steep northern wall and begins a steep descent to Brig clinging to the mountainside — a daunting environment for track widening, as the first picture of the original single track at the mouth of the 217m Lidenplatten Tunnel makes plain. The second picture shows structure work in preparation for a second track in the same vicinity. *BLS*

Below: The main arch of the well-known Bietschtal bridge on the southern Lötschberg slope was built in anticipation of a second track; only concrete and steel approach spans now need to be added. In association with bi-directional signalling on each line the extra track will raise the route's operating capacity by 150%, to the same level as the Gotthard's, and the BLS is ordering more Re4/4 locomotives to exploit it. But full realisation of this potential depends on Italian modernisation of the Domodossola yards south of the Simplon Tunnel. The Swiss Government exacted Italian agreement for this as a condition of its finance for the BLS doubling, but in 1980 the final allocation of the Domodossola bill was still unresolved.

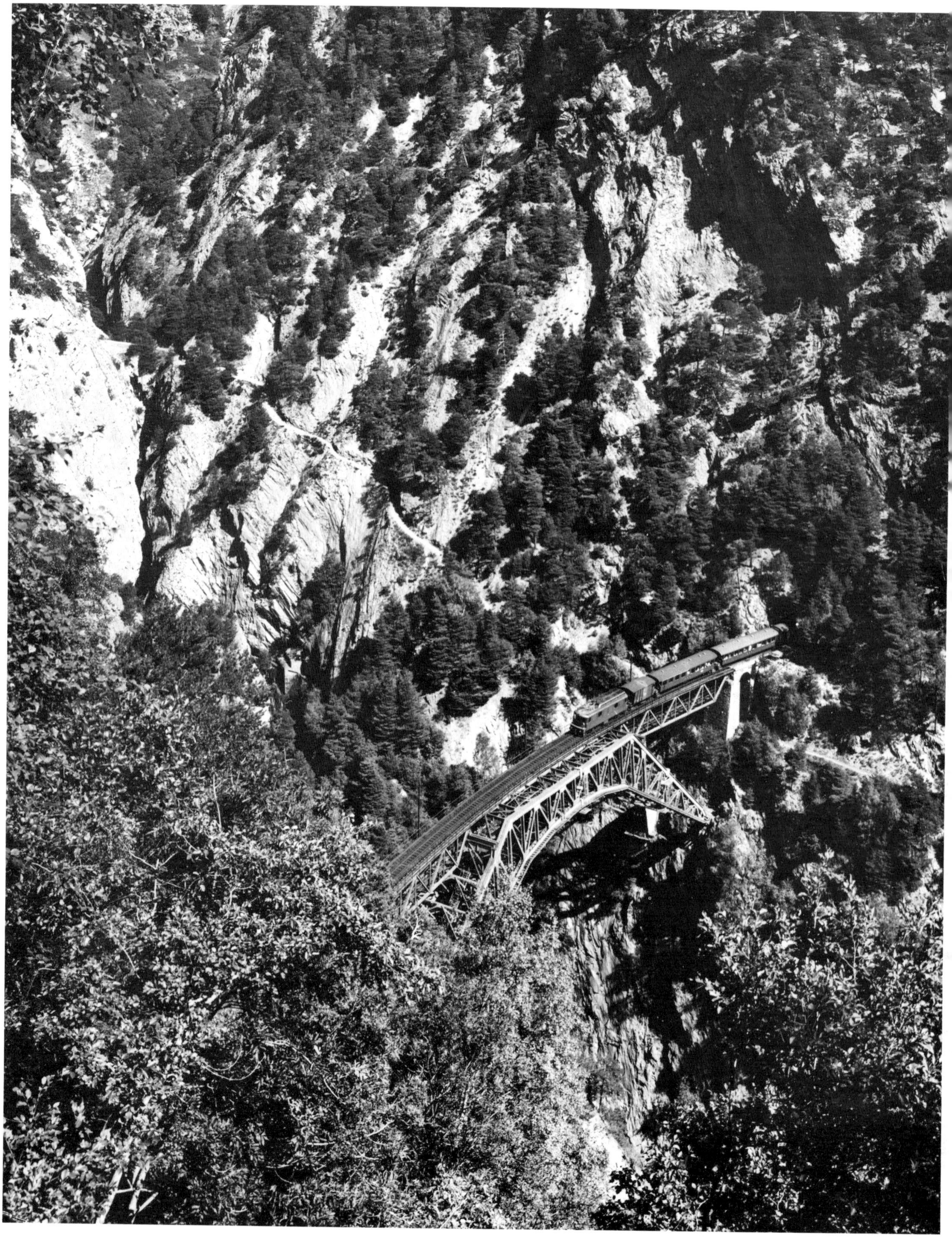

What's New in Traction?

The rapid, ongoing development of power electronics has given a new fillip to electrification, now a thriving industry around the world. Of the major railroading countries only the USA and Canada — and Britain, because of the Government's tight grip of BR's purse-strings — had little to show of electric traction progress in 1980.

Until late in 1980, North America seemed to be the only major railroading area of the world still doing sporadic electrification sums and finding the answers unconvincing. There, of course, the hurdle right at the start of the electrification course is the capital cost of installation, which has to be found from the private enterprise railroads' own resources. And with the average net return on US railroads' business hovering either side of 2% for some years past shareholders are apt to prefer more immediately productive investment.

Apart from a second high-voltage ac industrial 'merry-go-round' project, the only US surface electrification in view in mid-1980 was the extension of catenary from New Haven to Boston to allow of electric traction throughout Amtrak's Washington-New York-Boston corridor. But that was Federally financed under the North-East Corridor Improvement Project (NECIP), one of the rail revival schemes ranging from Amtrak to Conrail and grants to financially ailing railroads to upgrade their freight-operating plant which have already absorbed over $11billion of the US taxpayers' cash since 1970. And still more has been shelled out for urban rapid transit development.

Conrail, the Federally-funded body created in 1976 to rationalise (hopefully) and run the bankrupt, Penn-Central-dominated network in the North-east, needs to extend the ex-Pennsylvania catenary from Newark, NJ, to Pittsburgh, Pa. But consultants' forcast of a $1.2billion price-tag, including the cost of extra locomotives, made the massive Federal finance essential for the scheme's execution look unlikely to be voted. Even though Conrail has worried Congress ever since its creation through its chronic inability to operate within its budgeted means, the consultants' prediction that the completed electrification scheme would cut running costs by $84million in the first eight years of operation and secure an 18% return on the outlay over 29 years seemed bound to carry less weight than the size of the down-payment to fund it.

Much of the operational economy of electric traction derives, of course, from intensive use of fixed as well as mobile equipment. North American addiction to the irregularly patterned working of freight in mammoth trainloads obviously affects the equations.

No railroad on that continent, probably, had up to 1980

Left: The evolution of SNCF Bo-Bo *rapide* power — 5,500hp No BB16047, re-styled in Corail livery, the ac version of the first 1950s essay in the production of 1.5kV dc, 25kV ac and multi-voltage type employing virtually standard mechanical bodies and chassis (above); and No BB15013, the ac variant of the same principle applied in the late 1970s to the SNCF's range of thyristor-controlled 5,900hp Bo-Bos. The Netherlands Railways is acquiring a fleet of locomotives based on the latter type's 1.5kV dc counterpart, the BB7000. In 1981 No BB7003 of the latter type is to be rebuilt as a prototype 6,700hp machine with asynchronous three-phase motors.

Left and below: The French look is patent in these samples from the lengthy catalogue of French industry's traction exports — a Portuguese Railways 77tonne, 4,000hp Class 2600, an Alsthom type derived from French Railways successful Class 15000 and 17000 Bo-Bos, at the head of one of the system's supplementary-fare Lisbon-Oporto *rapidi*; and the 25kV 60Hz ac Type EU4000 Bo-Bo-Bo electric built for the Korean National Railroad by the 50 Cycle Group.

Right: The most powerful electric type in Belgium — one of the 25 7,000hp Class 20 Co-Cos with thyristor control, built for the SNCB in Belgium by La Brugeoise et Nivelles with ACEC electrical equipment.

studied the possibilities more exhaustively than Canadian Pacific, which had gone as far as arranging for special tests of the latest European thyristor-controlled locomotives on the nearest Scandinavian main-line equivalent to the winter environment of its trunk route across the Rockies. These trials convinced CP that electrification would substantially reduce haulage costs and size of traction fleet. But the present loading of the Rockies single-track line between Calgary and Vancouver is only 15 freights each way daily, of which the export shipment coal trains gross 12,700tonnes and need an aggregate of 12 front-end and helper 3,000hp diesels to cope with the 1 in 38.5 grade between Rogers and the Connaught Tunnel at 20mph. Small wonder that no top CP executive yet discerns a worthwhile payoff from electrification proposals.

Unexpectedly, however, it was disclosed in the second half of 1980 that a massive electrification scheme had been seriously pondered south of the 49th Parallel. The Federal Railroad Administration, an adjunct of the US Department of Transportation, made public a scheme to wire no less than 26,000 route-miles of the most heavily-loaded trunk routes in the country. Its accomplishment would put more than half of all tonnage currently moved by US Class I railroads behind electric traction, even though it would convert only 14% of the US trunk network. Before going any further one should emphasise that the FRA's ideas were aired before they had even been taken on board as declared policy by the Carter administration, and within months of a turnover of the Washington bureaucracy following Reagan's election. Whether a Reagan regime dedicated to a reduction of Federal expenditure and intervention will pick up the FRA scheme was a hazardous speculation when this review was written, but the four railroads chiefly concerned — Conrail, Southern, Union Pacific and Burlington Northern — all wanted to discuss it further.

The prospects of execution are likely to be dim because of the nub the FRA scheme was that the capital cost hurdle would be cleared largely with Federal funds. The FRA proposed that the electricity-generating companies, who would get their return from traction current sales, should meet the bill for getting the current to the catenary, the railroads the cost of electric locomotives and a share of the expense of resignalling and immunising telecommunications. The installation of catenary and any associated civil engineering would be Federally funded, but the money would be returned by the railroads in the form of a tonnage-related royalty on all traffic subsequently worked under the wires. That way the cost would not lumber the railroads' balance sheets with another fixed charge. The FRA calculated that the electrification would cost on average about £210,000 per single-track route-mile and £330,000 per double-track route-mile, and that its full scheme would cost £6.25billion in total.

US railroads' share of a national oil consumption is less than 2%. The completed electrification's likely reduction of that to 0.6% was obviously not the FRA's preoccupation. What counted was the prospect, first, of a national freight system insulated from further oil crises; and secondly, one with the extra operating capacity afforded by electric traction's characteristics to rescue road haulage in such crises.

The vulnerability of oil supplies, never mind the quadrupling of their price since 1973 and the certainty that ultimately they are finite, is the obvious motivation to electrify for countries without inland or offshore resources of their own. The relative cost of oil and electricity for traction is less and less a decisive factor (except for countries rich in hydro-electric resources — but most of these were the world's rail electrification pace-setters in the first half of the century). In most countries the cost of electricity has been allowed to chase the rising oil price, even where it is mostly generated in plant burning indigenous coal. A conspicuous example of that trend is South Africa, where the effect was a temporary indecision over pursuit of the railways' electrification programme.

Above: The remarkable Sishen-Saldanha Bay ore export line in South Africa, unusually electrified at 50kV 50Hz ac because clearance problems for the catenary were obviated by the semi-desert nature of the railway's route and the high voltage permitted a feed of the 534mile line with only six sub-stations. The ore customarily moves in trains of up to 200 four-axle wagons grossing just over 20,000tonnes — a 3ft 6in-gauge record which very few North American standard-gauge systems surpass for weight — behind a trio of 5,070hp thyristor-controlled Co-Cos, of which 25 were British-built for the operation by GEC Traction. *GEC Traction*

Right: One of the German Federal's five Class 120 three-phase electric locomotive prototypes. In 1980 one of them was tested at up to 143.6mph. *DB*

Below right: The Swiss Federal's new three-phase motor Class Ee6/6 1,330hp electric Co-Co, a heavy yard shunter. *SBB*

Other than disquiet at reliance on imported fuel, the most persuasive inducement to electrify is the steadily reducing real cost of working trains electrically as operators learn more science in rostering for continuous traction unit employment. Apart from reducing the number of units needed for a specific traffic demand — and thereby cutting the already low maintenance costs of electric as against diesel traction — this usually effects an operating staff economy too. In Spain, RENFE, for instance, has concluded that when all these considerations are quantified and aggregated, tonnage is moved by electric traction at 16% less cost than with diesel power.

Another consideration is that in the past few years electric traction technology has been advancing much the more rapidly. Electronics have been the dominating influence, pointing the way to energy-sparing (and maintenance-simplifying) control systems that achieve a steadily more precise adjustment of effort to each haulage task. The real cost of setting up an electrification, moreover, has been coming down through the refinement of lighter and cheaper catenary, and of simpler lineside feeder apparatus.

In June 1980 French Railways (SNCF) inaugurated 128 route-miles of 1.5kV dc across country from Bordeaux to Montauban, on the Paris-Toulouse main line just north of the latter city. Yet at the start of the 1970s conversion of this line, which carries no more than 11 expresses, four stopping trains and 18 scheduled freights each way per 24hr, was a very remote possibility (even though the former Mid Railway and subsequently the SNCF had its conversion seriously in mind in the 1930s). The SNCF's electrification seemed then to have run almost its full course. With the inauguration in May 1970 of some 40 miles more of 1.5kV dc to complete catenary between Dijon and Bourg, and with the 5,800-odd miles then electrified bearing three-quarters of SNCF's inter-city passenger and freight traffic, the traffic flows satisfying the SNCF's economic criteria for electrification of the time had all been met. In only one of the following years did the amount of electrification exceed 25miles; in 1974 a mere 2km of new conductor were strung up.

But all the factors summarised earlier dictated the draft of a drastically revised set of SNCF criteria in the mid-1970s. In particular the economy attainable through electronic power controls had been demonstrated by the SNCF's first thyristor type, the 5,900hp, 88tonne BB15000, once the irritations of thyristor circuitry's harmonic interference with signalling and lineside telecommunications equipment had been overcome.

Apart from its enhancement of adhesion and tractive efficiency through stepless acceleration, solid-state control vastly reduces the number of wearing parts and the frequency of contactor operation in the system. Additionally it greatly simplifies recourse to dynamic braking, limiting the stress on a unit's mechanical braking components. Its adoption, one should perhaps add, has been less rapid and widespread than one might expect from these virtues primarily because of the interference nuisance mentioned — which, for instance, will initially restrict the Swiss Federal's forthcoming Re4/4IV thyristor Bo-Bos to routes where lineside circuitry has been protectively immunised — and a solid-state system's additional weight, bulk and cost. But in the SNCF BB15000 these debits were offset by a halving of the maintenance requirement per locomotive in terms of man-hours, and by doubled wheel-tyre life as a consequence of dynamic braking, quite apart from much more efficient performance than that put out by a 5,000hp BB1600 on the same sort of work.

Two special considerations cemented a French decision of 1975 to electrify a further 2,500miles before the century's end, even though this would add only about 8% more inter-city passenger and 11% more freight to the electrically-hauled totals (in addition, the Paris suburban network would be totally electrified). One was the value of rail movement in raising off-peak current demand closer to the output of the country's nuclear power stations, which is much less easy to adjust to fluctuating demand than that of plant fuelled otherwise (this association of the SNCF with France's controversial nuclear programme provoked protesters to blow up four of the line's conductor supports on the eve of the Bordeaux-Montauban inauguration). The second factor was an SNCF accounting decision not to regard the fixed equipment as fully written off at the end of a normal life, but as having a residual value either as scrap metal or as the basis for reconstruction.

So it is that the pace of SNCF electrification has stepped up from 9miles in 1976 through 65 in 1977, 80 in 1978 and 96 in 1979 towards an annual target of some 185miles per annum in the 1980s. The principal lines scheduled for conversion in the medium term are the increasingly important cross-country routes from Lyon to Tours and Nantes, and from the Seine estuary at Rouen to Amiens and the industrial North-East; the main lines to Brittany and the Atlantic ports; and the route from Paris to Clermont Ferrand, the only significant radial from the capital whose expresses are still diesel-powered.

Britain, complacently gulping North Sea oil and hag-ridden by insular convictions that public transport should be self-supporting, was the only Western European country with vast tracts of dieselised main line still trying to make up its mind in mid-1980 that electrification was justified. Elsewhere Belgium decided in 1975 to put some 435 more miles under its 3kV dc wires, chiefly to convert the links between already electrified trunk routes. The Austrians have taken a similar course and early in 1980 their Federal Railway, the OBB, announced that it had listed 425 more miles for electrification by 1990 in a programme that included extension of catenary throughout the suburban area to the north and west of Vienna.

At the same time the Italian Transport Minister laid before the country's Parliament a £5billion 1980-5 plan to increase the severely overtaxed operating capacity of the national railways, the FS. As well as substantial double-tracking and upgrading of secondary routes, resignalling and the construction of a new £50million marshalling yard at Domodossola which the Swiss made a condition of the Lötschberg route's double-tracking, this Italian programme embodies almost 900miles of new electrification.

Several railways joining the electrification drive since the oil crisis have had to decide whether to continue with the dc of their first conversions or switch to high-voltage ac at the industrial frequency because of the latter's substantially cheaper traction current cost. Despite the easy versatility of its multi-voltage locomotives, the SNCF has so far preferred to stick with 1.5kV dc within the Paris-Marseilles-Bordeaux enclave, though it opted to extend from Marseilles to the Italian border in an isolated stretch of 25kV ac.

The last Western European country to embark on main-line electrification, Denmark, had since the 1950s been planning every essential fixed asset reconstruction to make provision for a 1.5kV dc when the Government eventually allowed it to electrify. That was the system operative on its only existing electrification, in the Copenhagen suburban area on the largely segregated *S-Bane*. But when six years of colloquy between the State Railways CDSB) and the Government was at last concluded and the Danish Parliament in May 1979 approved a rolling electrification programme, the DSB opted for 25kV ac. DSB's immediate objective is to electrify from Copenhagen to the Zeeland ferry ports, starting with the busy line northward through suburbia to Helsingör (likely to be finished in late 1984) and then turning to the lines to Korsor and Rodby in the south-west, probably in late 1982 or 1983.

In the later 1970s the Spanish national system, RENFE, dreamed of building a 25kV ac, 4ft 8½in-gauge 150mph passenger railway from Madrid through Saragossa to Barcelona and on to a meet with the SNCF at Port Bou. But for the present

that has been filed in favour of the infinitely cheaper possibility of up to 125mph on existing RENFE infrastructure — realigned where feasible — with the latest Talgo variant incorporating an automatic tilt-body feature (see page 17). The 1,725mile programme of additions to the existing catenary with which Spain immediately reacted to the Middle East crisis in 1974 has been executed entirely at the system's 3kV dc (to which most RENFE lines initially electrified at 1.5kV have been converted). This big programme was finished in 1980, but some 1,500 more track-miles are proposed for electrification by 1991. Neighbouring Portugal's only prewar electric line, the short Lisbon-Estoril system, was 1.5kV dc, but the limited main-line electrification launched in the 1950s was at 25kV ac 50Hz.

Yugoslavia, the busiest electrifier outside the Eastern Bloc proportionately to network size since the 1960s, switched to 25kV ac from the 3kV dc installed earlier in its north-western provinces under Italian influence. Within the Eastern bloc only Poland is sedulously persisting with 3kC dc, which covers over 3,700miles of the national system. Czechoslovakia made the switch from this system to 25kV ac even though it had over 1,000miles dc-electrified.

The most hectic electrifier in the whole world at the present time, the USSR, which claims to be stringing up catenary at the rate of some 500miles a year, had vastly more of its railways under 3kV dc when it took up 25kV ac. It has subsequently re-electrified some of them to try and rationalise its electrified network. More than a quarter of all the electrified track in the world is within the USSR's boundaries.

Outside Europe the list of railways embarking on or accelerating the pace of electrification is so long that one can only pinpoint some outstanding members of it. At the start of the 1980s Indian Railways' 3,000-odd route-miles of electrified track, chiefly 25kV ac, accounted for only 8% of the system and bore about a quarter of IR's traffic; moreover, of the £1,750million which the government allocated to railway investment under the 1978-83 five-year plan only £60million was earmarked for electrification. But now there is anxiety to double IR's carrying capacity by the century's end to keep pace with traffic forecasts. Two-thirds of all Indian freight that is mechanically transported moves on rail and private road haulage is closely controlled because of the inferior state of the road system. Accelerated electrification has to be one means to the objective, given the uncertainties over oil, and IR management is hopeful of government finance for a conversion rate of 300-350 miles a year, so as to have more than 60% of its traffic under the wires by the year 2000. The priority is to have all four major metropolitan areas of Delhi, Calcutta, Bombay and Madras, interlinked by electrified trunk route; at present only Delhi and Calcutta are connected by catenary, but Delhi-Bombay should be finished in this decade and work on the longest link of all, from Delhi to Madras, has begun at each end.

When the Indians took up 25kV ac at the end of the 1950s they imported almost all their fixed equipment and traction, but now their locomotives are home-built at the Chittaranjan plant. IR's first thyristor - contolled locomotive was turned out in 1980.

After tabling a long-range electrification plan in 1974 South African Railways (SAR) were taken aback by soaring current prices as its Government and the supply industry set out to recoup the cost of grid extensions in short order. In 1978 SAR found themselves paying at least 150% more to feed the Sishen-Saldanha Bay line — the remarkable 546-mile track which ferries export ore in trains of 20,000tonnes gross behind trios of GEC Traction-built 5,070hp locomotives — than the accountants forecast when the project was costed four years earlier.

But by the end of the decade independence of imported fuel had become one of South Africa's overriding concerns. In 1980 a five-year, £330million programme to convert some 1,135miles of the SAR was under way, with extension of catenary throughout from both Cape Town (presently it stops on this route at Beaufort West) and Port Elizabeth to de Aar high up the list. But all the new extensions would be at 25kV ac, not the 3kV dc which characterised SAR trunk electrification until the 1970s. SAR changed in that decade to 25kV ac for the line from Transvaal coalfields to the port of Richards Bay, north of Durban. Dc could not match up to the 9,000tonnes-plus loads of shipment coal envisaged as standard practice on this line —

Italy's latest in electric locomotives; (far left) the 5,360hp, 125mph Class E444 'Tartaruga' ('Tortoise'), of which a member heads the 'Ligure' TEE alongside an *Autostrada* between Savona and San Remo en route from Milan to Avignon; (left) the Class E656 'Caimano' ('Crocodile'), a 5,630hp Bo-Bo-Bo; and the newest in 1980, the 6,660hp, thyristor-controlled Class E633 'Tigra' ('Tiger') a B-B-B with variable-gear monomotor bogies, which the FS now contemplates boosting to an 8,000hp maximum output (below). The next FS move will be for two prototypes of a three-phase, asynchronous motor Bo-Bo design with a continuous 6,700hp output and a one-hour 8,000hp rating; intended for 125mph operation on lighter inter-city trains (a speed made generally permissible on the completed section of the new Rome-Florence *Direttissima* in 1980), it may be tested at up to 150mph. *Y. Broncard, FS*

Left: A model of BR's forthcoming Class 58 diesel-electric, which is to share mechanica components to the highest degree practica with a new Class 88, high-power Co-Co electric locomotive type.

Right: The first Australian-built electric locomotive — the Comeng Class 85 for Ne South Wales. *Comeng*

Below right: The bygone zenith of US railroa pursuit of high-power single-unit diesels; th TOFC freight on Sherman Hill, Wyo, is powe by a trio in which a centre EMD 3,000hp SD40-2 Co-Co is flanked by two of the EMD 6,600hp Class DD40X Do-Dos specially bui for Union Pacific in 1969-71, which becam known as the 'Centennials' in view of their delivery around the anniversary of the first U transcontinental route's completion.

which, incidentally, is to have its operating capacity further enlarged.

Besides astonishing the world with 3ft 6in-gauge operation of mineral trains grossing as much as anything on North American standard gauge, SAR is about to show a clean pair of passenger speed heels to a good many standard-gauge systems in the Western hemisphere. A huge re-equipment programme announced at the start of the 1980s (it proposed over 900 additional and replacement new locomotives in 1981-6) included 415 new passenger cars as the basis of a bid for the quality inter-city passenger market. At present that cannot be courted with speed, for 55mph is the general SAR line speed limit; only the super-luxury 'Blue Train' is permitted 70mph here and there, and the 'Blue Train' and the weekly Johannesburg-Durban 'Drakensburg' are currently SAR's only completely air-conditioned trains.

But the invention of the High Stability or HS bogie, a device with a measure of wheel-set self-steering sometimes described as the Scheffel cross-anchor bogie in tribute to the SAR Test Section chief who fathered it, has handed the SAR a speed tool which could revolutionise its competitive standing in the passenger market. In late 1978 an HS bogie-fitted coach was tested at up to 152mph behind a re-geared and specially faired Class 6E electric locomotive near Johannesburg. So on its principal routes from the Transvaal to Cape Town and Durban the SAR is now aiming — with some realignment — for electric passenger train operation at up to 110mph in favourable track conditions.

Australia is another major country where electrification has suddenly become an 'in' word under compulsion to eschew imported oil and make more of domestic riches in fossil fuels. Queensland Railways had had wistful hopes of expanding Brisbane suburban electrification into a main-line project, but the former's first stage — begun as a 1.5kV dc scheme — had aborted in 1960 for lack of money. Then the Whitlam Labour Government's Urban Passenger Transport Programme sparked its revival as a 25kV ac project, Australia's first, in the 1970s.

Completion of this first Brisbane phase in 1979 was quickly followed by one Australian commitment to electrification after another. Queensland endorsed main-line electrification as State policy; so did Western Australia, with the Kwinana-Kalgoorlie stretch of the Trans-Australian route as its first objective; and the Federal Government moved for catenary — almost certainly 25kV ac — throughout the country's busiest inter-State route, from Sydney to Melbourne. Meanwhile New South Wales was stringing up more 1.5kV dc wire in its Sydney suburban area. Another recent Australian development worth recording is that the country's dominant traction and rolling stock manufacturer, Commonwealth Engineering, has joined the world's electric locomotive builders, though the units it has been building for NSW Railways have Mitsubishi traction motors from Japan.

Japan itself is anxious to electrify some 3,000 more route-miles as quickly as possible to save oil, though all its most heavily-trafficked routes are already energised. China did not undertake its first electrification until 1958, when 25kV ac was applied to the rugged Baoji-Chengdu line and finished throughout its 422miles (which feature 1 in 30 mountain grades) in 1975. By the end of the decade little more than 2% of China's rail system was under wires, but five new routes aggregating more than 1,400miles were in the grip of electrification engineers.

The South and Central American countries have so far taken fewer definitive steps to electrification than one might expect, but Brazil and Mexico are conspicuous exceptions. Mexico was one of the area's biggest railway spenders at the start of the 1980s signing a mouth-watering deal with General Electric for a rolling programme of 600 to 1,000 new locomotives over the 1980s decade. Most of them will be diesel, but some will serve the 5,000 route-mile electrification plan the country's Transport Ministry wants to establish as a matter of urgency. The French consultancy, Sofrerail, has the engineering design contract for the first phase of the 25kV ac 60Hz project, which embraces the 217-mile route from Mexico City to Irapuato.

By 1980 thyristor control had become virtually a commonplace of electric traction design. The next product of the galloping development in power semi-conductors and control electronics promised to be a new age of the three-phase ac traction motor, thanks to new-found techniques for compacting the equipment to mutate a single phase current supply into a three-phase feed to the motors.

The benefits of the ac motor compared with dc are its simplicity, minimum of components subject to wear and requiring sophisticated maintenace, and its smaller size and weight. It is easier to adapt to dynamic braking and is not guilty of the harmonic wave interference with signalling and telecommunications circuitry which has modified some railways' initial rapture with thyristor-controlled dc motors.

8506
8506

UNION PACIFIC
6927

The other side of the balance sheet is the elaborate and expensive apparatus needed to maintain a precise control of the current feed's voltage and frequency, as both must be varied to suit the speed and torque required of the traction unit from moment to moment. But the resultant versatility in all conditions of drawbar load, line speed and track should justify the cost.

That is clearly the feeling of more than one European railway keeping a close eye on the performance of the DB's five prototype Class 120 three-phase electric locomotives, the outcome of years of research and development in ac motor technology by West Germany's electric traction industry. These machines took up work from Nuremburg depot at the start of 1980.

Each 120 has cost the DB almost £1million, R&D costs excluded, or almost 25% more than one of the preceding DB production series, the orthodox dc-motored 5,500hp Class III BO-Bo. But for its money the DB has a 7,500hp, 84tonne Bo-Bo which may cover all its trunk hauls with equal facility, from 100mph, 700tonne Inter-City passenger rakes to 75mph, 1,500tonne TEEM freights and — in multiple-unit pairs — 5,000tonne mineral trains. In December 1980 one of these machines was also put to the proof over the stiff grades of Switzerland's Lötschberg main line, while the testing of another at up to 143.5mph between Celle and Uelzen in its own country seems to have stilled early uncertainty that the Class 120, suitably regeared, would also be able to exploit the DB's rising mileage of 125mph Inter-City track without sacrifice of its heavy duty potential. However the DB has prudently decided to order a further batch of Class IIIs to allow of a longer evaluation before commitment to series production of the Class 120.

Meanwhile the Norwegian State Railways have taken the plunge and ordered six three-phase motor Class EL17 electric locomotives with 150kmph (93mph) capability plus five Class Di4 diesels with the same electric system. One should perhaps add that the Swiss Federal has been operating six 2,500hp diesel-electric heavy shunter Co-Cos with three-phase motors, its Class Am6/6, since 1976. To these in 1979-80 it added 10 similarly motored straight electric shunters, the Class Ee6/6II 1,330hp Co-Co.

The feasibility of three-phase motor traction has stimulated a British Rail research and development exercise of important economic promise if the device is perfected, and if it can be manufactured at competitive cost. This is an internally-moun axle motor. The basic idea is practical because of the ac moto compactness and obviation of brush gear, but BR's scienti were prompted by the production of large-diameter tubular ax for the Advance Passenger Train's hydrokinetic brake to try novel format: the squirrel-cage rotor is integrally mounted the inside of the wheel-set's hollow axle and the stator wrapped round a static axle fitting within the rotating wheel-s axle — in other words, the usual arrangement is reverse Prototype Tubular-Axle Induction Motors (TAIM) were bei tested on the prototype unit of BR's Class 314 suburban electr multiple-unit design in 1980.

When the Swiss Federal has satisfied its immediate need heavy Gotthard route power with delivery of the last of its 8 standard 10,600hp Class Re6/6 Bo-Bo-Bos in late 198 Western European development of the high-power six-ax electric locomotive will almost cease. Certainly nothi comparable to the DB 103 or the SNCF CC6500 — both 12 mph plus machines in the 8,000hp range — was in prospect mid-1980.

In Italy the FS pursues the articulated B-B-B layout that finds apt for the incessant curvature of its historic main line The draft of a high-speed Co-Co, the E666, has bee temporarily laid aside and to the surprise of many observers th FS has so far eschewed a higher-powered development of i E444 'Tortoise' Bo-Bos in favour of two fresh Bo-Bo-B variants, the 120tonne, 5,630hp 'Crocodile' E656 and th 102tonne, 6,660hp thyristor-contolled 'Tiger' E633 wit variable-gear monomotor bogies. Both are 100mph units, bu the FS hopes to prove the E633 fit for 125mph. However, th FS recently disclosed that it is working up the design of a 8,000hp locomotive with three-phase asynchronous motor capable of powering 12-coach trains at 125mph and 20-coac rakes at 100mph.

British Rail aims to build a new Class 88 Co-Co standardising its mechanical parts to the maximum possible wit a forthcoming Class 58 diesel-electric. But this newcomer' purpose is pre-eminently the avoidance of the freight double heading presently essential over the Shap and Beattock banks o the West Coast Anglo-Scottish route, because their slippery rail

Below and below right: EMD's 3,000hp Class SD40-2 in close-up. Now Co-Cos are tending to go out of US railroad fashion.

ın defeat the adhesion of a single Bo-Bo charged with ,000tonnes.

Earlier references to the SNCF Class 1500 and later to the B's Class 120 have indicated the combination of power and ›eed output now obtainable from a four-axle locomotive of less ıan 100tonnes gross weight. Another impressive example of :cent build is the thyristor-controlled Class 1044 which immering-Graz-Pauker unveiled for the Austrian Federal ailway (OBB) in 1977 after the latter's sampling of thyristors its 10 ASEA-built 4,830hp Class 1043s of 1971. Capable of a eak 7,250hp output as well as 100mph, the Class 1044 has reatly reduced double-heading over the OBB's Semmering, rlberg and Tauern mountain pass routes. The 91.4tonne M-7s which General Motors are building to the basic ASEA .e4 design for Amtrak in the USA pack a short-term punch of ,400hp.

No comparable advances are discernible in diesel traction, ecause for the past few years progress in raising engine output er pound of weight without prejudice to reliability or risk of neconomic maintenance costs has been meagre. But gains in educing the cost of diesel operation and maintenance have been ubstantial.

In the 1970s the pioneers of diesel locomotive operation, US ailroads, called off their chase of 4,000, 5,000 and even ,000hp single units and impressed upon manufacturers that eliability and economical maintenance were the only grails that ıattered. With long-haul passenger trains an Amtrak traction esponsibility, all the big operators were after units economically daptable to fast merchandise and container/piggyback trains n the one hand, and heavy block trains of coal, minerals and rain on the other.

In the past three years the outcome has been the domination of new construction orders by 3,000hp Co-Cos. They accounted or around 60% of the 2,000-odd locomotives ordered by North American railroads in 1979. Only the systems with easily-graded routes were buying new Bo-Bos in the 2,000-3,000hp ange; the rest were catering for any medium-power demands by ending existing units to the re-manufacturers.

But escalating construction prices and interest rates have dramatised the extravagance of this all-purpose Co-Co approach. Consequently all North American builders have the perfection of high-adesion four-axle designs as their top priority ıowadays.

Each of them has developed a creep-control device, of which the system devised by General Motors' Electromotive Division must suffice as an example. In this, true ground speed is verified by a Doppler radar unit beneath the locomotive which continuously scans the road-bed. Its reading is electronically compared with traction motor speed as detectable from current-voltage measurement and the motor's characteristic curve, and that automatically prescribes the power reduction or — *in extremis* — the degree of sanding necessary to restrain creep within the range for optimum tractive effort in the track conditions being encountered at the time.

EMD claims that the device will enhance adhesion by a third. It is a feature of EMD's latest 'Super-Series' Bo-Bo, the GP50, which with a new Series 645F design of 16-cylinder engine is offered at 3,500hp compared with the 3,000hp of its predecessor, the GP40-2. The 'Super-Series', one should add, also offers a six-axle unit, the SD-50.

Fuel economy is the other all-consuming concern of today's US railroads. Besides dictating new features in engine design and a reappraisal of traditional types of auxiliary in the context of their appetite for power, it has compelled railroad managements to take a stricter line on the way their locomotives are run. The shutdown of engines when a locomotive is booked idle for more than half-an-hour and the ambient temperature is keeping above 50deg F has become much more general practice. Steadily gaining favour, too, are 'Fuel-Saver' devices which allow the engineman of a multi-unit formation to switch some of his locomotives to idling and keep on full throttle only as many as are needed to sustain train speed when the load is rolling on favourable alignment. One manufacturer is offering an apparatus which performs this job automatically, since some railroads are reluctant to add to enginemen's preoccupations.

Railroads are more conscious than ever of the need to keep their maintenance routines in fine trim. If any of them needed a lesson, that came from sequence of trials at the Pueblo, Colorado, Test Centre track circuit in 1976. Two multi-unit formations of the same 3,000hp Bo-Bo type were put on successive trials. For three months on end a trio from one railroad hauled the test load without trouble. But a trio from a second railroad which had previously had a fairly high repute for the state of its traction made a very poor fist of the identical tonnage. They needed the addition of a fourth locomotive to complete their stint at Pueblo.

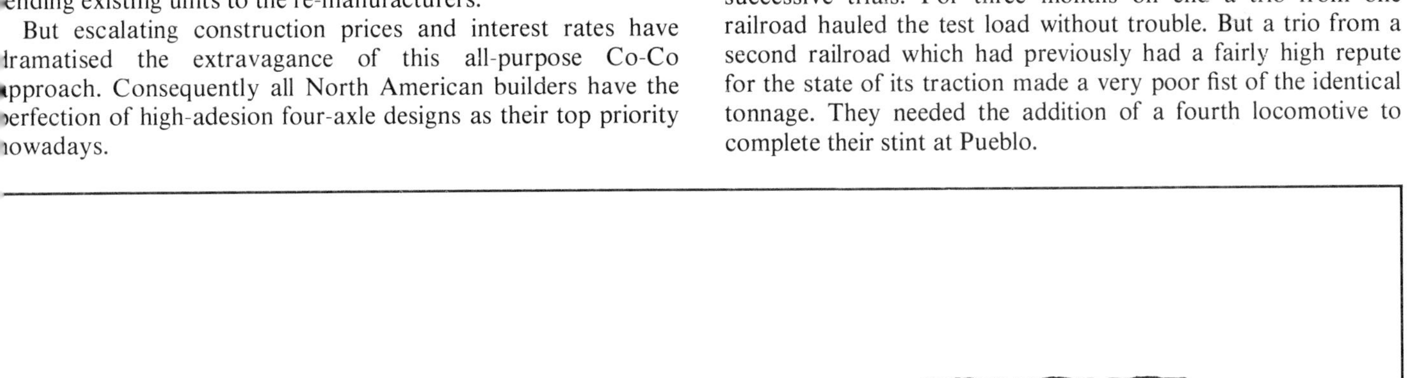

Right, far right and below: The advancing technology of EMD's general-purpose Bo-Bo diesel-electric design for North American railroads: the 2,000hp GP38-2 dating from early 1972, the 3,000hp GP40-2 dating from late 1974, and the new 3,500hp GP50, incorporating the latest EMD 645 series 16-cylinder, two-cycle engine.

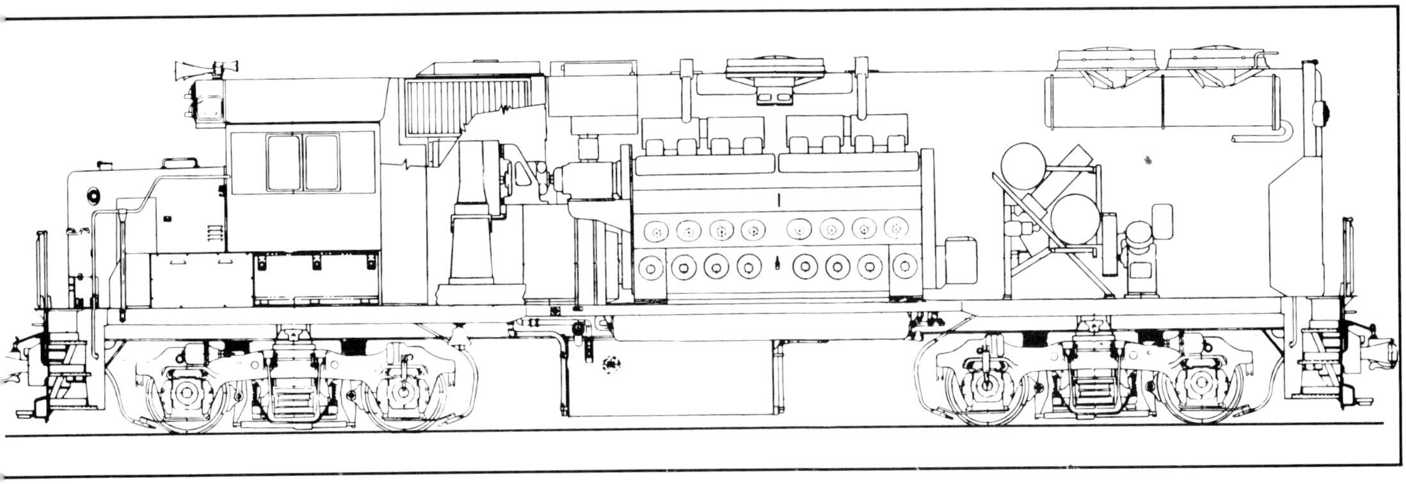

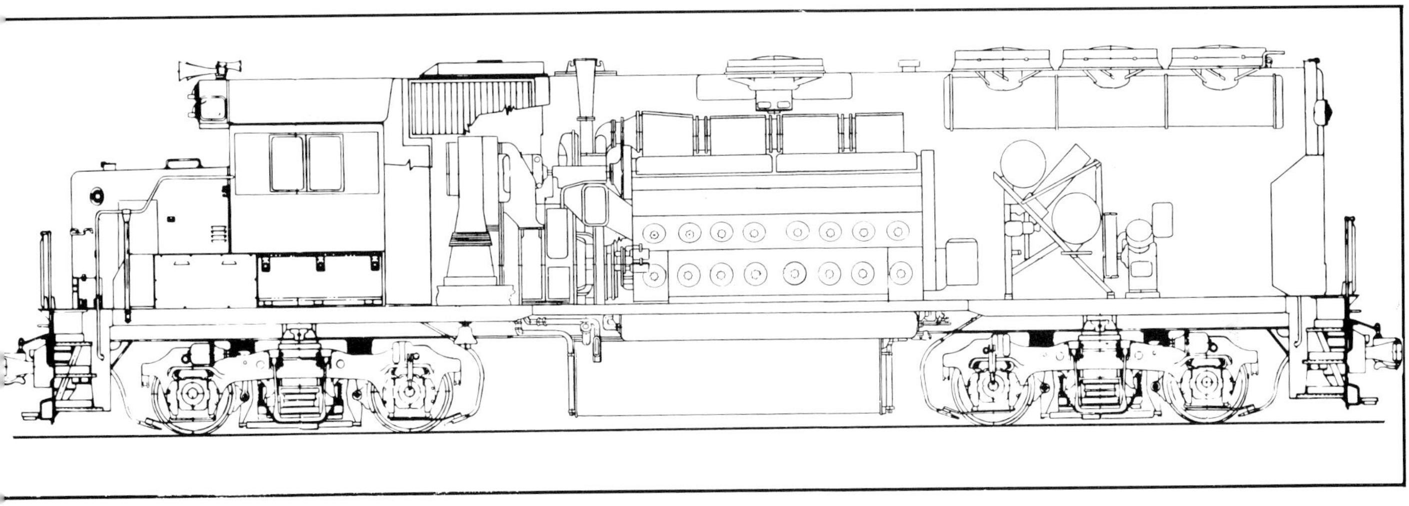

Left: EMD export model embodying the turbocharged 645 series engine — the 3,300hp, 110.4ton Type GT26CW model as supplied to the Moroccan Railways. It can be geared within a range providing 67,200lb continuous tractive effort and 65mph top speed at one end of the scale, 53,300lb and 83mph at the other.

Below left: The SNCF's most powerful diesel type, the 3,600hp 108ton CC72000 with alternator/rectifier transmission and monomotor bogies.

508 020

The 1980 Style in European Commuter Stock

Left and below: The interior and exterior of one of British Rail's new family of high-density electric multiple-unit types, the four-car Class 508 for the third-rail dc Southern Region suburban network: the train is passing Wimbledon depot on a Waterloo-Hampton Court service in March 1980. Acceleration rate is $0.78m/sec^2$, and seating capacity 320 per set.
Les Bertram

S1 Bochum
DB

Left: Driving trailer and second-class saloon interior of one of the DB's push-pull sets employed on the Rhine-Ruhr S-Bahn network. *DB*

Above and right: New in 1980 were five prototypes of a thyristor-controlled 'Pendolare' electric multiple-unit built by the GAI Group in Italy for the FS, which took up service in the Milan area. Each four-car unit has two 53.6tonne power cars with an aggregate 2,360hp output, two 30.3tonne trailers, and seats 344; maximum speed is 87mph and rate of acceleration 0.66m/sec^2 up to 60mph. *Breda*

Above: In 1979 the Danish State Railways took delivery of four prototype two-car units for its Copenhagen suburban system. Built by the Danish firm Scandia-Randers, two of the units have ASEA electric traction equipment, two GEC Traction; this includes thyristor control and regenerative braking.
GEC Traction Ltd

Right: The OBB's Class 4020, the new thyristor-controlled unit built by Simmering-Graz-Pauker which is taking over Vienna commuter services. All axles of the single power car are motored for a total output of 1,610hp and top speed of 75mph. Weighing 129tonnes in total, each unit has seats for 184 and standing room for 416 more.

The Dutch have a New Respect for their Railway

Energetic marketing and attractive fare schemes have stimulated a rising trend of passenger traffic which heralds a new 'age of the train' in Holland. But growing demand is highlighting the NS network's bottlenecks and redoubling its need of increased investment in both infrastructure and rolling stock.

The superb inter-urban highway system of Holland still teems with private cars. But Dutch political and public opinion is perceptibly veering away from more indulgence of private transport to increased support of one of the most impressive public transport operations in Europe. And the first effects are stretching the Netherlands Railways (NS) to the limits of its existing capacity.

Trends since the mid-1970s, the oil crisis — and especially the marked upswing of passenger business in the past two years — have vindicated all the warnings of the NS policy document of 1969, *Spoor naar '75* ('By Rail to 1975'), that within a decade demand would outstrip the existing rail infrastructure. For some years Dutch Governments were sceptical. As the 1970s progressed, however, the purse has been opened wider for such priority projects as the direct line from Amsterdam to Leiden and Dan Haag via Schiphol airport and a multi-track tunnel under the North Sea Canal to improve rail access to Amsterdam from North Holland. Investment funds have been promised early in the 1980s for one or two other vital enlargements of operating capacity, but a great deal more is needed if the NS is to cope with continuing increase of passenger journeys which recent results imply. And, one should add, which their own marketing ploys are making the more certainly predictable. The NS expects passenger demand to rise overall by at least 1.5% a year and wants to spend some £1,500millions to cater for it between now and 1988.

The short-term component of *Spoor naar '75* was a programme branded *Spoorslag '70* ('Rail Attack '70'). This established the most immaculate regular-interval inter-city service in Europe. The 40 principal Dutch population centres were interlinked by a rigidly patterned service of electric locomotive-hauled or multiple-unit trains on at least hourly frequency, but in many cases half-hourly.

In the Ranstad or 'necklace of cities' in the urbanised west of the country, an area roughly the size of Greater London which embraces Amsterdam, Haarlem, Leiden, Den Haag, Rotterdam and Utrecht, several of these inter-city services converge for sectors of their journey. That produces four domestic inter-city trains each way throughout the day between Amsterdam and

Below: The basic tool of the NS short-haul, fixed-interval passenger service — one of the snub-nosed electric multiple-units of mid-1960s design at Utrecht; the driving cab is just abreast of one of the sets of crossovers that divide main station platforms and simplify separation of multiple-unit formations into independent sections for differing destinations.

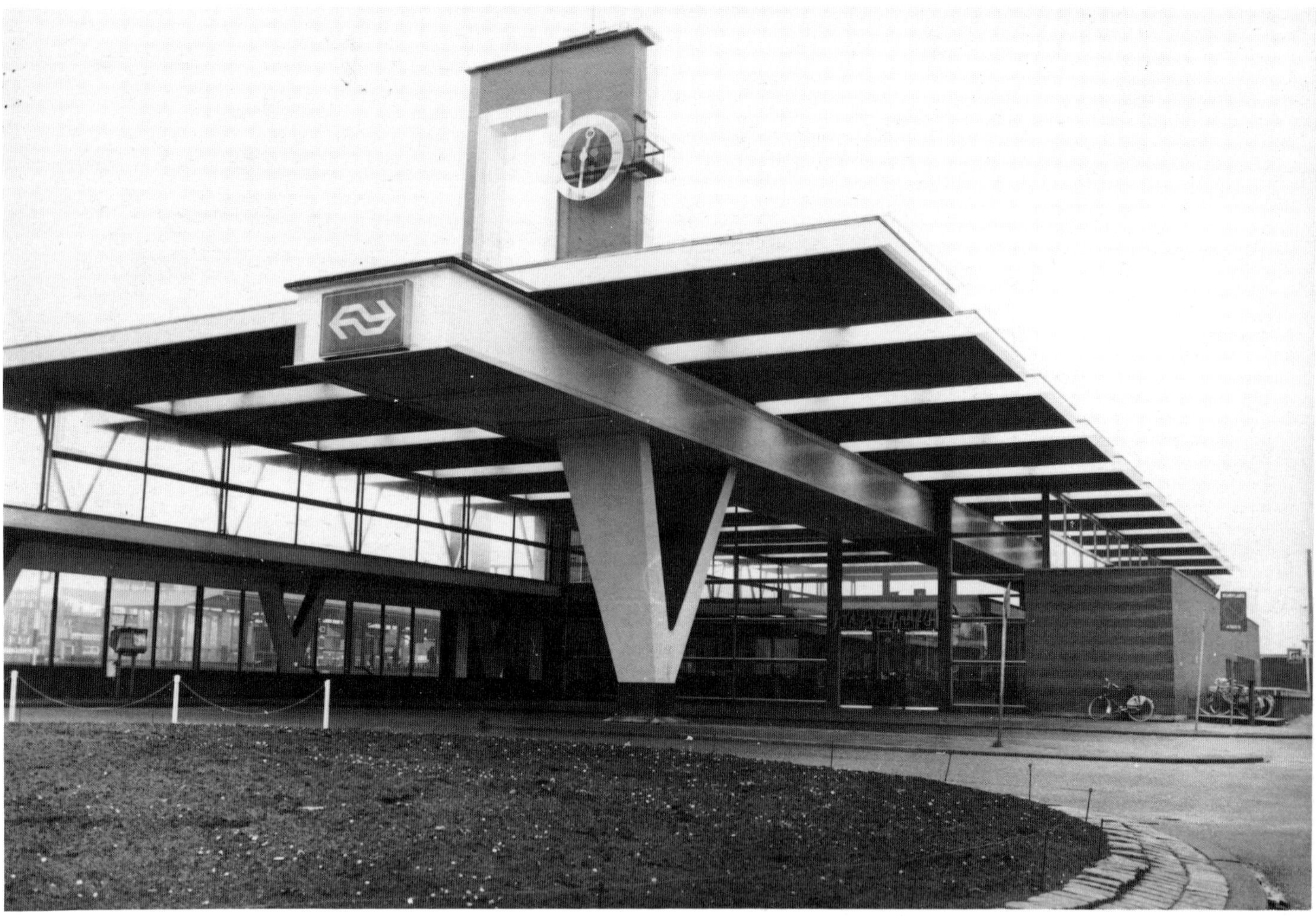

Above: An outstanding feature of the NS since World War 2 has been the striking architecture and neat layout of its reconstructed stations; this is Almelo.

Utrecht, for instance, plus the international TEEs and other workings which are superimposed on the internal service. Stopping services are similarly patterned.

The whole passenger service is tightly integrated for prompt interconnection so as to simplify all the likeliest journeys between pairs of Dutch towns and cities. And at the interchanges the station working is organised so all the frequently made connections are either cross-platform or between halves of a platform.

The intensity of present-day NS service would be totally impossible without the two-train capacity of almost all through platforms at main stations. The characteristic of these layouts is three reversibly signalled tracks between each pair of through platform faces, the centre line exchanging crossovers with the platform tracks at the mid-point so that trains can be berthed behind each other or depart in any required order.

Catching an NS train at a station like Utrecht or Amsterdam you need to verify from the platform notices whether it is leaving from the 'a' or 'b' half of its track just as carefully as the track number. Once on the platform you find that each half is served by its own independent set of the signalbox-controlled computer-based roller-blind train indicators which are one of the many impressive passengers aids at NS main stations (as the scope of control from signal centres spreads they are becoming standard furniture at wayside stations too). If you have gone to the wrong end of the platform its indicators will tell you nothing about the train you are after.

The other *raison d'être* of the NS through station arrangement, of course, is to simplify the assembly of multiple-units from different points of origin as one train for the next sector of their journey, or conversely their dispersal to different destinations. With Scharfenburg couplers which on impact automatically combine physical attachment with connection of all control and auxiliary lines this is a remarkably slick operation.

At Utrecht for example, every hour brings the arrival at 42min past of an inter-city mu from Den Haag, tailed 3min later into the same platform by another from Rotterdam. Just 6min are then allowed for coupling and the end-change of driver before the combined train reverses out to Amersfoort, Deventer and Enschede.

Extra trains are scheduled in the peak hours, but otherwise the timetable is precisely repetitive from hour to hour throughout the system. So is platforming at main stations. A regular Utrecht-Amsterdam traveller needs only to memorise eight minutes-past intervals, four for each end, and two platform numbers to have his whole service on instant recall.

By present-day standards the 1970 timetable was short on market research. Given that the NS is by Dutch Government definition a passenger railway first and foremost, it was as much an exercise to extract the ultimate in productivity from assets as an answer to carefully sifted public demand. It was executed with the minimum of special investment. The principal outlay was on extension of remote-control signalling from strategic centres in the busiest areas. The instant increase of each weekday's passenger working from 2,800 to around 4,000 trains was carried out without any expenditure on flying or burrowing junctions — and path conflicts on the flat are frequent in the complex Randstad network — or on additional running lines. And at that time the NS was calculatedly putting new lines and stations rather than capacity enlargement at the top of its shopping list with the Government.

How hard the NS passenger service drives its assets was highlighted in 1980 by the joint British Rail/Leeds University

Above: At the start of the 1980s the NS Inter-City service was still furnished chiefly by electric multiple-units of this 1950s design, many of them internally refurbished. *NS*

comparison of European railway performance. This showed that the NS gets substantially more vehicle-km from its mus than anyone else: 167,000pa for its emus against a next best of 121,000 by the SNCB (the BR figure is 107,000) and 154,000 for its dmus against a next best of 118,000 by the SNCF (BR scores 96,000). With its electric locomotives the NS records 182,000km a year in a table where BR is the runner-up with 154,000. As for passenger-km per vehicle, the NS puts up an average of just over 4million, 20% more than the nearest rival, the SNCF, and it is also ahead of all comers in annual mileage per passenger vehicle; here its figure is almost 50% better than BR's.

The 1970 timetable stemmed the drift away from rail as Dutch car ownership soared from some half a million in 1960 to around 4million in the mid-1970s. But it had far more influence on the structure of NS users than on numbers of passenger journeys. In the ensuing five or six years short-distance travel declined; use of the railway in the 25-50mile journey range showed little change; and the marked improvement was in longer-distance inter-city travel, where journeys of 90 miles and more climbed by more than 30%.

A number of factors have combined to alter these trends since the mid-1970s. The obvious but not necessarily the salient influence is energy concern and the escalating cost of petrol. Also significant is the continuing migration from the cities to new dormitory areas and the mounting strain of commuting to and from them by road, chiefly because of intolerable jams at the exits from motorways and parking space shortage in most cities. Then the vicious winter of 1978-9 inculcated a new respect for the train's all-weather availability (even if its punctuality was vulnerable). But not least effective have been the first fruits of the railway's 1975 translation of its Commercial Affairs department to a Marketing organisation.

The Marketing men soon recognised that they could not count higher speed as one of their short- or even medium-term weapons. The country was too small and its major cities too close to each other to make any sense of expensive, widespread track upgrading or resignalling for 100mph. A lift from 140km/h (87mph) to 160km/h (100mph) would gain insignificant transit time on most journeys and aggravate capacity problems by widening the speed band unless 100mph traction became standard. But a great deal could and must be done to improve the quality of train travel, the one aspect of NS inter-city operation where development had been virtually non-existent for 15 years.

NS stations are arguably the most well-equipped and stylish in Western Europe, but the emus and above all the locomotive-hauled inter-city coaches they host have become badly dated and uninviting by contrast with Mercedes, Opels, BMWs, Toyotas and the rest. The fleet must be renewed on a large scale. Over short distances especially more direct train services eliminating connectional changes, too, had become imperative. Another line of attack on the habitual car user the marketing managers envisaged was fare manipulation to stimulate consistent train travel.

The Dutch Government prescribes basic NS passenger fare and freight rates, but the NS can price below the maxima provided the gross income at the end of the day meets the Government's budgetary target. Because, as already remarked, the NS function is essentially that of passenger carrier half the total cost of the passenger operation is currently covered by state subsidy.

Left: The other principal component of the NS Inter-City service at the start of the decade was locomotive-hauled trains of 1950s vintage stock, hauled mostly — as here — by a 1200 class Co-Co.

Right: Exterior and first-class interior of the new NS Inter-City coach built by Talbot. *NS*

Nevertheless, each Government-authorised fare increase has some deterrent effect. NS policy now aims to limit it by weighting the bad news to the infrequent rail user's disadvantage. So single tickets took the brunt of a 1979 rise by 5% overall; annual season tickets holders were asked for only 1 to 2% more.

In 1978 the NS introduced a novel variant of the family card. Currently it offers a household of, say three, unrestricted travel, separately or together, the length and breadth of the NS for 12 months at a cost of about £540. The prime requirement is that one member of the family pays FL2,200 (about £495 for the first card. Once that is done, any other members of the household can buy their own card for Fl100 (about £22.50) more per person. Then they too travel free for twelve months.

The 1978 offer was aimed at potentially heavy or long-mileage users of the trains, and up to the 1980 spring about 55,000 had been sold on an average of three per household. Accepting that £495 is a substantial investment for any householder, in October 1979 the NS put on sale a second 'reduction card' designed for families spending between Fl1,000 and Fl2,200 on rail travel. If one member of a household buys this card for Fl375 (about £85) the rest get a card free; ownership then entitles every cardholder to purchase single tickets at half-price, returns at 40% discount and weekly or monthly seasons at a 35% discount. When the whole household is travelling together, only two have to pay and the rest go free. If the cards are well used, then every rail journey is far cheaper than the perceived costs of motoring. Up to last spring 29,000 of these new cards had been marketed.

A sign of new political attitudes to transport in Holland is the Government's more active role in coordination. This has not yet extended to compulsion on the non railway-owned bus undertakings to coordinate their operations with those of the NS, although licences for competing inter-city bus services — for example, from Breda to Utrecht and Nijmegen to Eindhoven — have been refused. However, the widespread juxtaposition of public road transport terminals and rail stations indicates a great deal of unforced cooperation. In addition to its rail service timetable, a model of clarity in presentation, the NS also produces a *Kleine Busatlas* which tabulates with the aid of excellent maps the operator, route, frequency and journey duration of every bus service connecting with trains at NS stations. That list alone occupies over 100 pages, which is clear testimony to the admirable scope of the voluntary public transport coordination.

The most striking Government move so far, is its sponsorship and introduction from 1 May 1980 of a multi-journey ticket valid on any public road transport and also on the railway for short-distance journeys in the conurbations. The whole country has been sectioned off in zones as a framework for roughly 4-mile journeys and each ticket is valid for 15 trips of that distance. The tickets are on sale in post offices and shops as well as at public transport installations.

For years past the NS has made as ample provision for park-and-ride as it could and at the end of the 1970s disposed of some 28,000 car places at its stations. In Holland, of course, park-and-ride has to take proper account of cycles as well as cars; one station on the new Zoetermeer line to Den Haag's dormitories has a cycle park with 1,000 spaces.

The NS was always eager to create more parking room. But by the end of the 1970s it had run out of redundant wagonload freight yards and it was balking at the average £225 or so that each new car place cost to create outside railway property. Rather than mount its own soapbox to campaign for more communal aid than it was getting in often reluctant contributions from some municipal authorities, the NS sagely bent the ears of the Dutch motoring and cyclists' organisations.

These bodies prevailed upon the Government to sponsor a 60-station scheme which will relieve the NS of any expense. The Government has earmarked Fl35millions (almost £8millions) to meet 80% of the bill; the rest will be found by the local authority beneficiaries. For the present, use of such parks will be free, but if they have to be enclosed motorists may be charged a small fee to cover the cost of protection. Promoted under a new 'P+R' pictogram in the standard NS format, the first 'P+R' facility was inaugurated at Schagen early in 1980; Amersfoort was to follow in the summer.

The initial impact of some of these marketing moves was

Above: A 'Sprinter' electric multiple-unit on the recently opened Zoetermeer line serving new dormitory suburbs of Den Haag. *NS*

Right: Interior of a 'Sprinter' second-class saloon.

patent in the Dutch railways' 1979 passenger results. Volume overall was between 5 and 6% up, but the global figure masked a 12% upsurge of peak-hour rail travel. With the added influence of the critical shortage of parking room in Amsterdam the most striking increase was one of almost 40% in first-class travel betweem Alkmaar and Amsterdam. On this route 1,000 more passengers overall inflated the peak-hour movement, a trend which prompted the NS in 1980 to borrow some SNCF Paris suburban bi-level cars for trial between North Holland and Amsterdam. Between Dordrecht and Amsterdam, too, there was a 20% uplift of first-class peak hour journeys as well as a 12% rise in second-class volume.

Inevitably, these 1979 trends, which were countered by squeezing in a few more peak-hour trains and lengthening formations on existing services, overtaxed the known bottlenecks in the Ranstad and disrupted peak-hour inter-city punctuality. Another factor in the congestion is that apart from more intensive passenger train operation NS tracks are nowadays occupied by more daytime non-passenger services.

The NS still moves the great part of Dutch post. The independent single-unit electric post cars, now being re-liveried from overall brown to a new scheme with broad postal red bands, used to work in multiple with passenger emus to a considerable extent, but in 1979 the NS decided to operate them independently so as to avoid delay to the tightly-timed and closely interdependent passenger timetable. These postal cars are shuttling between main centres as often as four and five times daily.

In the early days of the postwar Dutch interval passenger service the small size of the country made for an ideally segregated operation. The internal wagonload freight services could interlink every population centre in the country between one evening's passenger peak and the next morning's rush-hour. In the daytime the passenger trains could have almost free run of the system.

But no longer. The wagonload operation has contracted and 70% of today's NS freight working is in unit trains, either international or to domestic company contract. These have to be run to suit neighbouring railways' scheduling or the customer's industrial processes. And that can even mean, as I have seen at Utrecht, running a four-diesel rake of empty ore hoppers from the Saar back to Rotterdam through the height of the evening peak. (The changed pattern of freight working, incidentally, has also upset the nice, productive balance of electric locomotive provision whereby a proportion of the fleet could do passenger duty by day and switch to freight at night.)

Capacity problems will be exacerbated by passenger service developments to come in the 1980s. So far as the existing network is concerned, the NS is conscious that, if it has no scope for sensible increase of line speed, it must find other ways — apart from higher-quality coaching stock, of which more shortly — to improve its long-distance product. But at the same time shorter-distance travellers cannot be neglected; that is where, off-peak, the rail share of the market has been static, as remarked earlier.

The NS solution is to move from a two-train to a three-train category passenger timetable structure. The top grade will be the ototype that the NS has been field-testing under the brand-ame of 'Intercity-Plus' (which will not necessarily be the title of e final version) at peak business hours between Maastricht and msterdam, Heerlen and Den Haag, and Gronigen and Den aag. The prime selling-point, for which a supplementary fare is iarged on the first two of these three services, is fewer termediate stops than on the basic regular-interval Inter-City ains.

Thus the 7.34 'Intercity-Plus' from Maastricht stops only at ttard and Eindhoven and reaches Amsterdam Amstel, the eripheral cross-platform interchange with the Amsterdam letro, in 2hr 6min, whereas the hourly direct Inter-City trains all also at Roermond, Weert and 's-Hertogenbosch and take hr 23min. As extras the 'Intercity-Plus' user gets guaranteed ee station parking space, a guaranteed free seat reservation, nd free coffee and newspaper. The two 'Intercity-Plus' services) Den Haag, by the way, were in the spring of 1980 spring nploying the 'Corail' coaches which the NS borrowed from the NCF for appraisal during the formulation of its new ocomotive-hauled stock design.

The three-category structure is not yet beyond the outline age of planning. Still to be decided is which 20 to 30 stations ill form the 'Intercity-Plus' network. The choice is bound to be olitically sensitive, since the chain reaction will deprive some sser towns of their quickest peak-hour connections with the big ities. And at the end of the day the timetable — as well as assenger service closures — has to be approved by the Dutch Government. NS officers do not expect the full three-category service to be operational before 1985 at the earliest, by which time they may have been able to enlarge their operating capacity sufficiently to make room for 100mph running by the 'Intercity-Plus' trains.

Such a protracted time-scale is enforced just as much by the essential preliminary widening of bottlenecks. The revised timetable graph resulting from this timetable will create new ones. And some old ones will become more congested by additional services.

In 1986, probably, the new direct line from Den Haag and Leiden via Schiphol Airport will at last reach the Amsterdam city centre. A direct line avoiding the Haarlem detour was proposed in the last century, revived as a concept after World War 2 but not conclusively approved and funded by the Government until early 1974 — the first important sign that the state was persuaded investment in the NS infrastructure was becoming socially essential. The intitial postwar schemes did not envisage serving the Airport. The line of route was deviated that way in 1963.

Below: An NS ICIII electric multiple-unit for Inter-City service; the driving cabin is raised, cockpit-like, clear of a passageway to the opening doors in the nose from the passenger saloon; when two ICIII units are coupled the gangway between them is wide enough for passage of a refreshment trolley. *NS*

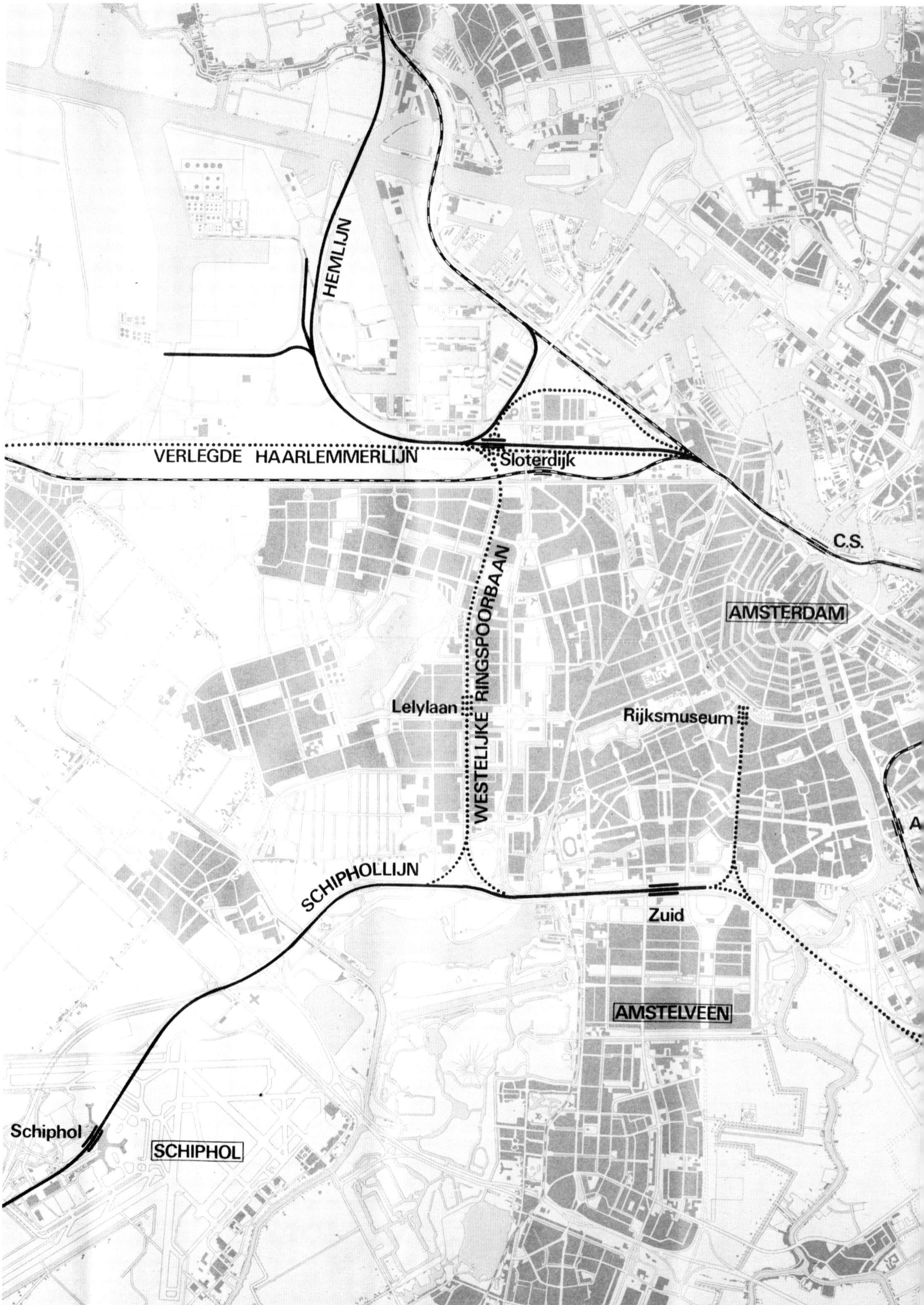
HEMLIJN
VERLEGDE HAARLEMMERLIJN
Sloterdijk
C.S.
WESTELIJKE RINGSPOORBAAN
AMSTERDAM
Lelylaan
Rijksmuseum
SCHIPHOLLIJN
Zuid
AMSTELVEEN
Schiphol
SCHIPHOL

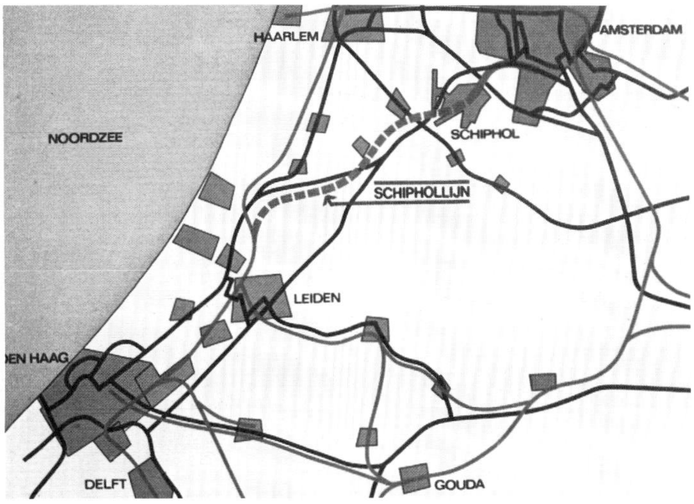

Above: The dotted line shows the location of the new Amsterdam-Schiphol-Leiden line in relation to the existing NS system.

Left: The existing main lines in the Amsterdam area, the Schiphol-Leiden under construction (note the distance of this line's initial Amsterdam Zuid terminus from the centre of the city), the Hem Tunnel line also under way, and the various new lines projected to integrate the Schiphol line with the rest of the system. Also shown is the abortive project to create a new central terminus at Rijksmuseum.

The 6 miles from a road-rail interchange at Amsterdam Zuid, beginning in the median strip of motorways then burrowing in the NS system's longest rail tunnel to a cavernous and palatial three-platform station beneath the Airport terminal, were opened at the end of 1978. A 20min-interval emu service sprints between the two stations in 6min, but as a tram ride from Zuid station to the Amsterdam centre may exhaust up to 30min the project so far is not doing a stunning business. Extension a short distance along the motorway to RAI, the Dutch national exhibition centre, for which approval was conceded in 1980, will not materially improve custom in the interval between events at RAI, one imagines.

West of the 3.6-mile Schiphol Tunnel the construction is forging ahead to a flying junction with the existing Amsterdam-Haarlem-Leiden route at Warmond, although there will be no physical connection between the new and old routes at this point. At Leiden a third platform is to be built to serve the Schiphol tracks, which will remain segregated until they diverge to Den Haag Central. On completion of the Schiphol-Leiden section in 1981 it will be commissioned with a four-trains-an-hour service, half Inter-City and half *Stoptrein*. That will infuse considerable zest into the passenger business, but realisation of the full potential obviously hinges on driving the line closer to Amsterdam's centre.

The NS hankered for a new city station close to the Rijksmuseum, at the opposite end of the main traffic axis to the Central station on the waterfront. But though the city's commercial interests were behind the railway, the city fathers refused the plan as detrimental to the fabric of Amsterdam. Instead a route has got to be created from RAI around the west of the city, for the most part adopting an existing goods line, to a multi-level intersection with the Amsterdam-Haarlem line (and possibly the Metro as well) at Sloterdijk, whereafter the line would fork into a connection with the Zaandam-North Holland line and an approach to Amsterdam Central.

The NS expects funds to complete this line to Sloterdijk by 1985. Also possible, but not before the 1990s, is another adaptation of existing goods lines to carry a second orbital route from RAI around the eastern side of the city to approach

Amsterdam Central alongside the route from Hilversum, and also to make connection with the new railway to Lelystad, in the reclaimed areas of Flevoland (one more of the Government's recent package of railway investment authorisations, on which work has just begun; completion to Lelystad is expected in 1988).

Meanwhile, capacity to operate trains to the neighbourhood of Amsterdam Central will have been enlarged by completion of the new Hem Tunnel line from Sloterdijk to Zaandam, on the busy route to North Holland. The present line is double-track and intersected by a swing bridge over the North Sea Canal. The new railway, which tunnels under the waterway, will have three tracks, all reversibly signalled (a widespread feature of NS main lines, which there is eagerness to make systemwide because of its value in facilitating maintenance, especially at night, when freights can easily run round possessions and allow much more to be accomplished during the week; NS is one more railway that is now taxed to find staff willing to do weekend work on the track). Beyond Zaandam the NS aims to double the Hoorn line by stages so as to exploit the extra capacity of the Hem Tunnel.

All this, though, will aggravate the already troubling shortage of capacity at Amsterdam Central, the busiest station on the NS. In the present timetable its 10 platform lines (most operated in two halves) and five through tracks handle 52 passenger arrivals and departures in each hour of the basic regular-interval service, but 66 in the peak hour. Practically all of these workings are terminal turnrounds. In the second half of the 1980s, plans envisage the basic hourly total rising to 74 and the peak-hour aggregate to 87.

The NS tried to wring more capacity from the Amsterdam layout by a revolutionary application of a computer complex to direct control of functions, not of relays governing the ultimate operation of apparatus. Fed with the timetable, the computer was to be in complete control of the layout and ancillaries such as recorded public address announcements and platform indicators, with human operators intervening only if the working got more than 5min off schedule.

But the Dutch did not have the same success as the Swedes (see pp99-105). Sadly the American genius brought in to create the system died with too many of his concepts committed to his own mind rather than paper. Even without that misadventure the project was soon proved over-ambitious; the huge range of priorities to be taken into account asked too much of memory banks. So for the present the NS has had to take up the book of life, turn to the page headed experience, make an entry and move on sadder but wiser.

Built on a raft-like foundation in a waterway, Amsterdam Central station is incapable of enlargement. The same goes pretty effectively for its approach lines from the west, which are hemmed in by the city. The solutions to the impending crisis are likely to lie in converting some present terminal operations into through workings, and in organising a through service between Den Haag, Leiden, Schiphol and the new railway to come in the Zuyder Zee polders, the Lelystad line, which will bypass Amsterdam Central by the putative eastern orbital route already described. This Flevoland line is presently expected to come into the operating picture in 1986 or 1987. Because it is a key social development with vote-catching significance and may eventually be projected as far as Groningen, its electrified double track will be engineered from the start for 100mph. To prepare for this addition to the network the NS is already seeking the Amsterdam city authority's consent in principle to a widening from four tracks to six of the exit from Amsterdam Central to the south-east.

Elsewhere the NS is enlarging capacity to the extent that its present resources can sustain (and also prospecting diversionary routes for its daytime freights). Double-tracking between Wijchen and Oos, for instance, will allow the 1981 inauguration of faster Intercity nonstops between Nijmegen and s-Hertogenbosch and also additional stopping trains to serve three new stations. The Leiden-Utrecht line, too, is being steadily doubled in sections as the money can be spared. Talking of new stations, the NS has opened over 30 in the past few years, most of them on main lines — another source of pressure on operating capacity.

A desperately-needed scheme which the Government has indicated that it should be prepared to endorse for 1982 is a four-track tunnel to bypass the crippling handicap of a double-track lifting bridge over the Nieuwe Maas between Rotterdam and Dordrecht, on the vital artery that leads to Roosendaal and Belgium in the south, and to Eindhoven, Venlo, Nijmegen and West Germany to the west. In scheming their systemwide structure of Intercity service connections NS timetable planners have to allow for a statutory 20min hoist of the bridge's lifting span every 2hr to allow shipping passage. What is more, maintenance of this and every other movable span in the total of 83 interrupting Dutch tracks comes entirely out of the NS civil engineering budget. Construction of the Willemstunnel to bypass both the Nieuwe Maas bridge and another close by over the Koningshaven is likely to take at least seven years, however.

The NS needs a great deal more than this to fit its infrastructure for the foreseeable traffic demands from 1985 onwards, however. It wants to extend modern remote-controlled MAS, already widespread and wide-ranging (Hook of Holland for instance, has lately been brought within the orbit of the Rotterdam centre), to the whole of the core system. In some cases station layout revision is a planned concomitant of resignalling. And the NS is also anxious to replace a number of flat convergences with flying or burrowing junctions; to add platforms to some key stations such as Dordrecht, Rotterdam and Ede; and to lay in additional running lines over several busy sectors. The priority under the last of these heads is to provide four tracks throughout from Den Haag to Rotterdam and possibly, in association with the new tunnel under the Maas, as far as Dordrecht. Next in line is four-tracking out of Utrecht towards Hilversum. Other signalling and telecommunications investment plans include extension of reversible working and renewal of the system's ATC apparatus.

For the past decade of so the amount of annual investment in the Netherlands Railways (NS) permitted by the Government has been virtually static in real money terms. Moreover, the Government has now and then dictated that the money be spent on political priorities rather than on what the NS deems urgent — for instance, railwaymen gnashed their teeth when they were required to electrify in the rural east of the country instead of getting on with the Schiphol line.

Although the Dutch people get a far more generous social deal through their railways than Britons, NS management seems just as hobbled by a Ministry of Transport as British Rail. More so in some respects: for instance, in the imposition of maximum charge levels, mentioned earlier, and in the need of Ministry approval to withdraw a freight service as well as passenger trains. The Government has in the past resisted an increase of railway expenditure with the argument that Dutch railwaymen cost too much (they are comparatively the best-paid in Western Europe). But it has refused closures, such as that of the little-used Ijmuiden passenger trains, as a way of saving cash for more useful objectives. 'It's much easier nowadays to get something opened than to close anything', one NS officer remarked to me.

Although Dutch Governments have been meeting half the cost of new lines and the present regime is considering arguments that one way or another its support should be even more openhanded, the Department of Transport keeps a very pedagogic eye on NS investment planning. No project costing more than Fl5millions (about £1.12million) can be launched without Government endorsement, and in 1980 the NS was doggedly resisting pressure to lower the limit within which it can

Left: Several vintage types of locomotive are being refurbished for extended service in the face of rising traffic demand; the Class 1100 Bo-Bos so treated are distinguished by new reinforced, bulbous noses, like No 1138 here calling at Amsterdam Amstel on a through train to the German border at Emmerich via Utrecht and Arnhem.

Below: One of the elderly NS diesel railcar sets principally employed on rural lines in the north of Holland. *NS*

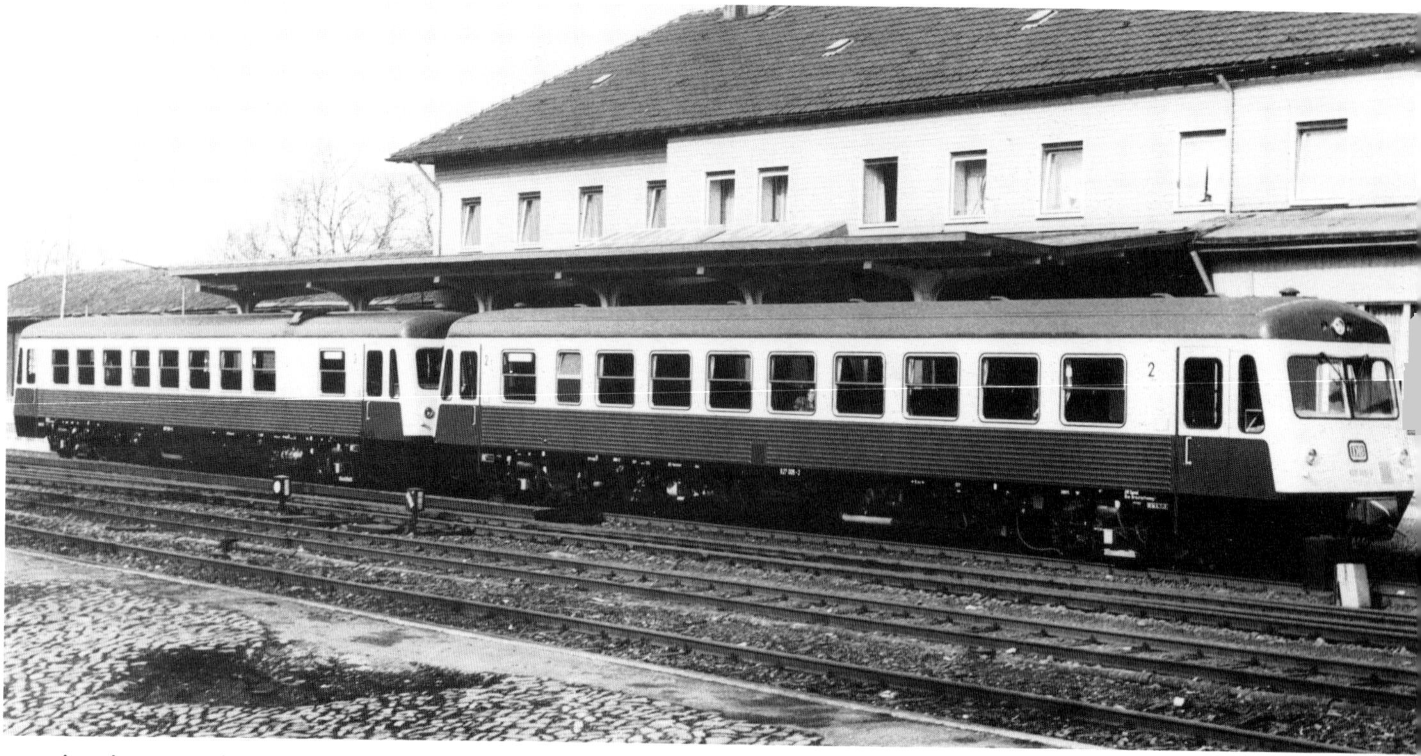

exercise its own judgement to a mere Fl1million (about £225,000). Like its counterpart on the British side of the North Sea, the Dutch Ministry has accumulated a considerable staff to appraise NS proposals and duplicate the work of the railway's own economists and planners.

However, a tide of Dutch public opinion in favour of more spending on the NS at the expense of the country's roads now seems likely to impel the Dutch administration to an increase of at least a third in the NS infrastructure investment allowance from the mid-1980s onwards. The political alignment on this issue in the spring of 1980 was a little complicated. Roughly 80% of the Dutch Parliament, composed in equal proportions of the Socialists and Christian Democrats, favoured much bigger investment in railways. But of these only the Christian Democrats were in Government, in a coalition with the Liberals. The Liberals were not pro-railway and the Transport Minister was a Liberal.

One area in which the NS has recently won endorsement for grand-scale and overdue modernisation is traction and rolling stock. Like BR, the Dutch have been confronting an alarming re-equipment bulge, because of the huge re-equipment programme that was the only course in the first postwar decade to get the railway back on its feet.

The bulk of the electric passenger service is still provided by the two- and four-car Inter-City emus of 1950s design; the snub-nosed lightweight two-car emus of the mid-1960s with enhanced acceleration which do *Stoptrein* duty (though I also noticed some of the 1946-style articulated emus still active and still in the old gold-lined green livery last spring). On the Inter-City routes not involving reversal on the way, locomotive-hauled rakes of the 1950s vintage stock, still painted in navy blue, predominated in 1980, but they are now being superseded by 226 new cars from Talbot of Aachen.

In 1980 I found the Inter-City emus steady and tolerably quiet riders considering their age and innocence of air-conditioning, but the locomotive-hauled stock — as one would expect — noisy and a poor competitive tool for the travel market of the 1980s. Both types of vehicle are entirely open saloon, but for non-smoking first-class compartments.

Wagons-Lits diners still function on international services, but the NS confines its domestic Inter-City catering to a mini-buffet operation, mostly from perambulated trolleys; so far as I could see, the restricted buffet saloons in the train-sets are now treated as general seating space. Average journeys are too short to make sense of a grander catering service, besides which major stations not only have, restaurants but often elaborate batteries of food and drink Automats in the platform waiting rooms.

The emus of the later 1950s have now to be kept going until 1985 and the last of them is not expected to disappear until 1995. Consequently a programme of technical improvement and internal refurbishment is under way as these units fall due for general overhaul. The revamped sets are distinguished by a lateral band of blue enclosing the windows, instead of the diagonal blue stripes on the overall body yellow which was the standard when the NS adopted its present house style. In Inter-City operation these emus average about 140,000 miles annually and the refurbished sets operate for 50 days between major depot examinations.

The future is likely to see switches from multiple-unit to locomotive-hauled Inter-City operation through revision of services to reduce the division or assembly of train sections en route. In the savage 1978-9 winter the emus' couplers were seriously vulnerable to malfunction and although NS engineers hope to avoid recurrence by devising a means of keeping the coupler heated many NS operators were soured by the experience.

The new generation of NS passenger stock was launched with the SGM or 'Sprinter' two-car emus, which have taken over the Rotterdam-Hook of Holland/Maasluis, Zoetermeer and Den Haag-Pijnacker-Rotterdam short-distance services. Besides some technical modification the further series to come will differ from the first batch in including toilets, lack of which has annoyed the public, and inter-car connection within each unit to help combat the universal menace of vandalism. 'They're the counterpart of the DB's ET420' emus, an NS officer said to me of the 'Sprinters'. I found them somewhat superior; just as sweetly-riding and quick off the mark to full speed, but incredibly quiet, with the traction gear so near-noiseless in the passenger saloons that a light wind whipping past the bodyside was the most obtrusive sound at speed.

Next to emerge were the prototype ICIII three-car Inter-City emus of entirely new design, of which seven units have for some months been covering Amsterdam-Utrecht-Nijmegen services. After protracted evaluation the NS was in the spring of 1980 coming to the point of series order. Frankly, on my ICIII journeys that spring I did not find the riding as smooth as in the

Above left: Replacements ordered for the diesel railcar fleet are versions of the German Federal Railway's Type VT627 twin-unit dmu.

Above: A heavy unit train of ore from Rotterdam in high-capacity bogie hoppers heads for Belgium behind a pair of electrics, with refurbished 1100 class Bo-Bo No 1158 leading. *NS*

latest Inter-City vehicles of BR, the DB and the SNCF, though the second-class saloon comfort was agreeable enough.

Both in the ICIII emu and in the 226 new locomotive-hauled coaches to essentially the same design as the emu trailer, except that the latter ride on SNCF-design Y32 bogies, the NS has taken a bold step in interior layout. Given the comparatively short distance of most NS Inter-City journeys, the NS believes it can use the same longitudinal spacing for both first- and second-class saloon seating. At least that eliminates a chronic criticism of British Rail's standard Mk III bodyshell, that because of spacing variation between classes body pillars are bound to block views from some seats. In the NS cars every seat back (naturally in first-class the lateral arrangement will be two-and-one, as against two-and-two in second) is neatly in line with a pillar. Another benefit of this move, NS men point out, is that second-class cars can be easily converted to first and vice versa if traffic demand varies, though that possibility will be limited by their Marketing department's insistence that in the new stock first-class accommodation must be a mix of compartment and saloon.

At the end of 1979 the NS got authority to increase its order for new Class 1600 electric locomotives from 30 to 48. Making their debut early in 1981, these machines are being built by Alsthom-Atlantique to the 6,150hp SNCF BB7200 design, following the NS evaluation on its own ground of a borrowed example from the French fleet. Since the green light for refreshment of the ageing NS traction fleet some pressure has been heard for revival of a domestic supply industry devitalised by lack of home orders, but the NS sees no rational alternative to buying where continuing business has fertilised research and development. Its engineers do not believe that three-phase technology is yet sufficiently proven to have justified its purchase in the late 1970s; but they expect to be buying it in locomotive orders for the later 1980s. Chopper control has been considered for the production series of ICIII emus.

Traffic demands have dictated refurbishing of the existing electric locomotive fleet for extended use. Now foreseen as serving until the mid-1990s are the home-built but American-influenced 3,000hp Class 1200, many of which are being submitted to a multi-faceted technical modernisation. Even the six surviving ex-BR Class 1500, the former Manchester-Sheffield EM2s, have been thoroughly overhauled for work until 1985-6, instead of going for scrap in 1981. The only complaint I heard of these machines is that they are underpowered and that procurement of spares is troublesome (one was cannibalised at the start of the 1970s). British Rail, it seems, has been trying to cajole the NS into an offer for its Class 76 1.5kV dc Bo-Bos since the Woodhead route closure and their redundancy became a foregone conclusion, but has so far met with smiling but firm refusal to be undermined by appeals to sentiment — the prototype won the soubriquet of *Tommy*, it will be recalled, through postwar loan to the NS pending completion of the Manchester-Sheffield electrification. Spares are also a worry with the Alsthom-built Class 1100 2,580hp Bo-Bos; nevertheless a number have been recently modified with reinforced cab-ends featuring a short bonnet.

A start has been made on refurbishing the Dutch system's elderly diesel multiple-units, but the NS has also ordered its own version of the DB's VT627 diesel-hydraulic twin-set for the non-electrified rural lines in the North. Here the Government has yielded to public pressure for retention of the train service, but the residents have been told that if they insist on trains rather than buses the train service must be operated as cheaply as possible. Since the railway unions are naturally jealous for the trains too, that may disarm their resistance to NS proposals not only to single-man the units in this area but also to induce the men to carry out some rudimentary maintenance chores themselves.

The NS version of the VT627 will be cheaper than its DB parent. A cardinal difference in the Dutch order of 71 cars, some for single-, others for twin-unit operation, is that each car is powered by a Cummins 280hp engine (built in Scotland, incidentally), whereas the DB twin-unit has a single high-powered motor car.

Forced to assemble a quartet of its 900hp Class 2200 Bo-Bo diesels to move the 4,000-5,000 tonnes gross ore trains regularly run nowadays from Rotterdam to the Saar, the NS urgently needs a new generation of diesels. Seeing nothing on anyone's shelf to suit them the NS mechanical engineering chiefs aim to assemble two new designs — a line locomotive of around 2,000hp and a heavy shunter of about 1,100hp — from proven components. In early 1980 they had the Henschel three-phase diesel-electric prototype on three months' trial, but simultaneously they were discussing orthodox dc-motor possibilities with Alsthom-Atlantique.

By 1982 the NS will be in the Light Rail Transit business with a 10.9-mile system now under construction from Utrecht southward to the expanding dormitory areas of Ijsselstein and Nieuwegein. The LRT is being built on a reserved right of way that encounters about 40 road intersections. Signalling will be confined to these crossings, where the WITAG method practised on the Rotterdam Tramways is to be adopted; in this system the LRVs activate the signalling as they approach each intersection. The articulated LRV units for the new line are being built to a new design by the Swiss firm, SIG.

Whereas the Dutch Government contributes roughly the same amount to meet the total costs of the passenger service as the NS secures in revenue within the ceiling set on its maximum fares, the state subvention for NS freight working is less than a third of the final bill. A previous administration set the NS an objective of making the rail freight services cover their avoidable costs by 1980, but the present regime has agreed with the railway that this is unattainable. At the same time it will not allow the NS to withdraw entirely from a domestic wagonload business that is almost entirely responsible for the shortfall. As already explained, the state regards the railway primarily as a passenger carrier; residual capacity is available for freight, which is consequently accounted on an avoidable cost basis.

Nevertheless, the NS has managed to push through a drastic rationalisation of its internal wagonload operation. Today it serves only 150 depots in Holland, as opposed to some 400 in the early 1960s. The freight books had actually been balanced by 1974, but since then inflation and recession have renewed losses.

The latest, major development in the streamlining programme has been the early 1980 commissioning of a new augmented yard — the first on the NS — with 36 sorting sidings at Kijfhoek, about 10 miles south of Rotterdam. The yard is plugged into the NS counterpart of BR's TOPS, so that its control is pre-advised of the consist and individual wagon data of all trains to be sorted. Within the yard, which was equipped by the US firm Wabco Westinghouse, the sorting process is computer-controlled and the detail of re-formed trains automatically transmitted to the central freight wagon data files of the computer bank at Utrecht.

The NS drive for remunerative freight trainloads is more bedevilled by the unfair apportionment of true costs than any other European railway's effort, Belgium alone accepted. Users of Holland's ramified inland waterway system pay nothing for their track, not even for negotiation of locks or lifting overbridges. If they did have to pay a fair price, independent analysts have calculated they would have to treble their tariffs to stay out of bankruptcy. As is, in the currently depressed transport market they have margin enough to undercut the railway with some ease. A previous Government hinted at moves to re-impose stricter controls on Dutch transport capacity, but nothing significant materialised. However, the administration of 1980 launched a fresh series of transport studies, and one of them was a re-examination of the infrastructure cost issue.

Price-cutting by the canal men and the navigable waterway from the Dutch coast right through Germany to Basle are main reasons why the NS has secured barely a quarter of the inland movement of containers to and from Rotterdam's Europoort terminal. So long as recession cuts their traffic in bulk minerals, containers are valuable space-fillers at any price for th waterway operators.

However, more and more Dutch firms are beginning to shar NS freight managers' conviction, not only that the barg operators are likely to dump their container business a unprofitable as heavy industrial traffic recovers, but also that th tide of regulation is veering in the railway's favour. Apart fror the fact that industrial relations in the giant Dutch road haulag industry are not as stable as in the well-paid railways, the 198 Government was hinting at stricter control of the road drivers working hours and at mandatory double-manning over th longest distances. Reaction from the Dutch counterpart of th CBI was strangely muted, possibly because of rising respect fo the growing efficiency of the international rail freight operation.

Certainly numerous bulk freight customers have bee switching to rail in recent months. Particularly marked — an for the most part captured from the waterways — is the growt of cereals traffic from France into Holland and from Rotterdar (imports in this case) to Belgium, France and as far even as Eas Germany.

Another conspicuous growth area is the movement of ore in huge unit trains. Apart from Dunkerque, Rotterdam is the only European port equipped to discharge the 250,000tonne ore carriers. The NS, as observed earlier, is shifting this in four-diesel trainloads of 2,270tonnes payload and 4,500tonnes gross to Saarland steelworks, and also running block trains to Belgium, France and as far afield as the Linz plants in Austria. If this traffic maintains its present growth rate it will exacerbate the NS capacity problems, since its operation cannot be confined to the nighttime.

Around 35% of the NS freight traffic now moves in privately owned or leased wagons, mostly the latter. New construction focuses to an increasing extent on specialist vehicles — so much so that some NS officers forecast the eventual extinction of the general-purpose open and covered wagon — and that redoubles the pressures for slick working, to amortise their high cost by intensive utilisation. One impressive privately-owned fleet on the NS consists of massive green-liveried tipplers operated for a firm which disposes of over 800,000tonnes of urban refuse annually via purpose-built and rail-connected loading and discharge plants.

Coal traffic, decimated when the Dutch mining industry folded, is now reviving and likely to become big rail business again. From about 1984 onwards a heavy tonnage is expected from a trans-shipment terminal now in the planning stage for coal imported by sea through Rotterdam Maasflukt.

At present NS container traffic, which in 1979 was 12.6% up in tonnage on 1978, is little more than one-eighth domestic. But in 1978-9 internal movement of containers by rail doubled, so with a substantial number of important industrial premises devoid of rail connection the NS has been studying possible creation of a Freightliner-type operation within Holland. Of its four current container trans-shipment terminals, only Veendam in the north is inland; the remainder are maritime, at Rotterdam, Amsterdam and Vlissingen. The concept being considered would demand new terminals in the south and east as well as in the north.

Road hauliers are gradually accepting that piggyback is their ally not their competitor in a high fuel-cost age. Thus shortage of specialist flatcars has been causing concern on the daily services operated to South Germany, Basle and Milan from the Rotterdam piggyback terminal as haulier confidence waxes and demand rises. NS freight managers believe that this business will get a fresh boost from the drive-on, drive-off capability for complete tractor-and-trailer rigs to be created by the new ultra-low-loading Talbot flatcars. If drivers can travel with their vehicles in passenger cars attached to the train, then they are on hand at destination not only to monitor and push through the load's processing, but also to canvas for a return load.

Cars by Rail — a Contrast

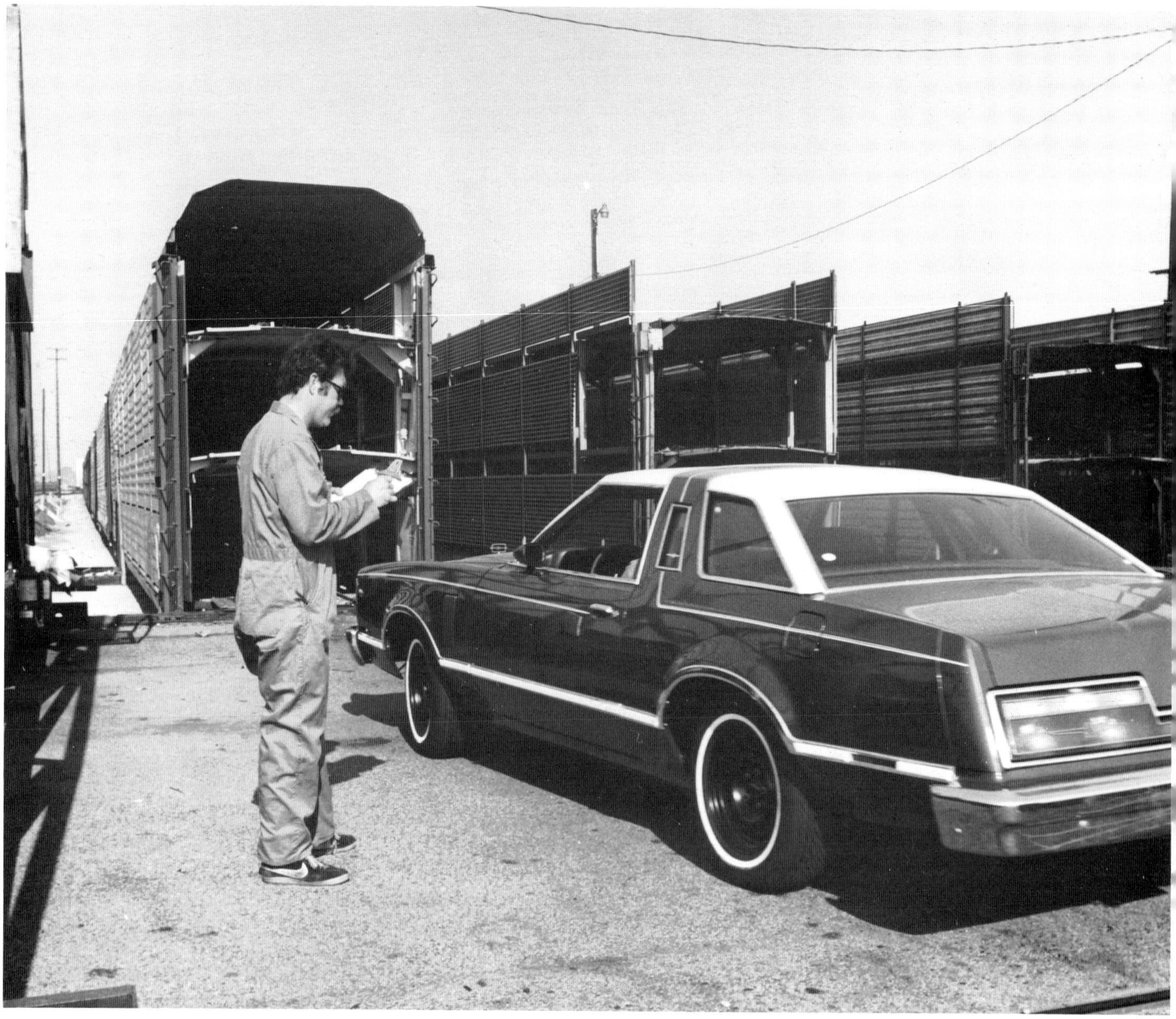

Previous page and above: In the past quarter-century motor manufacturers have realised the value of rail as a damage-free deliverer of new vehicles to distribution railheads. The 1979-80 recession seriously dented the traffic, especially in North America, but it has not inhibited technological development — a new 1980 variant was the shipping of Subaru cars from Japan to the USA market in containers, two per box, for inland movement from Houston by Missouri Pacific. The generous North American loading gauge allows rail movement of US-manufactured cars in tri-levels, both open and closed, as seen in these pictures of the Santa Fe's 'Autoveyor' yard at Amarillo, Texas, and of a Ford loading facility at Pico Rivers, California. *Santa Fe*

Right: In the UK the private wagon manufacturer Procor (UK) has contrived in its 'Procar 80' a vehicle that achieves the best payload/tare and payload/train length ratios yet within the BR loading gauge. Weighing 24.5tonnes and 79ft 5in long over buffers, with 75mph capability, the 'Procar 80' can carry 12 British Leyland Minis or, as seen here, a mix of 10 middle-market family saloons.

ꜱweden's Cheap-
ꟷare Plan Boosts
ɔoth Travel and
ꓤevenue

he Government-financed reduction of all rail fares in 1979 has imulated both a 35% rise in journeys and an increase in venue. As a result the Government is likely to smile on a nsiderably higher investment in the national rail system roughout the 1980s.

 the late 1970s Sweden acted to rescue its national railway stem, SJ, from the tail-chasing frustration of steady price creases to offset inflating costs and shrinking traffic on the ɔmmercial sector of the rail network. The outcome was ɔvernment financial backing for a revolutionary fare scheme, unched in June 1979, which lopped an average of 16% off the ɔst of rail travel. By the spring of 1980 the fare offers, coupled ith availability of a family railcard, had generated over 20% ore journeys overall, but a 35% improvement in long-distance il travel. Three-quarters of the new business was second-class.

Given the generosity of the scheme, the net revenue gain was nlikely to be startling. But some additional contribution to direct costs has been achieved from the 9% rise in gross venue, because the offers were weighted to stimulate off-peak avel and the big increase in demand has been satisfied rincipally through more productive use of track, traction and ɔlling stock. The surcharge of direct operating costs has been roportionally small.

Sweden's political parties have worried the issue of fair llocation of infrastructure costs to the various transport modes since the early 1960s. But they have never been able to agree a basis for apportioning the full road bill between different categories of user. Consequently as SJ management sees it, private motoring and bulk road transport in Sweden have been getting cheaper in real money terms.

Since the mid-1970s of course, the Swedes have been increasingly anxious to curb oil consumption. Where passenger transport is concerned the oil these past few years has been going not only into buses and cars but into a fast-developing internal air network. By 1979 at least 25 Swedish centres were interconnected by air services priced very competitively against SJ's first-class tickets. In contrast to this oil-consuming transport, SJ moved 90% of its traffic over the two-thirds of its system that works under hydro-electrically energised catenary.

Despairing of any agreement on the road cost issue, the Government proposed the alternative of a grant to SJ of at least £30 millions and up to twice that amount, to compensate the railways for their unique responsibility for all infrastructure costs in their commercial sector. Unfortunately this concept surfaced as the national economy came under severe pressure from inflation and recession, and Parliament cut the annual figure to about £15million.

Of this aggregate just over half was offered as Government underwriting of the cheap fare scheme. The rest was added to SJ's depreciation provision, to ease the limit on annual investment which had been denying the railways some much needed re-equipment — track doubling; track improvement for higher-speed and the new intercity rolling stock to go with it; ATC; track-to-train radio; at least 25% of the new freight wagons needed annually; the station modernisation.

The Government has effectively shouldered some of SJ's infrastructure costs as the result of a 1980 change in the detail of SJ's budgeting. Some items of track upkeep and renewal are now counted as investment, to which the Government contributes not only by the new provision just mentioned

Below: A typical SJ locomotive-hauled express of modern times, headed by an ASEA-built, thyristor-controlled Type Rc4 electric locomotive. The 200-odd locomotives of the Rc family average 140,000miles a year.

Left: One of the so-called 'Paprika' trains, the Class X9 electric multiple-units, which are the Inter-City equipment of some less busy routes such as Malmö-Helsingborg.

Right: The first-class accommodation of some of SJ's older passenger stock has a highly individual character: here, from top to bottom, are the first-class saloon, a first-class compartment and the second-class saloon of a Type AB7 composite.

(though at the time of writing that has been voted only until the end of the 1981-2 financial year), but also by loans on which the SJ pays no interest unless the railways are in financial surplus. Which, sadly, has not been recorded since 1975-6 and is not a betting prospect in the forseeable future.

Over some 4,350 route-miles of the SJ total of about 7,150 the Government foots the whole investment bill and also subsidises running costs. This is the trackage in rural Sweden which so far it has proved politically impossible to close in favour of bus transport under direction from Stockholm, though better luck is expected with the establishment of 24 Regional Transport Authorities to take over local planning throughout the country. The first is due to take up office in the summer of 1981 and completion of the scheme is expected by 1983.

In earlier years Swedish Governments pressed the SJ to run this unremunerative sector as basically as possible. One result is that SJ has probably the highest proportion of unmanned stations in Western Europe. That kind of economy has reached practical limits, so the Government has resigned itself to whatever bill results from running at least one statutory train each way daily to placate the local electors — even over a line stretching 467 miles from Gällivare to Ôsterund, where habitation averages about one Swede per square kilometer. One should add that within the sector of its system where SJ is mandated to operate commercially the Government meets staff costs at some stations where the Transport Ministry has overridden an SJ closure submission.

Despite this Government aid the SJ shares with British Rail the unwanted distinction of having to fund more of its investment from its own resources and loans than any other Western European railways. Even if it had much scope for enlarging those resources by up-pricing — and besides Government control of general tariff levels, it has lately had to contend with a Price Control Bureau's microscopic scrutiny of any detail variation it has attempted — SJ could not spend them as it pleased.

The Government proposes and Parliament has to approve the annual investment allowance, which since the mid-1970s has been that much lower than SJ's submission year by year. Furthermore, though SJ has to back its submission with a 10-year programme, the Government does not commit itself for more than a year at a time. Thus SJ's forward planning ha always to be speculative to some degree.

At least the politicians do not usually argue with SJ's order o priority. But it can happen. In 1980 Parliament was much mor interested in upgrading the long route through the sparsel populated heart of Sweden to the far north, a job which woul last well into the 1990s, than in the doubling of the route fron Stockholm to the south which SJ deems much more urgent t cope with economic demand.

The big increase in passenger traffic generated by the Jun 1979 fare scheme has set up some capacity problems t aggravate SJ's recent deprivation of adequate investment.

The fare scheme cut basic fare prices, but made them cheape still outside the peak weekdays, Friday and Saturday, if on bought an annual railcard. To stimulate persistent use of train these railcards were attractively priced at about £12 first- and £8 second-class. They helped to steer at least 35% of the new business to off-peak trains, but the high proportion of extra peak-day travellers put considerable pressure on SJ's coaching stock.

The strain was severe on the Intercity services, which attracted the bulk of the new custom. Here passenger journeys soared by 50% in the first few months of the new fare scales. Although the first of 150 new coaches rolled off the assembly lines as the scheme was launched, the vehicles they were to supersede had to be kept operational to cope with the boom. If train staff had rigidly followed the rules a good many passengers would have been turned away.

Simplified by SJ's possession of a Stockholm-based computer centre for seat booking and ticket issue throughout the Intercity network, seat reservation of 'X' category trains is obligatory. If one fails to reserve in advance, any spare seat on the train can be bought from its conductor, but after June 1979 latecomers found far fewer free seats and too many standing passengers had to be tolerated for SJ management's peace of mind. When I talked with SJ passenger men in the 1980 spring they were investigating the percentage of 'no shows' to see whether they dare indulge the airlines' habit of slightly overbooking train capacities.

SJ's Intercity service is a regular-interval operation, implemented on the principal routes by locomotive-hauled trains

Left: Second-class saloon of a refurbished Typ
B3 car.

Right: Exterior and second-class saloon interic
of SJ's newest Type B7 Inter-City car.

employing the redoubtable ASEA-built range of thyristor-controlled Rc Bo-Bos. Some lesser routes, such as Malmö-Helsinborg in South Sweden, are worked by the neat, low-slung Type X9 emus still familiarly known as the 'Paprika' trains, though the bright red livery which won them the nickname has since become the standard shade of the Rcs.

On the key routes from Stockholm to Malmö, Göteborg and Uppsala Intercity frequency is hourly, elsewhere mostly every two hours. Considering the line speed limit of 130kmph (79.6mph) thought necessary on straight, double track chiefly because of the high incidence of level crossings (see p99-105), SJ's Intercity trains are no slouches. For instance the peak evening express from Göteborg to Stockholm was in 1980 covering the 283.4 miles in an even 4hr, inclusive of calls at Skövde and Södertälje, which called for an end-to-end average of close on 71mph.

Now that ATC is to be installed system-wide, as described elsewhere in this book, and with the continuing reduction of the country's inordinate number of level crossings through bargaining with local authorities, SJ is hopeful that it can achieve some stretches of 100mph track in the foreseeable future. Any higher speed than that looks out of the question. Consequently the main hope of shortening journey times lies in an increase of speed where track conditions check orthodox rail vehicles.

Before 1981 was out SJ expected authority to order three prototype emus based on the experimental X15 unit, a four-car, 170 tonne, 4,500kW set with automatic body-tilting which SJ evolved with ASEA in the mid-1970s and which has been tested at up to 150mph. Given some straight track licence for 100mph, an X15 could cut the best Stockholm-Göteborg journey time, for instance, from 4hr to 3hr 20min for an average of 85mph throughout. But even without any easing of present speed limits the time saved through superior curving speed would be enough to warrant ordering X15s for the additional coaching stock SJ needs in any event

Accompanying illustrations indicate the quality of SJ's latest locomotive-hauled stock, but it has done an appealing job in refurbishing many of their predecessors. In first-class especially: here some of the older cars — which still ride very acceptably — splice compartment sections with a central lounge that features loose armchairs and an occasional table as well as bench settees against each lateral wall. Every SJ coach, incidentally, has in its vestibule a flask of drinking water and a supply of plastic cups.

When SJ first developed its regular-interval service it balanced greater frequency with shorter train formations and catering service was not a standard feature. But with the adoption of the aggressive new fares policy in 1979 SJ's management re-wrote their policy. For the next five years viability would not be the prime objective of train catering (which is furnished by one of SJ's subsidiary companies in vehicles owned by the railway). Any losses had to be kept within prescribed limits, but otherwise the aim was some form of catering on every Intercity train as one of rail travel's shop-window inducements.

The new policy had to be executed with the existing stock of catering cars, however. No new ones have yet been ordered, though SJ managers were pondering a case for new self-service vehicles when I was in Stockholm in the spring of 1980. Consequently the aim has been fulfilled mostly by a considerable extension of trolley service offering hot and cold drinks and snacks, which has proved encouragingly successful with the public.

At the same time available catering cars have been redistributed to present a coherent picture of service. All trains between Stockholm and Ânge, for example, are now trolley-served, whereas before the only catering provision on this route was a diner on one train each way daily. That has now been reallocated to make possible, amongst other things, inclusion of meal service on all trains linking Stockholm and Malmö, though not enough cars could be mustered to do likewise between the capital and Göteborg, as SJ would like.

One should add that the SJ timetable's knife-and-fork symbol does not connote a standard meal service. It covers both self-service cafeteria and full diner (these facilities are combined in some cars), although the cafeterias usually have a short list of basic hot dishes on offer as well as the predictable array of *smörgasbord.*

ÅK EJ PÅ
NEDERSTA
FOTSTEGET
5201

Above: Electric multiple-units with ASEA thyristor-controlled traction gear serve the Stockholm commuter network, which SJ operates under contract for the city authority. The SJ service has a primarily outer suburban role, leaving the city T-Bana, or Metro, to cover the inner suburbs with an integrated system of feeder bus services.

Left: SJ's heavy yard shunter and trip freight diesel is the Class T44 1,670hp diesel-electric Bo-Bo, created by Nohab in the late 1960s around a GM12-645E engine; one shunts the yards at Göteborg.

Below left: The Helsingborg yard is equipped with ASEA's version of the automatic, hydraulic retarder concept that obviates any energy input: the devices, seen mounted on the sleepers within the running rails, rise so that their curved scrolls apply appropriately graduated retardation or impetus to the flanges of passing wagons.

Sleeper travel on the SJ was — with one proviso — a bargain compared with the cost of a passable hotel before the fare remissions of the 1979 summer. They made it cheaper still. Moreover, the business traveller gets a powerful inducement to regular overnight travel from the SJ's 12-month pass which, once purchased, covers not only all first-class travel for the rest of the year but also sleeper berth occupation without further charge. The cost of this and other special cards was also cut in the 1979 summer revolution.

The qualification hinted at above is that the SJ prices overnight privacy very steeply to maximise occupation of the three berths per compartment in its existing sleepers. In the spring of 1980 a berth cost only £4.60 or so on top of the second-class fare when all three in a compartment were in use. Double-berth occupation incurred first-class fare and a fee of about £7 per berth. But for single-berth exclusivity the SJ exacted a swingeing £25 in addition to first-class fare.

Most population centres of significance have a sleeper service to and from Stockholm and the SJ's central reservation computer books around a million sleeper and half-a-million couchette sales a year. Some foreign cars penetrate the country, such as the DSG sleeper which has to take to the train ferry twice — between Puttgarden and Rodby from West Germany

Above: Compelled by the political collapse of closure proposals in the uncommercial sector of its system to renew its diesel railcar fleet, SJ is one of the numerous countries to buy a fleet of cars derived from the Fiat Aln668 design for the Italian State Railways. It is designated Class Y1 by SJ.

ɔ Denmark, and between Helsingör and Helsingborg from Denmark to Sweden — on its 'Hamburg Express' run from Iamburg to Stockholm. But the majority of the cross-border vernight workings are covered by the SJ's cars.

These are now heavy with years. Until recently SJ management did not expect to renew the fleet, envisaging that faster aytime transits with X15-type emus would slim the overnight narket. But opinions have changed, influenced by continuing igh demand and the service's healthy operating ratio (the SJ ars, incidnetally, are staffed by ordinary railwaymen/women rades).

Designs of a new 'Universal'-type car have been drafted, with oncern for convertibility of the compartments to comfortable itting room. The present SJ cars are uninviting quarters for the everal hours most passengers will pass awake on the 'Nordilen's' sleeper that pulls out of Stockholm as early as 16.32 on s 847-mile journey to the Arctic Circle at Kiruna, for instance.

In its 1979-80 financial year the SJ at last reversed the steady ownturn of freight tonnage since 1974, pulling in 6% more. This sector generates more income than passengers. In 1979-80 reight revenue totalled Skr2,731m, compared with Skr1,508m rom the commercial passenger network and Skr733m from the nviable passenger services which SJ is mandated to keep going.

In the immediate wake of the oil-price explosion the SJ lost lmost a third of its freight tonnage. That was a reflection of the ystem's dependence for more than 80% of its volume on three ommodities — ore, iron and wood, all very vulnerable to economic recession. When the Continental economy is buoyant the ailway revels in this traffic since it is predominantly long-haul. The ore is mined principally in Lapland, north of the Arctic Circle, and the timber industry is concenetrated around the north coast of the country. The remoteness of these areas is a nain factor in the 180 mile-plus average transit of an SJ freight consignment. The reverse of that coin is that any slump in these raffics obviously canes the overall SJ freight results disproportionately.

The railways' quest for general merchandise is hampered by he collapse of efforts to equalise infrastructure costs discussed earlier. Moreover, in the later 1970s when the Government and the SJ general management of the period locked themselves into a fruitless pursuit of rising deficits with draconian price increases, SJ freight tariffs jumped by 28% in 1976-7 alone.

SJ's scope for cost-cutting has now become limited. Through electrification, widespread extension of CTC, computerisation of data processing and drastic simplification of its rural railway working SJ has achieved impressive economies. Since 1950 its total staff has been cut from some 70,000 to almost 30,000 and their productivity, measured in traffic units per employee, has more than trebled.

But now SJ has got to resume recruitment, because an age bulge is showing. Swedish youth these days expects to start work at a high rate of pay — and in any event railwaymen get a wage that stands quite high in the Swedish industrial league — so that SJ cannot hope to sustain the marked recovery from its worst post-oil crisis deficit it managed in 1978-9 without charging more still for freight movement. Between 85 and 90% of that traffic is handled under term contract that is anyway immutable without a general tariff increase, which has to be Government-approved. Short of some fiscal action on infrastructure costs by the Government, SJ's one hope of competing for high-rated merchandise on fairer terms is that oil prices will rise faster than wage rates.

Nevertheless, a drive to regain ground with inter-modal techniques and special-purpose rail vehicles makes encouraging headway. SJ now operates between 35 container terminals, for instance, though by 1980 only the Stockholm-Malmö and Stockholm-Göteborg routes were generating volume enough for a dedicated container train service. Because so much of the traffic so far is handled in wagonloads, many of which ply between industrial sidings with cramped layouts, SJ has favoured a two-axle pattern of shock-absorbing container carrier.

Containerisation spearheads one SJ drive to integrate rail transport in the production and distribution processes of Swedish industry. Besides its role in the movement via double-deck transporters of SAAB car bodies manufactured at Göteborg to the firm's assembly plant at Malmö, the SJ has also captured a regular inter-plant movement of components in specially — and rather grotesquely-shaped containers.

SJ freight managers begin to suspect that their container traffic may be outstripped by piggyback, which they recently launched with a fleet of 25 Kangarou-pattern carrier wagons for conveyance of crane-loaded road trailers. At first road hauliers were disinterested, but by 1980 they were responding quite warmly to a new SJ piggyback tariff that priced a return trip between Stockholm and Malmö or Gotebörg very competitively against the cost of throughout road movement. The rate was higher than for container transport, but shippers were showing preference for piggyback because it gave them the easier option to return to road if the rail service started to dissatisfy. Apart from these two domestic services the SJ combines with the Norwegians in an Oslo-Göteborg piggyback working; and to that an overnight Oslo-Stockholm service was added in June 1980.

The SJ is backing Danish moves for a faster freight route between Scandinavia and West Germany that seems to have very attractive piggyback traffic potential. Stagnant national economies on both sides of the Oresund, the narrow strait separating southern Sweden and Denmark, have dulled the optimism of the late 1970s that both countries were close to agreement on bridging it or tunnelling under it to eliminate the train ferries between Helsingör and Helsingborg. Denmark is now emphatic that any money it can spare for such an enterprise will go first to bridging their Great Belt waterway, which bisects the country — and the DSB — between Sealand and Fünen; and no one genuinely expects that to take shape before the century's close.

The DSB is therefore evolving a plan for a new high-capacity ferry link, with each ship able to house a whole freight train of 50-60 wagons, that would bypass the intensive residential passenger operation between Copenhagen and Helsingör by plying between a southern Swedish port — possibly Malmö — and Copenhagen itself. If similarly-sized ferries were put on the Rodby-Puttgarden crossing to West Germany the SJ is convinced it could quickly fill a daily piggyback train direct to the DB's massive new Hamburg yard at Maschen.

Wagonload freight transits are monitored continuously by a computerised wagon tracing and control centre which SJ installed at Stockholm as long ago as 1968. Since then the apparatus has been elaborated to create a comprehensive data bank for management decision-making and forward planning.

As already remarked, for the past year or two SJ has been restricted by investment curbs to about three-quarters of its claimed need of new freight vehicles (and some of that construction has been Eurofima-financed — one of the rare instances of Government consent for SJ borrowing elsewhere than from the country's Treasury). In early 1980, however, SJ was hopeful that it would be allowed to accelerate its freight stock re-equipment through leasing.

Maximisation of payload potential is a priority in contemporary SJ wagon design. The SJ loading gauge is slightly more generous than the UIC gauge and this margin has been fully exploited in new vehicles for purely internal traffic, such as one for transport of wood chips. A prime concern in track work is fettling up for maximum freedom to deploy wagons built for 22tonnes maximum axle-loading.

Best-known of SJ's freight operations outside Sweden is the iron ore movement within the Arctic Circle from the ri deposits around Kiruna to the coast. They are served by a often steeply-graded single line of 294 miles running coast-to-coast from the Swedish port of Lulea, on the Gulf of Bothnia, to Norway's Narvik. Narvik is ice-free, but Lulea is not; during th five midwinter months the trains to the Swedish port can onl build up its storage capacity of 5million tonnnes. The Swedis sector was that country's first main-line electrification, in 191 except for the Greater Stockholm suburban area this is so fa the only stretch that SJ has been able, to within its circum cribed investment budget, to equip with the track-to-train two way radio communication it wants throughout its system.

The ore moves in unit trains formed either of three-axl hoppers with 42tonnes' payload capacity, or bogie hoppers tha can carry 80tonnes of ore. The latter, which (with the loco motives involved) are fitted with Russian-type automati couplers, are normally operated in 52-wagon formations. In th depth of winter temperatures plumb such depths that the wagon have to be warmed and heated by special apparatus before th congealed ore can be disloged for unloading.

In the 1960s Swedish industry conceived for this assignment breed of triple-unit articulated electric locomotive tha culminated in the 9,750hp Class Dm3a of 1967. These are sti the chief workhorses for ore haulage, but more recently ASEA has adapted its remarkable thyristor-controlled RC electri Bo-Bo for Kiruna line duty. Premiered with the Rcl series i 1967, then progressing through the Rc2 and Rc3 to the 4,900hp 78tonne Rc4 of 1975, this type dominates the working on SJ' main lines (besides which, of course, it has won export order from other European railways and — for construction unde licence — from Amtrak in the USA). Now ASEA has an Rc on the drawing board and is at work on a new asynchronou three-phase motor design, of which a prototype is forecast fo 1981.

Such a comprehensively electrified system as SJ has no cal for high-power diesel traction. Its modern locomotives of this genre are essentially freight hauliers or heavy yard shunters. Latest of them is the 1,650hp 'Class T44 diesel-electric 'hood', one of a range devised by the Scandinavian manufacturer Nohab around GM engines.

The collapse so far of attempts to prune the rural system has compelled purchase of 100 new diesel railcars. SJ has sensibly opted for one of the two European designs lately attracting export orders, the Fiat Aln 668 for the Italian State Railways (SJ has classified it Y1), rather than work up its own specification from scratch. The Danish neighbours have bought the other model in the UIC-gauge shop-window, the German VT627 of the DB, but the Fiat type has so far proved the more popular worldwide. By the end of the 1970s 15 countries dispersed over Europe, North Africa, Asia and Latin America had between them accounted for half the near-1,000 cars built, the Italian railways absorbing the remainder.

As 1980 progressed a new optimism was clearly pervading SJ. A prime factor was the Government's self-congratulation that the cheap-fare ploy had not only stimulated such as substantial increase in rail passenger travel, but had actually increased gross revenue — a bonus not anticipated. This emboldended the SJ to submit a claim for considerably higher investment in its 10-year-plan for 1981-90. Proposing an expenditure of some £2.2billions over the whole decade, SJ planned to spend half the total on track and signalling, including the spread of cab signalling and automatic speed control, and a considerable sum on new passenger stock, including a fleet of 40 125mph tilt-body train-sets. At the same time SJ management was echoing the warnings of its British colleagues: that unless the Swedish Government raised the railways' investment ceiling by about 30% line speed reductions on several routes could be inevitable because of inability to finance adequate track maintenance.

The Scandinavians Computerise their Signalling

round the world computers and micro-processors are bringing 'eadily closer the age of the fully-automated main-line railway. 'he recent installations of the Swedish signalling firm, LM 'ricsson, on the DSB and SJ, underline the progress already chieved. They include a remarkable computerised interlocking r the whole Göteborg station, yard and port area of the SJ.

)anish State Railways (DSB) might become the first European ailway system to control its entire network from a solitary ignalling centre. That is the ultimate objective of a resignalling lan based to some extent on DSB's experience since 1972 with entral control of its entire Copenhagen suburban electric etwork of 60 stations.

The Copenhagen installation is restricted to the 120 track-iles of the local lines radiating from the city's main through tation which carry the electric multiple-units. At present these re the DSB's only electric traction, but their tracks are not eserved. They are the access to some freight depots and yards, hough most of the freight traffic is confined to the night hours vhen the passenger service is either sparse or closed down.

Normally between 60 and 70 trains are in action imultaneously on the whole electric network of seven branches nd the core section through the heart of Copenhagen. Outside he peaks headway is 4-5min between trains, but in the rush-our it closes up to 2min. Providing the working proceeds to imetable pattern, route-setting and regulation of the trains are ntirely automatic; the two signalmen who share the central ontrol room with two traffic regulators, one each for the orthern and southern sectors of the system, merely sit and nonitor their big illuminated track layout diagram.

Because the suburban lines are used by other traffic they are block-sectioned for orthodox lineside signalling, but all the emus are equipped with continuous cab signalling and an automatic speed control system known as HKT. When HKT is operative — which is regarded as the suburban lines' normal signalling — the lineside signals are switched to a neutral aspect of two diagonal yellow lights. The emu drivers are governed entirely by their cab signals unless they encounter a lineside signal showing a red aspect.

HKT commands are transmitted in coded frequencies over a looped conductor laid between the running rails, and detected by antennae mounted beneath the cabs of driving vehicles. The system has a capacity for up to 15 different messages, which allows for automatic control of emu train speeds at five levels graded from 20 to 90kmph maximum.

Consequently the HKT-governed emus work to a much shorter block sectioning, which will admit three and sometimes four trains to a single section of the lineside signalling system. But the tracks may be used successively both by emus with HKT cab-signalling and a freight locomotive without, so the apparatus has to embody a device that progresses advance indication of each working's description through the block system.

The emu drivers have full control of their trains unless they infringe the HKT-prescribed limit at any point. That ceiling is indicated continuously on an inset in their driving desk speedometer. If a speed more than 5kmph in excess of that commanded by HKT is held for longer than about 6sec without a service brake application, emergency brakes come into action automatically. Every driver also has a two-way radio communication with the CTC control room.

The HKT signalling is actuated by track circuiting and the state of the individual station interlockings, which are normally controlled by LM Ericsson UAC 1605 computers in the Copenhagen CTC centre. One computer stores the working timetable. From this it originates train numbers, prepares instructions for the remotely-controlled platform train indicators at stations, issues routing instructions to its companion CTC computers, then checks actual train movement and track circuit operation against the CTC computers' memory as a basis for actuating the train decription displays of the control centre's illuminated track diagram.

Two CTC computers govern the interlockings on the basis of instruction from the third, the Train Describer Computer just

Left: An electric multiple-unit pauses at a central Copenhagen station, the last stop before arrival at the Danish capital's main station. To the right of the picture are the main DSB tracks to Helsingör.

A
KLAMPENBORG
Lægecentret
Frlheden

eft: Continuous cab signalling and speed ontrol on the DSB's Copenhagen suburban ystem: the looped conductor which transmits he commands to trains is visible between the unning rails.

Right: One of the two signalman's consoles in he Copenhagen suburban network control entre, facing part of the illuminated route liagram of the system. When train working is n schedule his function is virtually confined to nonitoring operation as recorded on the route liagram.

described. Normally one CTC computer runs the northern half of the system, the other the southern sector, but in an emergency either one can operate the whole network. They feed the route-setting, track occupation and signalling indications to the illuminated diagram.

At selected stations the apparatus automatically monitors timekeeping and details any delinquent train on VDUs built into the desks of the control centre. The traffic controller can then step in and, through a simple keyboard of push-buttons, modify the stored traffic plan at any interlocking to get the working back on schedule. Any specific train's whereabouts can be highlighted by a 'paging' device that locates it with a flashing light on the track diagram as well as printing out the details on the traffic controller's desk display.

On his VDU at the back of the room, moreover, the controller can get an immediate close-up of any area of the system where he wants a detailed look at the traffic picture and the identity of trains in its neighbourhood. Needless to say, the control desks have the facility to insert additional trains into the working ad hoc, or conversely for cancellation of services.

At present the DSB's main-line system is ruled from 15 signalling centres with widespread CTC. Now that the Danish Government has approved a rolling electrification programme (see pp57-70), and the DSB has elected to execute it at 25kV ac, not the 1.5kV dc of the Copenhagen suburban lines, much of the signalling will need re-engineering on that count alone. Sensibly, the opportunity is being seized to start a concentration of control on just two centres.

The jurisdiction of the centres will be demarcated by the Great Belt waterway which separates the country's Zealand and Fünen islands and makes train ferries the only link between the eastern and western halves of the DSB. One centre will be located near Copenhagen and dispose of some 3,100 route-settings over 300 route-miles of railway. The other will be at the gateway junction on the east coast of Jutland, Fredericia, and embody around 6,600 possible route settings in its territory of 550 route-miles. The work will proceed in step with the electrification, the first stage of which will hopefully be operational between Copenhagen and Helsingör, the train ferry port for Sweden, in 1984.

New interlockings will be necessary throughout the system. Controls are to be kept as simple as possible, so that at crossing stations on the single track which characterises so much DSB trunk route in rural territory, for example, a complete route in either direction can be set up in either direction with one button-push.

The primary objective of the resignalling, given so much single line, is more efficient train working. Denmark is currently burdened with too much unemployment to make labour-saving a virtue.

The CTC itself will be fully computerised , but the DSB plans to associate with it a wide range of computerised data processing. The new centres will generate a whole range of operating information, from detail of freight wagon movement to mileage of locomotives and rolling stock as a basis for scheduling periodic overhauls.

The two-centre CTC scheme is not to be the ultimate in DSB resignalling. In the spring of 1980 a discussion paper was already circulating in the railway's Copenhagen HQ outlining concentration of the job on a single centre for the entire network.

DSB's neighbour, the Swedish State (SJ), is also in the forefront of advanced signalling and train control technology. As in Denmark the specialist supplier principally involved is the Swedish firm, LM Ericsson.

Ericsson's first computerised CTC installation anywhere was in Stockholm. The first part of it was commissioned in 1971 and in its final form it supervises just over 340 miles of track in and around the capital. Unlike the Copenhagen control, Stockholm's covers all movement, passenger and freight, intercity and local, so that the potential for automation has been more constricted.

As at Copenhagen, the Stockholm centre is served by three interconnected computers. One processes train descriptions and their indications on the centre's illuminated track diagram, while the other two transmit remote controls to the outlying interlockings.

The layout in the immediate area of the city, which includes Stockholm Central station and nine satellite interlockings, is worked from signalling control keyboards within the same premises as the CTC console. The rest of the territory is partitioned for remote control through automatic route-setting in accordance with train descriptions by one of the other computers — which, as at Copenhagen, are arranged so that in an emergency one can assume the total responsibility.

Altogether the Stockholm apparatus has a capacity for 36,000 CTC indications and the ability to supervise 4,000 track circuit berths.

Though modern rail signalling and traffic control systems make growing use of computers, most engineers insist that fail-safe requirements, if nothing else, demand the retention of relays for the final actuation of signals, points and so on in an interlocking. In 1974, however, SJ and Ericsson decided to develop a system in which interlocking logic was written into a computer programme. The first installation was finished at Göteborg in 1980; a second is under way at Malmö.

The risk of a programmed fault which has deterred so many signal engineers is avoided in the Ericsson method by double-checking. All the interlocking calculations are made by two separate programme systems which are set to tackle the data and the addressee specifies in different ways. Their output is then compared in fail-safe relay apparatus for any discrepancy, total absence of which must be proved before the commands are allowed to reach equipment on the ground.

The first part of the Göteborg project was operational at the start of 1979 and completion was scheduled by the end of 1980. In the spring of 1980 SJ officers told me they were very satisfied with the innovation.

Right: At the rear of the Copenhagen suburban network control room the traffic regulators' desk is fitted with VDUs on which they can call up selective views of the traffic situation in any part of the system.

Below: SJ's control room from which the whole of the Stockholm area is operated by CTC.

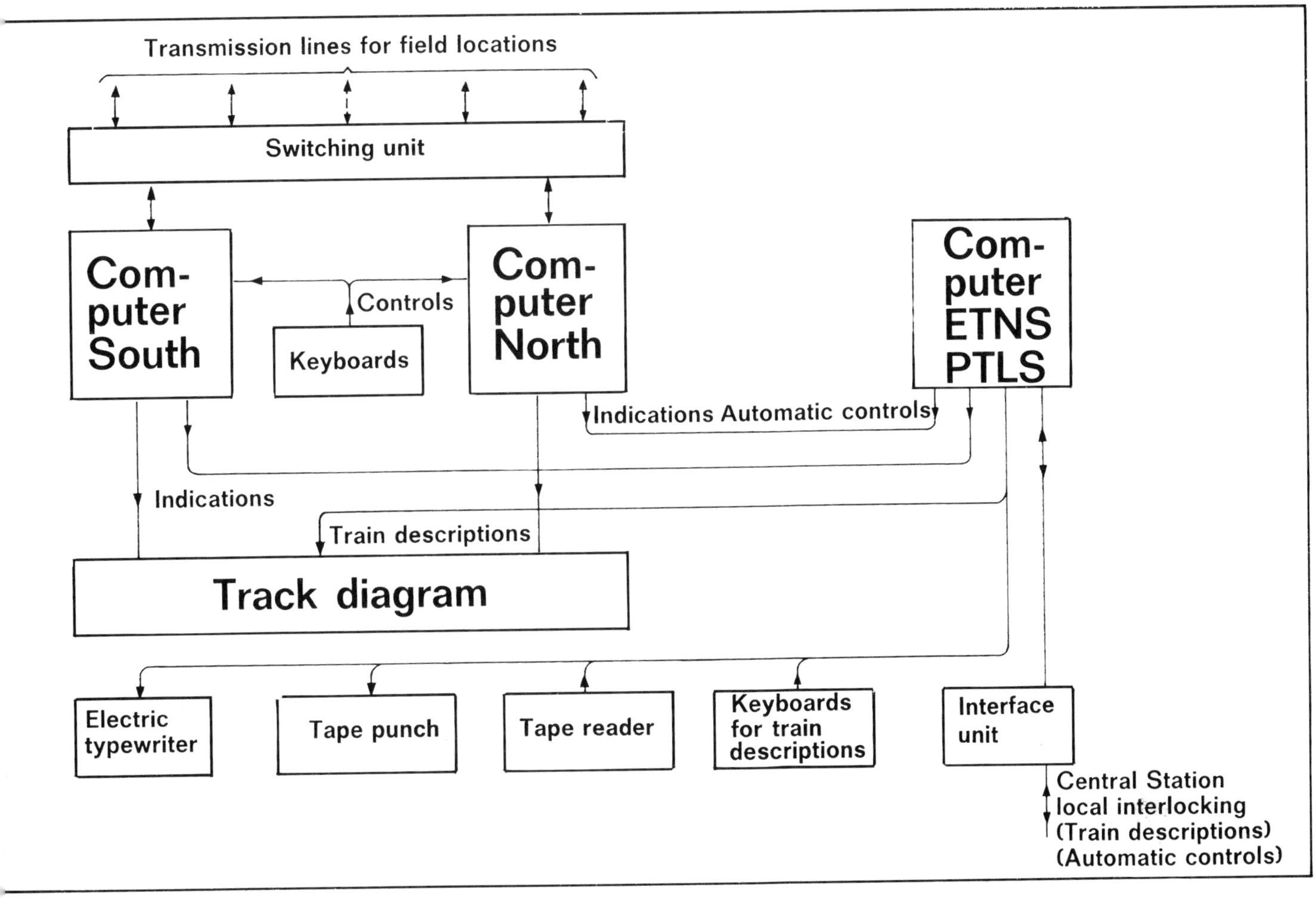

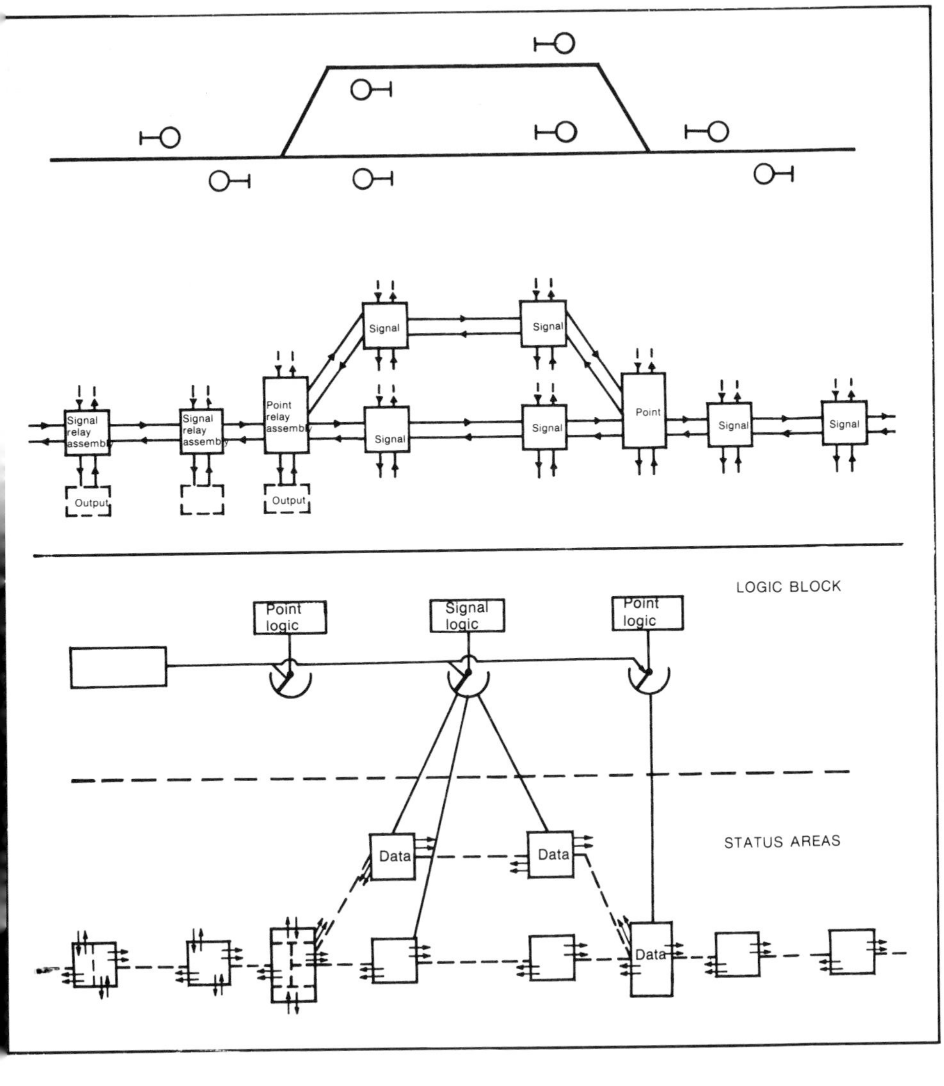

Above: the basic arrangement of the Stockholm CTC computers and peripheral units. The ETNS/PTLS computer processes the train descriptions and their indications on the centre's illuminated track diagram.

Left: The essential difference between a relay interlocking system and Ericcson's System JZS750. In the upper diagram, showing a specimen geographical relay interlocking, individual logic has to be provided for each piece of equipment in the area. With System JZS750 operating the same track layout and signalling, the logic is common, shared by all items of the same type, but each individual piece of apparatus has its own status area.

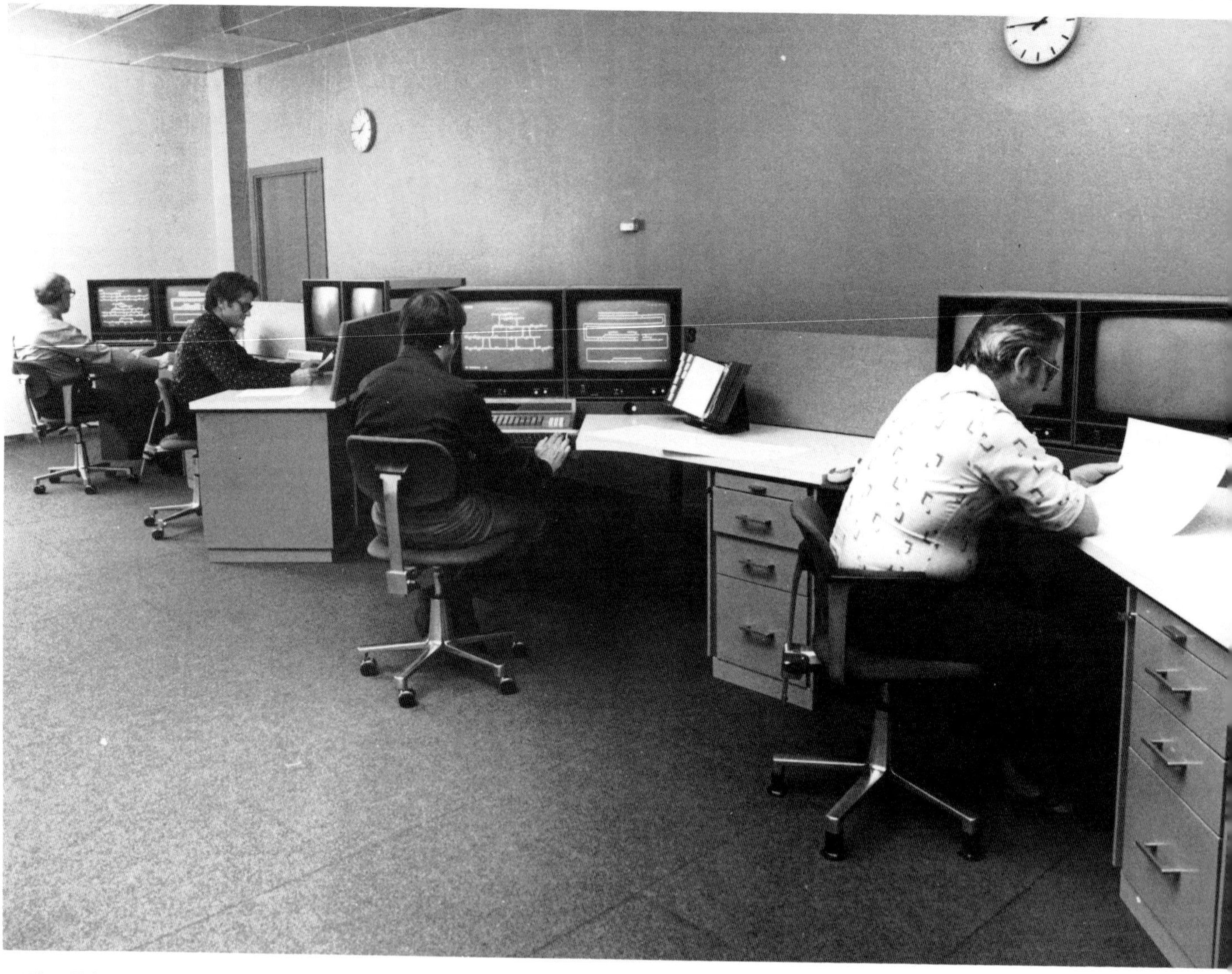

Above: The operating room of the computerised Göteborg signalling centre. Note the absence of any panoramic route diagram of the whole area under the centre's control.

Above right: Close-up of a Göteborg operator's desk. At the front of the desk is the alpha-numerical keyboard on which the operator route-sets by picking out appropriate route codes. The left-hand VDU reproduces the whole area under his control; on the right-hand VDU he can call up enlarged views of the traffic and route status in a specific sector.

The Ericcson System JZS750, as it was designated, greatly simplifies any modification of the interlocking dictated by layout alterations or the introduction of new safety devices. The chief problem has been the need to retrain maintenance staff in a totally new technology.

One Göteborg feature that SJ is unlikely to repeat is the size of its computerised plant. The traffic and rail geography of the area, which centres on Sweden's principal deep-sea port, is complex. The city's terminal station (the restaurant of which, incidentally, has a fascinating and eclectic gallery of railway models and vintage posters, including some issued by Britain's 'Big Four' in the 1930s) is the hub of five routes: to Stockholm; Malmö; the Norwegian border and Oslo; Boras; and Strömstad. Within the control area are two marshalling yards, six public freight depots, several private sidings outside the dock area, (the largest of them catering for a Volvo plant), and a tracery of lines catering for sidings and docksides in the harbour area.

SJ and Ericsson decided to bring all this within the orbit of a single interlocking. That incurred a heavy expense in computers. The rapid progress of micro-processor development makes smaller interlockings preferable in future applications of the technique.

The computerised interlocking is not connected directly to each item of apparatus on the ground. Outward commands to point, signals, etc and the return indications of changed status are channelled through local concentrators, between which and the central apparatus transmission passes serially at the rate of 2,400 bits/sec. At one specimen location seven strategically placed concentrators share the actuation and reception of responses from about 200 pieces of signalling equipment. Thus cabling is reduced to a minimum.

Another benefit of a computerised interlocking is that it simplifies miniaturisation of the control centre displays — an advantage of growing significance as signalling installations encompass ever wider territories. The control room at Göteborg has no panoramic reproduction of the entire layout under its control, only colour VDUs at the operators' desks.

Each operator sits at a desk facing a compact keyboard and two VDUs. One VDU reproduces the entire area under the operator's control, the status of its apparatus and the description of trains occupying track circuit berths. On the other VDU the operator can switch to an enlarged view of a limited area. He

orders his routes by picking out their relevant codes on his keyboard, then pressing an 'execute' key. If the interlocking proves the route unavailable, it will be automatically stored until found safe for setting, which will then be accomplished without further action by the operator.

Ericsson is also the manufacturing protagonist in the Automatic Train Control system which SJ is to extend to its entire system within the next five years. This has been an SJ objective for some time but until recently it was put out of reach by Government curbs on investment.

Economic pressure has also been instrumental in the SJ's option for the despatching system on some of its unremunerative lines in the sparsely populated north of the country. That led to accidents which in turn generated Parliamentary pressure for ATC. The SJ management then reinforced the case by winning union agreement to single-manning of traction as the norm provided ATC and track-to-train radio were standardised. (Present SJ rules provide for double-manning for journeys of extended duration or on trains above a specified length, and as a general principle in Arctic conditions). So at last the work has begun.

Continuous ATC was obviously a pointless luxury in Swedish traffic conditions. SJ therefore adopted the intermittent Ericsson JXG700 system, which affords a substantially wider range of information than most of its kind. In the first phase of the SJ scheme it was commissioned throughout the Stockholm area in 1980.

In general the system employs a pair of closely-spaced, track-mounted beacons at each information point. The beacons need no local current supply. Normally inert, they are energised by a transmitter in each passing traction unit. From that input they store enough energy and transmit their message fast enough to repeat it eight times while the receiver of even a 185mph locomotive is within their range. A microprocessor on the traction unit decodes the message, relates it to such parameters as the train's weight, length, maximum speed and braking capability (which in some cases have been manually switched into the device by the engineman before the start of the journey), then actuates the appropriate visual displays or audible warnings in the cab, or if necessary issues its own braking commands.

Usually the first track device, known as a 'synchronised beacon', has the variable message capacity, based on the aspect of the signal which encodes it and the nature of that signal. The second is a location marker, which may also signify the distance between a distant and home signal or between warning of a restriction and the start of the slack itself. Sometimes a third beacon will offer supplementary route information — for instance, on gradients.

Main-line SJ speed is circumscribed by the system's predominance of single track — only 10% of the network is double-line — and its plethora of level crossings, which average as many as two for every route-km. The nuisance is aggravated by the high proportion of occupation crossings. To equip these with properly protected gates would be prohibitively expensive, so the Swedes have excluded all level crossings from the ATC scheme.

Exhaustive tests have convinced the SJ that the ATC is proof against every extreme condition of their operational environment. The beacons have functioned properly under trial blankets not only of snow but also of iron ore and even when immersed in water.

Double-Deckers

Left: The most eye-catching bi-level stock of the moment is that designed and built by Hawker-Siddeley Canada for the main-line short-haul services on Canadian National tracks that are financially sponsored by the Toronto Area Transit Operating Authority under the GO Transit brandname. Highlighted by an unusual two-tone green-and-white livery is the lozenge-shaped body, conceived to combine an aerodynamically-effective outline with room for pantographs should a multiple-unit customer be found. The GO Transit trains, one of which is seen against the Toronto skyline, are diesel-powered push-pulls.

Below: Upper and lower levels of a GO Transit double-decker. Seat coverings are bright blue, contrasting with red end-partition walls and off-white sidewalls and ceilings.

T
2

Two types of double-decker electric multiple-unit built by Comeng for the New South Wales State Railway Authority in Australia; the suburban and the interurban version, with a view of the upper deck of the interurban type. *Comeng*

Double-deck stock increasingly equip the SNCF's Paris suburban services, mostly in push-pull sets, but an electric multiple-unit version is in production. The interior views show the vestibule of the Type VB2N stock for inner suburban routes and the upper deck of the recent Type VO2N vehicles for outer suburban operation.

The Modern Equipment of Switzerland's Narrow-Gauge Railways

The great majority of Swiss private railways perform a vital social function all year round and offer their public some of the highest-quality rolling stock seen on the world's narrow gauge.

Close on half Switzerland's total railway mileage is operated by around 100 private concessionary companies. Among them are key links in the country's standard-gauge network, such as the Bern-Lötschberg-Simplon artery from the shore of Lake Thun via the Lötschberg Tunnel to the Rhone valley and Italy, and the Bodensee-Toggenburg/Sudöstbahn route across country from St Gallen to the Gotthard junction at Arth-Goldau. But the great majority are narrow-gauge, in some cases an association of contiguous systems to realise economies of scale. Since 1939 the merger trend has been more and more warmly encouraged by the Federation and more particularly by the Cantonal administrations which have statutorily to underwrite the operating costs of many of these local railways.

In the spectacular Alpine regions no less than in the flatter, more urbanised areas of the country the numerous private railways fulfil a crucial public-service function. The 242-mile metre-gauge network of the Rhaetian Railway, for instance, winding and climbing through the clefts of the mountainous Grisons, the 'Canton of 150 Valleys', transports over 700,000tonnes of freight a year and features special-purpose refrigerated and sliding-wall, palletised traffic covered vans in its wagon fleet. Freight traffic in summer and early autumn so taxes the Rhaetian's single-track Chur-St Moritz main line that it has to thin out its passenger timetable; however, the railway's summer passenger traffic, even in August, does not reach the figures recorded in the peak winter sports quarter from January to March. From April to June the Rhaetian exemplifies the economic problems of the narrow-gauge systems serving Switzerland's mountain territory, Denuded of tourists passenger traffic contracts to about half that of the first quarter and freight — in April and May at any rate — runs some 25% below the tonnage total of the midsummer months.

Even in the high mountains, though, the baseload, year-round local passenger traffic is of a scale and significance to demand timely renewal of rolling-stock and embodiment of the latest technology in new equipment. The same goes naturally for

Below: A two-car train-set of the SZB/VBW system — the SIG design of the mid-1970s which set a new style for Swiss narrow-gauge rolling stock.

systems with a more conspicuous commuter role in urbanised Switzerland, such as two which were close kin to tramways in the suburbia of the Swiss capital, the Solothurn-Zollikofen-Bern (SZB) and Vereinigten-Bern-Worb (VBW).

After protracted debate from the late 1950s onward the Bernois eventually steeled themselves to lay out some £25million and project the 1,200V dc metre-gauge SZB below ground in the centre of the city. The SZB's original surface route to a terminus in Bahnhofplatz, outside the main standard-gauge station, was superseded by a new segregated double-track route from Worblaufen running on the surface close to the Aare river for the first 2.5miles, then bridging the water on a new reinforced concrete bridge before diving below ground for the final 0.75mile to a new four-platform station below the massively rebuilt Hauptbahnhof. Simultaneously the VBW's former city tramway current system of 850V was revised to the SZB's 1,200V and its route modified to funnel its Berne trains into the SZB at a new Worblaufen station.

An integral component of the reconstruction was the provision of new rolling stock capable of a high-density, one-minute-headway operation between Berne and Worblaufen in the rush-hours. In the off-peak the frequency of the two companies, which are closely associated, is normally 15min over this sector, beyond which their routes diverge. Local bus schedules are coordinated with the train services.

This was the stimulus for the Swiss rolling stock builders SIG to create, with Brown Boveri traction gear, an attractively sleek new pattern of Swiss narrow-gauge multiple-unit — an ingenious mix of Metro and Light Railway Vehicle bodywork concepts to combine streetcar ease of access and exit at near-

Left: Cab layout of an SZB/VBW Type Be4/8 motor coach.

Below left: The passenger saloon of an SZB/VBW Type Be4/8 car seats 68.

Right: The Montreux-Oberland-Bernois (MOB) version of the SIG design, Type ABe4/8.

Below: The MOB Type ABe4/8 unit incorporates a first-class saloon with seats for 17.

street level platforms with the ambience of travel in a comfortably furnished commuter train. The exterior livery of orange and white was the choice of that characteristic Swiss device, a referendum of local public opinion.

Of 12 two-car sets furnished by SIG, the VBW nominally took seven and the SZB five, but the sets are rostered indiscriminately between the two companies' routes as best serves the cause of averaging mileage throughout the fleet (the norm for each set is about 56,000miles a year). A mark of Switzerland's statutory provision for the financial support of essential private railways was the payment for nine of the sets jointly by the Federal and Bern Cantonal Governments. Even at mid-1970s price levels each two-car unit ran up a bill of over £500,000, which multiplied by twelve was way beyond the two companies' resources. Nine more units have since been added to the fleet.

The characteristics of the SZB/VBW operation demanded commonly predictable performance on every working. Hence the new Type Be4/8 rolling stock was shaped as power-car/trailer twin-sets capable of mu working in formations of up to three units, not as power cars to haul an optional number of trailers. The power cars were all-welded steel, but the driving trailers in all-welded aluminium alloy to help keep the total unit weight down to 47.5tonnes tare, which confronts a continuous 400hp rating in the four traction motors, one per axle of the power car. A feature of the Be4/8 design was its triple braking provision: dynamic; discs on each axle, electro-pneumatically operated and blended with the dynamic brake for the final stages of deceleration; and an electro-magnetic track brake on the power bogies only, for emergency application. Top speed of the Be4/8 is 75kmph (47mph).

No Swiss private railway is of a size to generate a large-scale vehicle order. Consequently Swiss suppliers are concerned in their design work to eschew any bodywork frills that inflate set-up and other non-recurring costs, or which entail a penalty in excessive manufacturing man-hours. The front-end of the Be4/8 is an object lesson in the achievement of appealing aesthetic style by very simple shaping.

Each SZB/VBW, unit seats 136 in fibreglass seating with removable cushions and has standee room for a further 84. The two wide entrances per side of each car have plug-in sliding doors with associated folding steps. The doors are passenger-operated under release from the driver's console (the sets are one-man operated), but once opened will close automatically after a 2.5sec interval if detector devices conclude that no passengers are entering or leaving the car.

In 1977 the basic SIG design was adapted to the requirements of two more companies, the Montreux-Oberland-Bernois (MOB) and the Chemins de Fer Fribourgeois (GFM). The metre-gauge MOB is the most direct rail link between the Swiss shore of Lake Geneva and the Bernese Oberland. Straight from platforms alongside the Swiss Federal's in Montreux station it springs up the mountain range walling in the north side of the lake on the steepest grade in Europe entrusted to pure adhesion — 7 miles of continuous 1 in 14.5 that steepen to a last half-mile at 1 in 13.7 before the railway bores through the Col de Jaman and breasts its summit, 2,246ft above Lake Geneva and 3,658ft above sea level. Thereafter the MOB winds more gently down

Above: An MOB train hauled by one of the system's 1,200hp motor-coach twins of the 1960s threading the beautiful valleys down to Zweisimmen.

through remote and delectable mountain valleys to an end-on junction with the Bern-Lötschberg-Simplon's branch from Spiez at Zweisimmen.

In the course of improvements executed with financial aid from the Vaud and Bern Cantons in the late 1960s the MOB acquired from SIG a quartet of 1,200hp two-car units, with both vehicles powered but also incorporating seating room for 18 first- and 86 second-class passengers. With an all-up weight of only 58tonnes apiece these times had the margin of power to haul two or three bogie passenger trailers on the 39.2mile run over the mountains between Montreux and Zweisimmen.

But in addition to the 10 or so daily through trains over the whole mountain route the MOB also operates a short-haul service between Montreux and Les Avants, the village famed for its narcissus fields high above Lake Geneva. Hence, partly, the MOB's 1977 recourse to an initial quartet of two-car multiple-units in the Bern mould, though with a substantially different seating pattern. The MOB sets, Type ABe4/8, accommodate only 82 second-class travellers and include in the driving trailer a first-class saloon with room for 17.

In 1979 the MOB procured two examples of a three-car version, with an aggregate of 600hp for a total weight of 65tonnes, to reopen service of Lenk. Throughout the 1960s the future of the Lenk branch, which reverses out of Zweisimmen to the mountain-girt village at the head of the lyrically beautiful Simmental, was cloaked in uncertainty. Its infrastructure relentlessly deteriorated as the authorities weighed up the balance of converting the line to a standard-gauge extension of the BLS branch from Spiez to Zweisimmen, or of transferring its traffic to road transport — increasingly a menace to many o the Swiss minor railways. So unkempt had the line become, i fact, that in 1975 its use was limited to freight.

Eventually a determined MOB management coaxe agreement from the Federal and Bern Cantonal administration in May 1978 to finance the line's metre-gauge rehabilitation These bodies put up two-thirds of the £4.3million cost o re-routing the branch out of Zweisimmen on a new alignmen obviating four level crossings, of relaying its throughout with heavier 36kg/m rail, and of equipping it with automatic bloc signalling. Regenerated, the branch resumed passenge operation in September 1979.

The Lenk branch was rebuilt for 50mph — as much a 68mph, in fact, for suitably geared traction — over two-thirds o its length, and the MOB procured two new SIG three-car unit for the revived service. Each set accommodated 35 first- an 115 second-class passengers, and cost roughly £800,000; the bi for one unit was met by the MOB, for the other by the Federa and Cantonal authorities.

A striking MOB innovation of 1979 was Western Europe' first air-conditioned narrow-gauge train-set. In 1977 the MO had taken from its coaching stock a 1911 vintage passenge trailer and in its own workshops — which normally dea exclusively in overhauls, not coachbuilding — transmuted it int a dome-roofed observation car with deep side-windows an extra glazing let into the camber on each side of the roof centre The enthusiastic public reception of the conversion soo persuaded the MOB to rebuild three more antiques in the sam fashion.

In the summer of 1979 the four conversions were assemble with two of the system's 1944-pattern articulated Bo-Bo-B locomotive/baggage cars and premiered as the 'Panorami Express', the whole liveried externally in cream and a darke blue than the MOB's standard for the rest of the railway' equipment. All year round this rake makes a daily round fro

Left: The MOB's air-conditioned 'Panoramic Express'.

Below: First- and second-class saloons of the 'Panoramic Express'.

Above: One of the Täsch-Zermatt shuttle push-pull sets of the BVZ, with thyristor-controlled, 1,485hp locomotive power.

Montreux to Lenk and back, reversing en route at Zweisimmen. Travel in it incurs no supplementary fare (the train is freely open to users of the Swiss Holiday Card) and the cars offer both first- and second-class accommodation.

From the entrance doors of the revamped cars one steps up quite sharply to the saloon, the floor of which is about a foot above the narrow-gauge car norm to give passengers the full benefit of the deep windows. The comfortable seating is modelled on French Railways' latest pattern for its 'Corail' inter-city equipment. The MOB's curvature is fierce — it is pinched at the sharpest to a 130ft radius — so the air-conditioned cars' riding is not tested by pace, but their smooth and peaceful negotiation of the tightest bends is very impressive. The interior decor is gracious, not least in the lavatories, the spaciousness and fittings of which shame the comparable rooms of some European standard-gauge inter-city vehicles.

En passant, it is worth remarking that the 'Panoramic Express' cars are now and then harnessed to relics of an earlier essay in metre-gauge luxury, the 'Golden Mountain Pullman'. At the end of the 1920s Germany's Mitropa company had flouted post-war agreements demarcating its sphere of operation and that of Wagons-Lits by infiltrating restaurant cars on to the Rhaetian Railway, on the disingenuous pretext that it had not been explicitly barred from the Swiss narrow gauge, only from the country's standard-gauge system. In the spring of 1931 the Wagons-Lits company riposted somewhat desperately by inveigling the MOB to run a Pullman train, for which Wagons-Lits extravagantly constructed the closest metre-gauge approximations it could manage to the florid magnificence of its contemporary standard-gauge cars. Every Pullman hallmark was reproduced in the smaller scale, not forgetting the genre's characteristic leaded, oval-shaped lavatory windows — but the bay windows of the 'Golden Mountain' cars' saloons had no precedent.

Though the Pullman train ran in connection with a standard-gauge Pullman service between Paris and Interlaken it was a commercial fiasco that never saw a second season. The majority of the cars found their way into ordinary Rhaetian Railway stock, but lately the MOB has refurbished a bar-car and a saloon in their original interior splendour for deployment on charter work. On a 'Panoramic Express' journey in the summer of 1980 I found the two Pullmans attached to the train for a special party journeying from Zweisimmen to Lenk and back.

From its summit at the Col de Jaman, a watershed between tributaries of the Rhone and Rhine, the MOB curves with daunting sharpness down to the Sarine valley and a junction at Montboven with another recent purchaser of the smart SIG electric multiple-unit design — GFM, the Fribourg railway group. This 61-mile system was a 1942 amalgamation of the standard-gauge Bulle-Romont and Fribourg-Morat-Anet Railways and the metre-gauge Gruyère Railway, which traces an inverted 'U' from Palézieux, on the Swiss Federal main line from Lausanne to Fribourg, round through Bulle and Gruyère to Montboven. The Gruyère line's two modern multiple-units, all second-class, are clad in an agreeable orange and grey.

Early in 1979 the SIG Bern multiple-unit design also re-equipped two associated metre-gauge lines in the Ticino Canton, south of the Alps, the Lugano-Ponte Tresa (FLP) and the Centovalli. The Centovalli is an international railway that traces a spectacularly sinuous route from Locarno across the mountains to the Italian rail centre of Domodossola; it is jointly

Above: An FOB push-pull train on exposed, high-altitude stretch of the route which new Furka Tunnel will obviate.

owned by the Swiss Ticino Transport Authority and its counterpart on the Italian side, which goes under the unprepossessing acronym of FART.

The FLP serves a vital commuter purpose for the mountainside suburbs to the north and west of Lugano, an important centre of Swiss commerce as well as an affluent tourist centre, and it was the first Swiss railway to lay on a regular-interval timetable back in 1968. The late 1970s acquisition of five SIG Be4/8 two-car units (two more were supplied to the Centovalli line) was one component of a thoroughgoing reconstruction of the line, its catenary, its signalling and its stations to enhance the railway's appeal as an alternative to compounding the congestion of the roads in the Lugano area. The investment included provision of a 54-space car park at the Ponte Tresa terminus. The works complete, the FLP service was relaunched in the spring of 1979 under the slogan '20×20', signifying a strict 20min interval service taking only 20min for the journey, whereas in the peak hours traffic jams can drag a car drive from Ponte Tresa to Lugano out to 40min or more.

One of the most operationally advanced of Switzerland's metre-gauge railways is the 17½-mile Brig-Visp-Zermatt (BVZ). It was the first in the country to equip its whole route for CTC, under which its entire — and busy — service is controlled from a command post at Brig; and all BVZ traction units are equipped with transmitter-receivers for radio communication with the Brig control.

Single-line throughout except for passing loops, the BVZ nevertheless shifts over 2million passengers a year and has carried over 95,000tonnes of freight in the same period, but in the latter sector its business has dropped to around 50,000tonnes in recent years. Its through trains are powered chiefly by 1,600hp twin-units with saloons for 12 first- and 100 second-class passengers. These can cope with a trailing load of five or six standard lightweight passenger cars despite the route's slopes of 1 in 8 and 9 where the rack (of which there are four sections) comes into play.

The most intensively worked section of the BVZ is the last 4miles from Täsch to Zermatt. Zermatt itself is still kept inaccessible to motor vehicles, but in 1971 the Cantonal highway was projected as far as Täsch, which promptly became the key motoring railhead for Zermatt — a fact only too plainly advertised by the hideous disfigurement of the narrow, mountain-walled valley floor at Täsch with a car park sizeable enough to content a Los Angeles shopping precinct. Between Täsch and Zermatt, therefore, the basic BVZ service of 11 Brig-Zermatt passenger trains each way daily is augmented by a frequent shuttle of push-pull trains. To enlarge the operating capacity over the Täsch-Zermatt section the BVZ installed an automatically controlled passing loop at Kalten Boden, enabling the line to deal in this sector with trains accommodating up to 2,000 passengers per hour each way in the height of the tourist season. The current system of the BVZ, incidentally, is 11kV ac 16⅔Hz.

For the Täsch-Zermatt shuttle the BVZ commissioned from SIG in 1975 a quartet of six push-pull trains. Each comprised a 48.7tonne, 1,485hp Bo-Bo locomotive with SAAS thyristor control, SLM bogies with combined adhesion and rack traction gear; four all-welded light alloy trailers with dual-class seating, of which the first-class car tared only 11.8tonne, the second-class 13tonne; and a 13.8tonne driving trailer of similar

construction. The equipment was arranged for a maximum speed of 40mph over the adhesion-worked stretches of the sector. Total cost of this shuttle equipment, plus two diesel-electric shunting tractors ordered simultaneously, was almost £5million.

The BVZ is budgeting a fresh £5million of investment improvement in the 1980s to reconstruct its Zermatt station. The railway was originally conceived for summer working only, but the upsurge of winter sports around the Matterhorn after World War I spurred the company to undertake all year-round operation. Given the steepness, narrowness and high mountain walls of the valleys the line threads, that entailed erection of avalanche shelters aggregating over 1.5miles in length.

There is already an avalanche shelter over the running line, though not over the adjacent goods yard, at the threshold of Zermatt station (it succeeds a tunnel surmounted by another repellent intrusion of oil-engined transport into this arena of breathtaking natural beauty — a heliport). Now the BVZ intends to safeguard winter operation at the terminus by reconstructing the whole station under cover. The shelter will embrace a new station building with ticket office, buffet-restaurant and baggage room; three passenger tracks, one pitted for vehicle maintenance; a freight depot served by its own track; and an oil depot siding.

At Brig the BVZ makes an end-on junction with the Furka-Oberalp Railway (FOB), the last of the significant Swiss narrow-gauge systems to open its account, in 1926. The FOB traverses wilder terrain than any other Western European railway, funiculars apart, in its $60\frac{1}{2}$-mile course from Brig to Disentis, which takes in the quite uninhabited Furka and Oberalp passes between the Rhine and Rhone valleys and forces the line up rack-equipped grades as steep as 1 in 9 to a 7,088ft summit in the Furka Tunnel. Nevertheless, the FOB is crucial to the country's defence strategy, because it communicates with the Swiss military redoubt in the mountains around Andermatt.

Even Swiss adaptability to hard winters cannot guarantee reliable year-round operation at the FOB's altitudes and at present the Furka section of the line from Oberwald to Realp is shut down annually from October to April inclusive. But in 1971

Above left: *Zernez*, one of the Rhaetian's Type Ge4/4II Bo-Bos with a 2,300hp one-hour rating and 56mph top speed from which the design of the FOB's new Ge4/4III is derived.

Left: A Rhaetian train headed by one of the line's 65tonne Class Ge6/6 Bo-Bo-Bos, with a 2,400hp one-hour rating, negotiates the Landwasser Viaduct.

Above: First-class saloon of a modern Rhaetian coach.

the Federal Government concluded that year-round communication with Andermatt was essential and decided to finance the boring of a 9.6mile tunnel that would bypass the exposed neighbourhood of the Furka Tunnel, eliminate the stiff climb to it, permit adhesion working all the way from Andermatt to Oberwald and thus slash 30min off journey times. The job was launched in 1973.

Most uncharacteristically for a Swiss civil engineering project, the Furka Base Tunnel project was seriously underestimated and a political tempest erupted in Bern as its halting progress disclosed some gross miscalculations. When the tunnel is ready for operation — a conclusion now anticipated in May 1982, much later than initial forecasts — it will have cost at least three times the original estimate.

The tunnel is single line, but two crossing loops are being installed within the bore. In association with the project Oberwald station has been considerably enlarged and endowed with a buffet, since this will be the terminus of an important new FOB service — a push-pull shuttle for accompanied cars of the kind run by the standard-gauge systems through the Lötschberg and Gotthard Tunnels (in the latter instance, until the recent commissioning of the Gotthard road tunnel, whereupon the rail shuttle was abandoned). The road over the Furka pass is as impenetrable as the present railway throughout the winter, so that the car-carrying shuttle should substantially augment the FOB's traffic.

The FOB has been engaged in a considerable programme of investment of its own since 1976, in preparation for the greatly increased workload completion of the tunnel seems certain to generate. Block signalling with colour-lights is being steadily applied to the whole route and all traction units have radio links with the railway's traffic control posts at Brig and Andermatt. And the traction fleet has been updated with four new SLM-built Type Deh4/4II locomotives for push-pull passenger service, to which have just been added two striking new machines specifically conceived for the tunnel's car-carrier trains.

The design of the two new Type Ge4/4III Bo-Bos, built by SLM at Winterthur with electrics by Brown Boveri, is based on the same suppliers' highly successful, thyristor-controlled Class Ge4/4II Bo-Bos for the Rhaetian neighbours. Each Ge4/4III weighs only 49.5 tonnes, but its stubby structure packs a one-hour rating of 2,280hp. To go with the Ge4/4IIIs the FOB has formed a pair of car-carrying rakes each comprising eight flats (six of them roofed) and a driving trailer, which when fully loaded with road vehicles will gross up to a maximum permitted load of 350tonnes, which the Ge4/4III is arranged to run through the tunnel at up to 55mph. In anticipation of increased 'classic' passenger business the FOB has also taken delivery of 26 new SIG lightweight passenger cars so as to have on call a fleet of 14 modern push-pull formations with an aggregate seating capacity of about 3,000.

Completion of the Furka Base Tunnel means, amongst other things, that the celebrated 'Glacier Express' can become a year-round operation instead of summer only. This is the jointly-operated train which traverses the whole length of the BVZ, FOB and RhB (which meets the FOB end-on at Disentis), covering the 187 miles in just under 8½hr, though transit time is of little consequence on a journey of such consistently stunning scenic splendour. Moreover, the Rhaetian graces the train between Andermatt and Chur with a full-blown restaurant car, the tableware of which features wineglasses idiosyncratically moulded with inclined steams so that their contents are safeguarded when the steepest gradients tilt the car's tables.

Hong Kong's British-Made Metro

Right: The winter of 1979-80 saw the opening of the first 9.3mile section of the Hong Kong Mass Transit Railway, its so-called Modified Initial System (MIS). Unique in the world because of its design for a greater loading of passengers per track than any other — a peak-hour throughput of 800 passengers a minute at some stations is envisaged — the line is part underground, part on the surface, and crosses the harbour in an immersed tube almost a mile long; the latter was fabricated on shore in 100m double-track, prestressed concrete sections, which were then towed out and sunk into position. Principal contractor for the track work was Henry Boot of the UK.

Left: All but one of the underground stations were built by the cut-and-cover method. They are capacious, mostly extending for about 890ft, with a width just over 65ft and a height of more than 80ft. Fare collection and ticket checking are automatic and passenger movement is largely supervised by closed-circuit TV at both concourse and platform level, to reduce the staff requirement.

Below left: The initial 210 cars for the MIS were built by Metro-Cammell with GEC Traction 1.5kV dc electrical equipment and the same suppliers have the order for 150 cars for the system's 6.7mile Tsuen Wan branch, now under construction. Both contracts were won against powerful competition, from Japan especially, but also from Germany, Canada and Australia. With completion of this extension and the likelihood that by the 1980s the system's daily passenger load will exceed 2million, the air-conditioned stock is likely to be operated in eight-car units with a crush load capacity of 3,300 a train, 400 of them seated.

Left: The trains are single-manned, but from the moment of starting to halting are controlled by a comparatively simple automatic system, operating through coded frequencies transmitted via the running rails.

Below: A train emerges from tunnel north of Kowloon Bay take the elevated section of the MIS to its eastern terminus at Kwun Tong. The cwr is laid on a continuous reinforced concrete trackbed — it was laid by a train specially devised for the project — to reduce the maintenance requirement under the intensive train service.

The New Railways of French and German Cities

Massive investment is creating railed transport systems that make a simple matter of cross-city travel as well as journeys from the suburbs to any point in town. How is it financed? And how much does it cost the taxpayer and the passenger?

Development of railed passenger transport in European cities at the outset of the 1980s is dominated by the huge projects of Paris and West Germany's biggest conurbations. As impressive as their physical scale is the apparent readiness of both countries' citizenry to be adequately taxed for the creation of an efficient, convenient and environmentally sympathetic public transport system.

The extent of public financial support even for the day-to-day operation of RATP, the Paris Metro and bus authority, contrasts sharply with the provision for London Transport. RATP's 1979 balance sheet for its whole undertaking, road and rail, shows that ticket revenue covered no more than 38.2% of total expenditure of Fr6.4billion, or over £600million (it met no more than 58% of the wage bill on its own). Just over 9% more of the year's total outlay was paid for by ancillary RATP activity, such as advertising space-selling in its vehicles and stations.

No less than 52.4% of the bill was publicly funded under the two main headings. One was a statutory indemnity related to levels of traffic and a theoretical commercial fare; the other was repayment for discounted travel at less than the actual standard fares fixed by the public authorities. Under the second of these headings RATP is reimbursed not only for the reduced fares statutorily available to such categories of traveller as mothers, scholars and the militarily disabled, but for the fare savings of journeys made on season tickets such as the bi-modal 'Orange Card'. Finally, the RATP's account is balanced with a comparatively small subvention credited to its operation of a few services categorised as irredeemably deficitary.

The RATP's public financial support is by no means wholly derived from the Ile-de-France Region, the supreme local government authority for the Paris Region. In recognition of its power to fix RATP fares, the State bears 70% of the cost of the compensatory indemnity mentioned above, which as explained is the nominal difference between break-even fare levels and the shortfall of actual revenue against expenditure at the fare levels stipulated; local authorities contribute only 30% of the indemnity. For the past few years a large part of the reimbursement for loss on discounted fares has come from a special tax on employers in the region, in sensible recognition that it is their choice of office or factory site which primarily determines the pattern and volume of commuter travel. Every employer of 10 or more in metropolitan Paris has to pay out the equivalent of 1.9% of his total wage bill; in the rest of the Paris transport region the tax is 1%. The final result is that on average 53% of the full cost of every trip on RATP services is subsidised, to the extent of 26% by the State, 15% by Ile-de-France employers and 12% by local government.

Cursory study of the financial performance of RATP's rail services in isolation yields some more intriguing facts. In 1979 the standard second-class Metro fare, for a journey of any length, was Fr1.50 (the same at the time as the *minimum* 15p fare for very short distances in London Transport's mileage-based, graduated fare scale). But no more than 42.5% of Metro users were paying full fare. As many as 40% were travelling on an 'Orange Card', the weekly or monthly bi-modal 'rover' ticket offering unlimited travel within a given zone or zones on the RATP's Metro, deep-level RER underground, buses and SNCF

Left: The Type MP73 rubber-tyred stock of RATP's Paris Metro.

Above right: The latest steel-wheeled equipment of the Paris Metro — a Type MF77 train-set at Miromesnil.

Right: The effectively simple style of recent RATP Metro station furnishing exemplified at Saint-Denis-Basilique, terminus of one of the recent Metro extensions, in this case of Line 13 on the north side of the city.

MIROMESNIL
un apparteme
construction

SAINT-DENIS-BASILIQUE
(HOTEL DE VILLE)

Above: Strikingly liveried in white with black window band and doors and cab front picked out in red, the first unit of Paris M179 'Interconnection' stock starts trials.

Right: Two examples of the remarkably spacious architecture of the underground interchanges in the 'Interconnection' area of the RER: the buffet area of the RER platform at Gare de Lyon and, on the floor above, the big concourse distributing passengers to the Metro and the SNCF.

suburban lines and road coach routes (a specimen monthly second-class 'Orange Card' covering two adjoining zones was then priced at Fr70, or about £7 — a remarkable bargain). As a result RATP's *average* take for each Metro trip — irrespective of length, remember — was put at Fr1.21, or significantly less than the *minimum* price of a London Transport journey.

Even on a full-fare ticket, in the summer of 1980 it was costing more than three times as much to take the London Tube from Waterloo to Kings Cross as to ride the Metro across Paris from the Gare du Nord to the Gares de Lyon, Austerlitz or Montparnasse. On the RER system only 41% of users were paying full fare, with the outcome that even on these costly new lines the average journey receipt was only Fr1.80, or roughly 18p.

Further comparisons with London Transport are instructive. RATP's total 1979 support from public funds towards coverage of gross operating costs of roughly £638million compares with London Transport's 1979 receipt of £134.6million towards its year's operating bill of £520.5million. The LT figure, however, includes a depreciation and renewal grant of £59.9million, so that the UK capital's actual fares support was much smaller than that of Paris.

On the investment side RATP in 1979 laid out approximately £217million, mostly on its rail services, as against LT's £100.4million. LT's money came entirely from the State and the Greater London Council. RATP found 26% of its investment cash from its own resources, obtaining a further 20% — or about £47million — in roughly equal grants from the State and the Ile-de-France authority, and the rest in long-term borrowing chiefly from the fund for Economic and Social Development and on the open French market, but to the extent of some £27million from the Ile-de-France authority.

At the same time the SNCF has been investing £75-100million annually in the Paris area, in its effort on the one hand to cater for the steady rise in long-distance commuting as Parisians move from the centre to an over-expanding suburbia, and on the other to contribute to the great joint RATP/SNCF scheme to drive full-size commuter lines across Paris and interconnect them with the Metro in the city's heart. Since the mid-1970s the combined investment in the rail services of Paris, SNCF and RATP, has been each year in the £250-300million range, over half as much again as the comparable figure for London.

The idea of reshaping the standard-gauge suburban railways of Paris as a 'regional Metro' first surfaced in the 1920s, along with schemes for express tramways which aborted. Up to 1939, however, the only step taken had been the electrification in 1935-9 and transfer to the Metro company of the Sceaux line, in the south-western suburban sector, which was earmarked for projection across the city to an end-on junction with the northern surface commuter system.

The postwar upsurge of private motoring, the drift of residents from central Paris and the creation of new dormitory towns impelled the city to revive the regional railway scheme in earnest. A master plan of 1960 sanctified the 'regional express Metro' concept as the RER and soon the mammoth 'Interconnection' project was under way. In stages up to 1977 a brand-new, deep-level, standard-loading gauge RER line was constructed from the eastern to the western suburbs via

SORTIE
SAINT-GERMAIN-EN-LAYE
DIRECTIONS
BOISSY-SAINT-LEGER
MARNE-LA-VALLEE

Left: A rubber-tyred train of the Marseilles Metro.

Right: The first train-set of the fully-automated and unmanned Lille Metro emerges.

La Defense, Châtelet-les-Halles and Gare de Lyon, and the Sceaux line — which was wholly absorbed by RATP in 1964 — was projected 1.5miles underground from its former Luxembourg terminus to a junction with it at Châtelet-les-Halles, in the first stage of forging the north-south link.

The east-west line is the RER's Route A, which now forks into three branches in the capital's western outskirts — St Germain-en-Laye and Poissy — and two in the east, Poissy St-Leger and the Marne-la-Vallee line to Torcy. Since its opening it has accumulated a daily traffic of over 250,000, more than a third of whom travel to and from the key city-centre interchange of Châtelet-les-Halles. Line B is the Sceaux, Line C a semi-circular route in the south-western quadrant of the city lately created by carving out a 500yd connection between the Orsay and Invalides termini so that RER trains can run from Versailles RG into Paris, under the Left Bank and out again to St Martin d'Etampes, Dourdan and Massy-Palaiseau (on this last route providing a vastly improved service to the station shared by Orly Airport and the Rungis market).

The next step is the link-up between the northern and south-eastern suburban networks of the SNCF, which entails the massive rebuilding of both the Gare du Nord and the Gare de Lyon and their approach tracks. With or without the Interconnection reconstruction was inescapable at Gare du Nord, because the dormitory growth on that side of the capital has been the most marked in recent years, to the extent of adding 6% annually to commuter travel; and also because the additional route to Roissy for Charles de Gaulle Airport, which runs a 15min interval service, has swollen Gare du Nord's daily tally of departures and arrivals by 20% to over 1,200. Since the terminal's Inter-City services are also quite appreciably peaked, new flying and burrowing junctions had become ineluctable to segregate express and suburban flows. That consideration helped the accountants considerably to justify the £120million cost — at early 1970s money levels — of combining the Gare de Nord modifications with a subterranean connection between the terminus and Châtelet-les-Halles.

Just as essential, irrespective of Interconnection schemes, was a restructuring of Gare de Lyon, where the impending regular-interval 160mph Paris-Lyon TGV service would have made intolerable the original station's grossly inadequate capacity to segregate peak-hour flows of commuters from long-distance passengers. Gare de Lyon has now become a four-level edifice. At the lowest level is RER Route A, threading a superbly spacious subterranean station — its appointments include an elegant platform cafeteria — and above that, opened in October 1980, a new four-track SNCF suburban station that has relieved the pressure on the main, ground-level station which is top of the pile, with the Metro immediately below it.

While the new Gare de Lyon suburban station was reaching completion tunnellers were absorbed in the final stages of an RER connection from Châtelet-les-Halles to Gare du Nord's new four-track sub-surface suburban station. The latter was being built *ad initio* for through working, so that upon completion of one platform and its flanking tracks SNCF and RATP would at the end of 1981 preface the interconnection service proper by projecting some Sceaux Line B trains onward from Châtelet to make a cross-platform interchange with certain SNCF Roissy line services re-routed to the semi-finished underground Gare du Nord station.

Ultimately trains tracing four different itineraries between the SNCF's northern suburban lines and south-west Paris — one of them directly connecting the city's main Charles de Gaulle and Orly airports — will thread an intensive service straight through the Gare du Nord-Châtelet tunnel. In the peaks each route will be operating at 10min headway, so that each tunnel track will then be carrying 24 trains in the hour. But that fulfilment is now unlikely until early 1983, partly because it was always the intention to programme a substantial running-in period of connection at Gare du Nord to allow RATP and SNCF staff to accustom themselves to each other's practices and equipment, partly because the financial collapse of Franco-Belge, constructors of the purpose-built Inteconnection multiple-units, had decelerated the latter's delivery.

These new multiple-units, classified M179, are being supplied alike to RATP and SNCF and appear in slightly different liveries according to their ownership. Their design had to comply with a very complex specification to satisfy the differing parameters of the RATP's RER network and the SNCF suburban lines in numerous particulars, such as platform heights, clearances, signalling and other control systems. Also essential was a power pack capable of sharp acceleration in face

of gradients pitched as steep as 1 in 24 in parts of the Interconneciton.

The M179 is a dual-voltage, aluminium-bodied, four-car unit, designed for normal operation in twin-sets with an aggregate seating capacity of 856 and standing space for 824 more. Thyristor-controlled traction motors endow it with an acceleration rate of 2.8ft/sec^2 and it is equipped for regenerative braking under the 1.5kV dc catenary of the RATP system and rheostatic braking when it is working with the 25kV ac of the SNCF's northern suburban lines. The driver has public address communication with his passengers, but the unit is also equipped for pre-recorded tape broadcast to its occupants of certain standard, frequently repeated announcements.

The next step in RER development, probably around 1984, will be connection of the SNCF's Cergy line to RER Line A, the east-west transversal. The new town of Cergy, north-west of the city just beyond the Oise river, which is programmed for a 300,000 population by the next century, was once in mind for service by hovertrain, but more rational counsels prevailed. Though neighbouring Pontoise is on a suburban route from Gare du Nord, the sensible decision was taken to avoid clogging that terminal's approach tracks with a new commuter flow and to plan for Cergy's workers ultimately to have direct rail access to the unsightly office complexes of La Défense, to the west of the city centre. Pending further RER development, that entailed an interim connection of Cergy to the Gare St Lazare suburban network, which was achieved by stringing together, revamping and electrifying some existing freight and passenger segments of route, then adding an elegant new steel bridge over the Oise to attain Cergy. The present Cergy route rubs shoulders with RER Line A at Nanterre-Université, where in due course it will be plugged into the latter via a connection roughly a mile in length.

The final phase of the great Interconnection Plan as presently constituted will be a break-out from the new underground SNCF suburban terminus at Gare de Lyon to a junction with the neighbouring RER Line A. Then the Gare de Lyon-Châtelet underground section will be ready to become a short stretch of RER Line D, which will link the SNCF's south-eastern Paris suburban system out to Melun with its northern line to Orry La Ville by through train.

By the end of the 1980s now fewer than 11 different outer suburban branches on all sides of Paris will have through RER trains interconnecting with each other and with the Metro at the Châtelet nerve centre of Lines A, B and D. And in all some 3million people will be benefiting from a rail service easing them from suburbs to the heart of the city with greater speed and facility, probably, than any other world capital can offer on such a widespread scale.

At this climactic point of the RER development the pressure on the tunnel double-track sections at the system's core between Gare de Lyon and Châtelet, and thence to Gare du Nord, will be acute. The expectation is that over the first the flow each way will be 48 trains in the hour, over the second 42, and that therefore provision for operation at headways as pinched as 1min is essential. Some of the heat has been taken out of the open-line working by building four-track stations at Gare de Lyon and Gare du Nord, which will stop a queue of trains forming in the tunnels to wait for platform space. At the crucial Châtelet station four platforms are served by seven tracks; this is arguably the most breathtaking underground station in the world, with its battery of 34 escalators interlinking the elegant RER platforms with the Metro and with a huge concourse 820ft long and 260ft wide.

By the end of the 1880s, with the full Interconnection service on all routes commissioned, the Châtelet junctions are likely to be the busiest in the world in the morning and evening peaks, processing as many as 144 trains in the hour. Such a throughput of trains on conflicting routes would be almost impossible to signal conventionally — research indicated that it would be impracticable unless block sections were only 80m long and the signalling five-aspect. The RATP-SNCF solution is to hand the Interconnection trains over to fully automated control under a species of moving block system, based on extremely short track circuits, in the affected area from Gate de Lyon to Gare du Nord, and also on the Sceaux line approach to the Châtelet intersection. With this method trains can be safely controlled at headways so tight that one train can be admitted to a platform as its predecessor is pulling out. The system, one should add, is a refinement of the fixed Automatic Train Control system already widely applied to the RATP's Metro lines.

Needless to say, the intensity of the projected throughput at Châtelet predicates computerised traffic regulation. The key area will be supervised by a central computer with the means to interrogate other computers monitoring the progress of trains on the branches beyond the city limits, within which the central computer oversees all working. When the central computer learns that a train is behind time, it will automatically transmit a message to the driver to adjust his speed to regain programmed time at the threshold of the central area: or, if the delinquent is beyond schedule redemption, automatically adjust its pathing to keep it clear of the central area until there is a usable gap in the timetable.

Alongside the great Interconnection enterprise RATP energetically pursues extension and modernisation of its Metro system. This now stretches several limbs beyond the traditional city limits of Paris — the 1979 projection of Line 7 to Fort d'Aubervilliers was, in fact, the 14th extension beyond those boundaries. Two Metro projections finished in 1980 — of Line 13bis by 1.7miles and Line 10 by just over a mile — cost a total of £64million.

Worth a final Interconnection note is the SNCF's adaptation of its ticketing procedures to avoid any fare issue or collection difficulties on through journeys when its suburban network and the RER are physically integrated. Whereas RATP's Metro charges a flat fare for any journey, RER scales are graduated, so that from the inauguration of RER Line A that system has ticketed its passengers via vending machines, the issues of which have to be dated and checked at automatic entrance and exit turnstiles. The SNCF was not prepared to shoulder the expense of a similar apparatus at all its suburban stations, given their very disparate levels of passenger business. Moreover, the SNCF declined to debar suburban passengers from buying a long-distance ticket with a component of local Paris travel at the start of their journey.

Within these self-imposed limitations the SNCF devised a system compatible with the RATP's. The main-line railway's suburban ticketing, season as well as ordinary, is being altered to a magnetically-encoded size according with RATP's, but only the main Paris stations and the suburban stations which together account for about 90% of the SNCF's commuter business are being equipped with the full RATP panoply of entrance and exit turnstiles. At other stations the automatic installation will be confined to entrance barriers, supplemented by spot checks at exits. At the least-used stations and those in the remote suburbs there will be automatic barriers, but passengers will have to validate their tickets (which throughout the network will be capable of pre-purchase in quantity, as in RATP territory) before travel — a practice to which Frenchmen are now accustomed since the SNCF adopted an open-station policy in 1978. As for through long-distance passengers from the suburbs, they are to be issued, in addition to their main ticket, with a magnetically-encoded but otherwise valueless coupon to get them through the barriers; they have, of course, to validate the main ticket and for this reason a validating machine will remain part of every SNCF suburban station's furniture.

The employment poll tax which largely funds Parisian railways' season and inter-modal 'rover' tickets was applied in Lyon and Marseilles — in both at the rate of 1% of the payroll — to fund their new Metros, the first sections of which opened in late 1977 and early 1978 respectively. In both cases the levy is enforced throughout the conurbation, even though the Metros are as yet limited to the city centres, on the grounds of widespread benefit through the provision of interchanges between them and other modes. In Lyons the proceeds of the tax completely bridged the gap between a Government grant of some £30million and the full £150million bill for the initial stretch of Metro. Marseilles got a bigger 25% Government contribution to its inaugural £125million investment. Lille — to the irritation of both Lyon and Marseilles — has been blessed with a much bigger Government subvention because its soon-to-open Metro is making the audacious technological leap to fully automatic, crewless train operation from its D-Day. This city has spurned any fall-back safeguards; its trainsets are being built without any driver's or attendant's cabin.

All three of these recent French city Metros employ the rubber-tyred system of certain Paris Metro lines (which has also been exported to Montreal, Mexico City and Santiago), but not to the extent of standardising car design. The proximity of Lyon's water table to ground level forced SEMALY, the Metro's construction company, to carry out cut-and-cover extraordinarily close to street level (to the benefit of passengers who have only a short stairway descent from street level to platform), which stunted the height of the loading gauge. But though the Lyon cars were thus restricted to a 3.4m height above track level, the track-bed was excavated generously enough for a car width of 2.89m. The Marseilles Metro, on the other hand, is in bored tunnels, which narrows its car-width to 2.6m but gives them an ample height of 3.55m above rail. Both systems had to incur gradients here and there steeper than 1 in 20, the Lyon line to negotiate hazards like the Rhone and a main city sewer, the Marseilles Metro because of that city's sharply contrasting contours; this factor and concern to avoid vibrational disturbance of the cities' fabric strongly influenced both administrations' choice of rubber-tyre technology, despite the latter's markedly higher first cost.

The inaugural 5.8mile Lyon Line A from the SNCF's main Perrache station through the city's hub on a spit flanked by the converging Saone and Rhone rivers, then eastward across the Rhone to the suburban perimeter at Bonnevay, is already culling well over 150,000 passengers daily and attracting a steady increase of patronage. More than £50million is currently being spent on extension of Line B, which by the end of 1981 will constitute a 2.5mile branch from Line A via the SNCF's new TGV station at Part Dieu to Jean Marc. A third Metro route, Line D (Line C is the city's old rack railway, which has been extended to integrate with the new Metro) is under way for opening from Bellecour to Parilly in 1984.

The Lyon Metro is arranged for automatic train control by an Alsthom system comparable to that devised for London Transport's Victoria Line, but it has eschewed automatic fare collection. Its stations are open, but with a difference that Lyon passengers have to validate their tickets in station machines before boarding a train. Marseilles, on the other hand, has embodied automatic fare collection in a full, computerised automatic train operation system, but with manned trains. The computer, regulating traffic as the timetable and prescribed headways dictate, controls a train's movement from the instant the train's attendant closes his doors at one station to re-opening them after halting the unit at the next stop; the coded commands passed through the track circuiting allow of 12 different speed levels, which are digitally indicated in the attendant's cab.

The Lille Metro's 15-station line, now due to open in the spring of 1983, is a unique concept in Europe. As already remarked, operation will be totally automatic. The basic plan is to operate a very intensive service with limited-format trains. Normally each train will be a single two-car unit with 160-passenger capacity, running at peak headways of no more than 60sec and possibly less between stations that in some instances are only 750m apart. Station stops of no more than 14sec duration are envisaged, under the surveillance of closed-circuit TV cameras transmitting to VDUs in the central control room, and passengers will not gather on a conventional platform but in a concourse with doors which will automatically open opposite those of a train when it has come to rest.

Two more French cities have opted for LRT development. First in the field is Nantes, which has gained the seal of Government approval for a 6.8mile line that in due course should open the State purse-strings for a financial contribution to infrastructure and rolling-stock costs. An important side-effect of the enterprise is the chance it affords French industry to reak into the booming worldwide market for LRT rolling-stock longside its considerable gains of full-size Metro business — in Iontreal, Mexico City, Santiago, Rio de Janeiro, Atlanta, 'aracus, Sao Paulo and Cairo. The Nantes City Transport uthority anticipates a start of construction in 1981, with ompletion in 1983. Strasbourg is the other potential LRT uilder, with a scheme for an initial 5.8mile line heading south om the city's main station and commercial centre.

In the second half of the 1970s West Germany invested the uge sum of £5billion in rail transport. A considerable part of hat was absorbed in the continuing refinement of urban ystems, notably the German equivalent of the French RER — he S-Bahn (*SchnellBahn*) which knits the DB's suburban etwork together by trans-city links that interconnect with the nner U-Bahn systems in handsome interchange stations. State id for S-Bahn development is on a more generous scale than for lmost any other rail improvement in Europe. For an approved cheme the Federal Government is obliged by statute to put up 0% (since early 1972; before that the proportion was 50%) of he infrastructure cost; local authorities furnish almost all the est, leaving the DB's resources to cover little bar the design and upervision of the works and the acquisition of rolling stock.

Four of the five S-Bahn schemes — Hamburg, Munich, 'rankfurt and Stuttgart — are shaped around the costly thrust f a standard-gauge railway through the sub-surface heart of the ity to set up through services between suburbs on opposite ides of the conurbation, or in the case of the Rhein-Main etwork, between neighbouring towns and cities, such as Mainz nd Wiesbaden, and the heart of Frankfurt as well. Only the Ruhr S-Bahn, which interconnects the territory's major centres, s primarily a surface system on existing infrastructure.

To take Stuttgart as an example of the financial grandeur of hese schemes, the ultimate cost to the public authorities of its S-Bahn infrastructure alone, when the network has been further xpanded by new lines now under construction — notably to Stuttgart-Echterdingen airport — will top £400million. But in Stuttgart and its suburban hinterland of the Middle Neckar Valley, aggregating around 1.5million people, the S-Bahn is only one component of an integrated public transport development entailing more formidable investment.

Besides re-orienting bus services to feed the S-Bahn and bracketing the whole area with a zonal — and substantially subsidised — fare scheme to simplify and stimulate multi-modal door-to-door travel by public transport (the authorities are also creating over 16,000 park-and-ride places to help keep private cars out of the city centre), Stuttgart has embarked on a transformation of its tram system. In the city centre the trams have already been dropped below ground to ease surface congestion and allow the reservation of the entire main shopping street as a pedestrian precinct. Now this metre-gauge *Strassenbahn* system is to be progressively converted into a standard-gauge *Stadtbahn*, at a cost for the first phase up to 1985 of a further £250million-odd, inclusive of an initial tranche of 45 new two-car train-sets.

At both Munich and Stuttgart the suburban S-Bahn branches converge an aggregate of 24 trains per hour each way on the double-track city centre tunnel. Many of the branches, moreover, are quite lengthy and well studded with stations — the average distance from one extremity of a cross-Munich S-Bahn route to the other is about 50miles. Consequently a sophisticated traffic regulation apparatus is almost obligatory to

Below: A Düwag-built articulated three-car unit of the Hannover Stadtbahn at the system's Waterloo station.

Frankfurt/Main equipment (left) the latest Type U3 twin-unit of the city's U-Bahnen, a 64-seater introduced in 1980, which can operate in multiples of up to four; and the Düwag-built Type P8 triple-unit of Frankfurt's Stadtbahn (below).

Bottom: Another Düwag Stadtbahn type — the Type GT8s of the Düsseldorf Rheinbahn, a triple-unit with two Düwag monomotor bogies aggregating 400hp and seats for 51 and room for 87 standees. Maximum speed is 44mph.

Right: A DB Type 420 electric multiple-unit on Airport S-Bahn service at Frankfurt/Main's main station.

maintain a smooth peak-hour train flow through the underground downtown bottleneck. Moreover, S-Bahn trains share tracks with main-line passenger and freight over more than half their networks.

The S-Bahn traffic control centres of both Munich and Stuttgart employ an elaborate computer-based information apparatus devised by Standard Elektrik Lorenz. Entry of any train into the S-Bahn control area is reported to the control computer complex, with details of its type and reporting number, via the train-describer system interconnecting each city's electronic signalling centre with fringe signalboxes. Thereafter the traffic control computers, automatically interrogating the outlying interlockings, continuously monitor the train's progress against its timetable schedule. Simultaneously the computers deduce from the train's point-to-point times its speed, from which they project the times of its probable occupation of track circuit berths ahead. In other words, the complex has the facility not only to issue a detailed, real-time picture of the traffic state throughout the S-Bahn network, but also a prediction of the consequences of that state as the trains' paths start to converge at critical junctions.

Each regulator in the control centre has a battery of colour VDUs which purvey him two types of information. One set displays the real-time traffic picture throughout the regulator's area, showing not only the topographical detail of each interlocking and its occupation state, but against each train description number its scheduled time at that interlocking and the minutes, if any, by which it is running early or late. The other VDUs reproduced time-distance coordinates against which the computers are continuously projecting the trains' theoretical progress ahead of their actual position in the system. Each theoretical graph-line is drawn in a different colour — passenger and freight trains are differently colour-coded too — to that of the line representing the train's timetable path, which is also displayed for comparison. Should the regulator want a permanent record of any specific traffic situation he can summon up a print-out, since the apparatus is continuously recording events on magnetic strip. The benefits of this apparatus in helping the regulators to anticipate conflict at nodal junctions is obvious. Patent, too, is the adaptability of the system to a high degree of automated signalling and train control should the DB opt for widespread application of a technology that has been on trial since the late 1970s.

Efm-Flughafen
DB
420 567-0

Left: The S-Bahn in the city centre at Frankfurt/Main's Hauptwache station.

Right: Two views of the DB's Stuttgart S-Bahn control room, equipped by Standard Elektrik Lorenz AG. The colour VDUs on the back wall reproduce the real-time traffic situation throughout the network, identifying each train individually; the VDU on the operator's desk answers his enquiries of the computers — for example, a request to project forward in time the progress of a particular train and show up potential locations of path conflict with other trains.

Above: Co-ordination in Hamburg — the interchange between the city's U-Bahn Line 3 and 15 bus services at Billstedt, a station used by some 30,000 people daily. The buses are traffic-controlled by radio from a local centre.

In the past decade or so West Germany has been the chief protagonist of Light Rail Transit in Western Europe. Here again, approved city schemes qualify for a 60% Federal infrastructure grant, as exemplified by Bonn's contribution to the £200million-odd Hannover needed up to 1985 to fund construction and equipment of the first three lines of a projected four-route, 56-route-mile network. The first two routes are already operational and the third is taking shape.

Outside the heart of the city the system is a *Stadtbahn* on a reserved right-of-way, for the most part on a new infrastructure but to some extent sharing the thoroughfare of streets and roads. In the inner city, however, it is a pre-*U-Bahn* — that is, it dips underground in tunnels built to Metro standards, is fully signalled with the back-up of automatic train control and serves fully-equipped stations with raised platforms. Again, a prime objective of project is to clear wheeled traffic from the city centre and create scope for pedestrian precincts.

The Hannover *Stadtbahn* is one of the numerous systems now supplied with LRVs by the Dusseldorf firm, Düwag. The Düwag portfolio shows a number of variants on the basic LRV theme, for it is only in the past few years that LRT entrepreneurs around the world have begun to grasp the sense of sublimating their itch for idiosyncratic detail and of buying off-the-shelf designs proved by the pioneers of the current LRT boom.

The Hannover vehicle is a standard-gauge, articulated, triple-unit on three disc-braked bogies, of which the outermost are monomotor, thyristor-controlled, each with a one-hour rating of 290hp to deal with a tare weight of 38.8 tonnes, approximately 60% of which is available for adhesion, with the backing of an anti-slip device. Scharfenburg couplers allow units to be coupled for operation in multiple. As is apparent from the accompanying diagram, the short central unit adjoins its neighbours in almost full-width vestibules, so passengers have ease of movement from one end of the set to the other. Each doorway has folding steps which retract to form a firm platform when the unit is serving full-height platforms.

The advantage of the *Stadtbahn* over the *Strassenbahn* — the traditional street tramway — it has superseded is not merely shorter transit times. The vastly superior punctuality possible on the reserved right of way, besides its impact on the public appeal of the service, improves vehicle productivity and thus helps to enlarge a route's passenger-carrying capacity. On its initial *Stadtbahn* lines the Hannover Transport Authority, USTRA, reckoned the advance to range from 55 to as high as 75%.

And what, in 1980, did it cost to use one of the West German conurbations' impressively organised, integrated public transport systems? Take one of the biggest, Frankfurt/Main, where the transport authority, FVV, manages an aggregate 330 route-miles of *Stadtbahn/U-Bahn, Strassenbahn* and bus services in concert with the DB's 14 radial S-Bahn routes. The city itself and the whole hinterland of the Rhein-Main S-Bahn scheme out to Mainz, Wiesbaden, Hanau and Darmstadt are divided into tariff zones grouped in four concentric rings, and pricing is based on journeys within one zone, with supplements for each additional zone entered in the course of a journey. Central Frankfurt constitutes a single zone, which conveniently for air travellers protrudes a finger to take in the S-Bahn's Airport station.

Monthly season tickets of two kinds are on offer — *Grosse*, available seven days a week; and *Kleine*, which does not allow travel between 03.00 on Saturdays and the start of the following Monday. From Mainz to the centre of Frankfurt is approximately 25miles, a journey spanning five tariff zones between that embracing Mainz and Frankfurt's central zone. So a *Grosse* monthly season for travel between Mainz and Frankfurt's commercial heart builds up thus; basic price of DM25 plus five times DM14 for each intermediate zone and a special DM26 for the Frankfurt central zone, total DM121, or about £29 at the exchange rates prevailing in the 1980 autumn. A *Kleine* monthly season rate for the same journey, assembled in the same fashion, works out at DM100.50, or about £24. A supplement of DM36, or roughly £8.50, on either ticket buys first-class travel in the DB's S-Bahn trains on the route (one ought perhaps to add that the FVV tickets are not valid in the DB's supplementary-fare main-line trains between Frankfurt and Mainz). In the context of West Germany's contemporary cost of living, the country's metropolitan public transport is clearly an appealing bargain.

Canadian Pacific Merry-go-Round

Left: The most remarkable circuit operation of unit trains has been generated by the appetite of Far Eastern countries, Japan in particular, for Canadian coal to generate electricity. This is Canadian Pacific's movement of over 12 million tonnes a year from the Kootenay River coalfield in south-eastern British Columbia over the Selkirk mountains for shipment from the West Coast at Roberts Bank, near Vancouver. The trains gross over 12,700tonnes and make a round journey of some 1,400 miles. To surmount the mountain grades, which peak at 1 in 38½ on Beaver Hill from Rogers to the Connaught Tunnel, these trains need the power of a dozen 3,000hp diesels dispersed in groups at the front, rear and in mid-train (the last 'slaves' remotely radio-controlled from the leading power unit). This train is threading the Thompson River Canyon. *Canadian Pacific*

Above: A CP unit train circles the unloading area at Roberts Bank. The operation involves 11 train-sets, each of which completes the 1,400mile round trip in 85-90hr.
Canadian Pacific

Right: The rugged Calgary-Vancouver stretch of the CP traversed by these trains is arguably the busiest single-track route — or mostly single — in the world, on the score of tonnage carried, which since the mid-1960s has swollen by over 150%. In recent years CP has spent heavily to increase its capacity by installing some 15 miles of second track in difficult mountain locations, the new line graded more easily for the advantages of loaded westbound traffic. To reduce still further the need of adding assistant locomotives over the mountains CP is now debating the expenditure of $300million on 20 miles more of new line, including a tunnel just over eight miles long below the present Connaught Tunnel, to bypass the stiff slope of Beaver Hill on easier grades.

America's Cities Take to the Rails

One after the other, US cities have been showing little reluctance to bear extra local taxation to finance the development of railed urban transport. For approved schemes there is 80% assistance from Federal funds, but even pre-Reagan Washington was taking a harsher attitude to the high cost of full Metros. Consequently the US market for Light Rail Transit has been widening. But will Reagan ring down the curtain even on LRT?

There are few more cogent testimonies to the train's new-found significance in American transport planning than California's change of front. Two decades ago European rail lobbyists were constantly pointed to the US West Coast as a model of civilisation which had already proved the passenger train superfluous in the 20th Century's second half. But since the early 1970s California's Department of Transportation (Caltrans), once exclusively dedicated to road building and maintenance, has taken on a mandate for all forms of transport. Under the energetic lady who has headed it since 1976, Adriana Gianturco, Caltrans has financially supported the '403(b)' development (see pp31-41) of Amtrak services between Los Angeles and San Diego and in the San Joaquin Valley between Oakland and Bakersfield that in four years have been doubled in both frequency and patronage. At 1980's close the Los Angles-San Diego trains were recording almost 100,000 passenger a month.

Ms Gianturco aims to hoist public transport's share of all Californian's trips from the present 2-3% to 10% by the end of the 1980s. 'People like trains', she told the US trade paper *Railway Age* early in 1980. 'They ride them. They want them. We've tapped a popular emotion'. And with the $350million the Californian Senate has made available for rail passenger transport in 1980-82 — generated by a quarter-cent petrol tax — she is intent on adding or expanding short-haul commuter operations to the longer-haul corridor workings mentioned above.

The biggest project on the Caltrans list is a five-year, $105million plan (80% of the capital investment cash would hopefully come from Washington under the provisions of the Urban Mass Transportation Administration (UMTA) legislation) for a progressive take-over of Southern Pacific's Peninsula commuter operation between San Francisco and San Jose. This covers an area where two-way commuting potential is developing fast through the extraordinary spread of the electronics industry in what has become known as 'Silicon Valley'. Even without the stimulus of improvement, use of the area's SP trains rose 40% between 1979 and 1980. Caltrans aims to intensify that operation from 44 to 48 trains daily and with new bi-level cars to boost daily ridership from 20,000 to around 50,000.

Moreover, Los Angeles, world-famed as a city which surrendered itself totally to the private car, was firmly set to build the first 18-mile line of a new Metro in June 1980, whem UMTA confirmed that it would pay $12million towards the initial engineering study costs of the sponsoring Southern California Rapid Transit District (SCRTD). Ultimate cost of the

Below: Most ambitious of the latest US full Metros is Washington, which has created some of the most airy underground stations yet seen.

inaugural line, to run from the heart of Los Angeles via Hollywood to the San Fernando Valley, is put at $2billion, of which California's 20% share — assuming UMTA continues its 80% funding — would come from State and local County petrol sales taxes. Downtown terminal of the Metro is to be the city's Union station. This Caltrans plans to redevelop as a multi-modal centre, housing amongst other modes the 2.9-mile 'People Mover' system thence to the city's Convention Centre — one of four 'People Mover' demonstration projects which UMTA endorsed for various US cities in late 1976.

'People Mover', one should interpolate, is the now almost universally adopted American tag for the technology of compact, crewless vehicles running automatically at close headways along guideways which, in the nature of the concept, can be woven comparatively cheaply through city downtown areas because of the lightweight cars' aptitude for sharp curvature and steep gradients. A pioneer US system operates at Dallas-Fort Worth — in addition to some experimental projects — but the most advanced examples so far are those due to be commisioned in 1981 in the Japanese cities of Osaka and Kobe, with two thirds of their cost met by the Japanese Government.

In Europe, the venturesome authorities of Lille, the first in the world to go irrevocably for crewless Metro operation by building train-sets devoid of any driver/conductor cab, has nurtured a People Mover system plan for some time, but its realisation is still some years away. And in the UK the British Airports Authority proposes to interlink Gatwick Airport's old and new terminals with a People Mover. A second system, this time the British Rail-developed Maglev People Mover, to be built by Metro-Cammell, is to be installed between Birmingham International and the nearby Birmingham Airport, but the one exciting most world interest at the start of the 1980s was that of Canada's Urban Transport Development Corporation (UTDC), sure of contracts in Hamilton and Vancouver on home ground and in the running for more business in Los Angeles and Detroit (Reagan permitting).

To revert to California, San Diego will open in mid-1981 the cheaper alternative to a full Metro — Light Rail Transit (LRT) — which has attracted a growing number of US cities since President Carter's denunciation of some Metro projects as unnecessarily elaborate, wildly extravagant and unlikely, if such over-indulgence continued, to win unquestioning UMTA support. Long before that Presidential démarche San Diego had in fact rejected a $1.2billion Metro network scheme as economically untenable. The subsequently formed San Diego Metropolitan Transit Development Board decided to avoid the wearisome rituals of obtaining UMTA finance. Instead it took the cheaper course of converting to LRT 14miles of all-but-abandoned Southern Pacific track which ran from the Mexican border near Tijuana almost to the heart of the city, straight through one of its most urbanised approach corridors. By the addition of 1.9miles more of track through San Diego streets this line could be led up to Amtrak's San Diego station.

The whole transmutation should be complete in just $2\frac{1}{2}$ years for an infrastructure cost, including purchase of the derelict line, of a mere $86million. Almost 90% of that money, again, is coming from a proportion of California's petrol sales tax which the State legislature earmarked for rail transit schemes throughout its territory in 1974, and the use of which in San Diego is the prerogative of the city's MTDB.

San Diego's cars — like those of Canada's pioneer LRT systems in Calgary and Edmonton — are by one of the European front-runners in LRV construction, the Düsseldorf form that is now part of Waggonfabrik Uerdingen and trades as Düwag. Electrically equipped by Siemens, the two-car articulated units are a derivative of Düwag's highly successful U2 type for the Frankfurt U-Bahn in its own country.

The modern LRV is a sophisticated traction unit. Most operators now opt for articulated sets for a number of cogent reasons: easier adaptation to restricted clearances and service of tightly curved stations; simplification of passenger supervision by a single driver-crewman, because of his throughout view of the accommodation; higher passenger/tare weight ratios, with consequent reduction of track wear and energy economy; and simplification of the drive and braking systems. In Germany especially the trend is increasingly to eight-axle, three-unit sets. In both two- and three-car designs only the outer-most bogies are customarily powered.

Light Rail Models from Europe

Far left, bottom: Two types of Düwag twin-unit for the Frankfurt U-Bahn in West Germany. On the left is the U2 of the late 1960s, a design adopted as the basis for the North American LRT systems of San Diego, Calgary and Edmonton; on the right is the 1980 Type U3, with thyristor control and regenerative braking.

Left: August 1980 saw the opening of the inaugural 12-mile Haymarket-Tynemouth section of Britain's first Light Rail Transit system, the 1.5kV dc Tyne Metro, a planned 33.4mile network centred on Newcastle-on-Tyne. The two-car train-sets, built by Metro-Cammell, have a 50mph capability and seat 84 with standing room for 125 more. The aim is $2\frac{1}{2}$min-headway operation in the downtown Newcastle area. Trains set their own routes automatically; each driver sets up his train description and route on cab controls before starting, and this information is absorbed by an underfloor transponder which is interrogated at key points by trackside apparatus controlling junctions, reporting to the control centre's illuminated diagram and actuating station train indicators. This is Ilford Road station.

Below: LRV Austrian style — this three-car unit produced by SGP for the Vienna-Baden route of the Vienna Local Railways (WLB) is Austria's first reversible articulated type for interurban operation. Weighing 35.4tons, it has room for 64 seated and 130 standing passengers, and its two 255hp motors are arranged for a maximum speed of 50mph. Up to three units can be driven in multiple.

Above and right: LRV Swiss style — a non-articulated two-car bogie unit for the Forchbahn of Zurich by a consortium of Swiss industry — Schindler Waggon, SWS and Brown Boveri. The two cars gross 42tons and seat 86 with standing room for 144. All axles are powered, each bogie being monomotored.

Top right: The Chicago Transit Authority's (CTA) 89.4-mile network of rapid transit lines includes the seven elevated lines of the pre-World War 2 area and city-centre subways and new radial surface extensions constructed since 1940. Its present annual ridership of about 725,000 is 15% greater than the tally before the 1973 oil crisis. This is a celebrated elevated section junction at Lake and Wells Street.

Since the rapid evolution of power electronics a number of operators — Hannover and the Vienna, Linz and Graz authorities are examples — have opted for thyristor control, despite the higher cost and weight of the traction gear, and have exploited its facility for rheostatic and regenerative braking, in conjunction with special devices to absorb the regenerated current when the network is not under other load. Energy savings of at least 25% have been recorded where blended rheostatic/regenerative braking is employed on intensively-operated systems that can accept the regenerated current.

The Düwag Frankfurt U2 twin-set is standard gauge, has a tare weight of only 31tonnes, but can accommodate 64 seated and 97 standing passengers. It is powered by two 600V dc motors with an aggregate one-hour rating of 402hp and has a top speed of 50mph. But Düwag offers more muscular models. Its articulated twin-set for Cologne, for instance, has a pair of motors with a combined one-hour rating of 630hp, endowing it with a power/weight ratio of 16.2hp/tonne and an acceleration rate of 1.2m/sec^2, with a top speed of 62mph. This type has room for 72 seats and 108 standees.

The line between the Light Metro car and what the Germans term a *Stadtbahnwagen* — the modern streetcar — has become very fine-drawn. The most obvious distinction is the *Stadtbahnwagen*'s usually lower floor, for ease of street-level boarding and dismounting. However, while Düwag's U2 is designed for exclusive operation at raised platforms, the blurring of another distinction, that between *U-Bahnen* and *Stadtbahnen*, by the dropping of tramways below ground in German city centres and their service by platformed underground stations has enforced flexibility in *Stadtbahnwagen* entrance/exit provision. Thus Düwag's Type P8 *Stadtbahnwagen* for the Frankfurt system has at every entrance retractable steps, so that it can load either from the surface or from a raised platform. That saves the expense of building platforms at lightly-used stops, moreover. The steps can be controlled by the driver or their deployment made an automatic function of the signalling system at stops where their use is essential.

To return once more to California, this was of course the arena for the over-ambitious, riskily inexperienced attempt to achieve a fully automated Metro, the Bay Area Rapid Transit (BART) system of the San Francisco-Oakland territory. More than a decade after its opening BART has overcome its basic problems — unreliable track circuitry; the incompatibility of the train-sets' programmed deceleration with the signal spacing; and train-set malfunctions — but it has yet to be operated to the intensity of its original specification. Nevertheless extensions of the network, including direct service of San Francisco airport, have been included in a 20-year, $1.7billion programme to expand the region's rapid transit rail service.

One must concede, however, that the imaginative audacity of the BART concept in the 1950s was instrumental in reawakening North American interest in rapid transit railways and in promoting the 1964 UMTA Act's Federal support of further schemes, provided they were integral components of a total public transportation package. The most spectacular product of that legislation to date — though one which with BART was chiefly responsible for President Carter's stricture on extravagant over-design — is the Washington Metro.

The final cost of the five-line, 98 route-mile Washington system is put at around $7.5billion, of which almost a third had already been laid out on the 35 miles and 38 stations operational

cta 7012

by early 1980. Perhaps the most stylistically exciting of all latter-day Metros for the spacious ambience its architects have created at the sub-surface, fully air-conditioned stations through unpretentious use of simple stonework, ingenious lighting and concern for uncluttered sight-lines, the Washington Metro has survived well-publicised early traumas with its complex automated devices to surpass initial user projections. By 1979 its annual carryings were already closing on 25million.

Besides making generous provision for private car-Metro transfers — by the mid-1980s parking lots at the system's out-of-town stations will aggregate room for some 30,000 vehicles — the Washington Metro planners were the first in the US to integrate a thorough-going re-orientation of city bus routes as Metro feeders in their scheme *ab initio.* Combined bus-rail journeys are simple despite the Metro's 'stored-ride' Automatic Fare Collection (AFC) system.

The 'stored-ride' method employs automatic change-giving machines, which accept $1 and $5 notes as well as coins, dispense magnetically encoded cards covering travel at optional values up to $20. Entering the platform, the passenger slots his card into a barrier 'reader', which marks the originating station of the journey. At his destination station the exit barrier 'reader' automatically calculates the distance travelled and deducts the cost from the stored value of the farecard. If the passenger has over-travelled the residual value of his card, the exit gate will not release him and an illuminated sign will point him to an 'Adfare' machine, which for the necessary surcharge will re-encode his card so that the exit barrier will accept it. A passenger intending to complete his journey by city bus has only to obtain a transfer ticket from a machine near the platform of this starting station.

Conceptually elegant and also convenient for the regular rail user, the 'stored-ride' system has caused come — but not all — its practitioners a good deal of pain. In the US its malfunction was one of BART's numerous plagues in the first North American application, and Washington seems to have had chronic trouble, so much so that in the 1980 summer the Transit Authority's chief formally asked his Board to write off the $52million cost of the apparatus, which he complained was costing twice as much to operate as the kind of token-worked turnstiles adopted in New York, and to scrap the Metro's mileage-based and off peak-variated fare scales for a Paris-type flat fare. The resultant drop in revenue, he implied, would be balanced by the maintenance saving through scrapping 'stored-ride' AFC.

The Washington Metro train-sets, fully air-conditioned and capable of 75mph maximum, are manned by a driver-conductor, but normally they move entirely at the direction of a computer-based Automatic Train Operation (ATO) system. The inaugural Washington Metro fleet of 300 cars was US-built by Rohr Industries, but with the exit of that firm from the rail supply business — and, in fact, with Budd the sole surviving US passenger car builder of consequence, but to its loudly-trumpeted irritation very hard put to match the bids of major

Left: Newest cars in the CTA fleet of over 1,100 cars are the air-conditioned Type 2400 by Boeing-Vertol, which operate in two-car sets; here a pair ride over one of the CTA's latest articulated buses at Wells Street and Wacker Drive. Renewal and 'winter-proofing' of the elevated lines — they were virtually immobilised for several days in the fierce blizzards of early 1979 — is a CTA priority. In the past few years Chicago has planned more than it has executed, partly because of successive changes in State and city political leadership, partly because of argument over priorities and the resultant inability to make firm requests for UMTA finance. The latter apart, the city now has some $765million to spend on urban transit from money earmarked for an abandoned Interstate highway scheme.

Right: Interior of a CTA Series 2400 train-set.

Below: In the 1960s Chicago pioneered the integration of motorway and Metro extension; this is the Jefferson Park terminus of the 3.9mile extension of the West-Northwest route's Milwaukee branch down the median of the Kennedy Expressway, completed early in 1970. Major CTA project of 1980 is the long-planned continuation of this line for seven miles to a terminal within O'Hare airport, the world's busiest. Hurrying over the CTA station to the left is a commuter push-pull on Chicago & North Western tracks, where Chicago's suburban commuters travel in the largest (248 cars) of three double-deck fleets operated under the aegis of the Chicago Regional Transportation Authority (RTA). RTA, which spends over $60million a year to maintain 14 services operated on its behalf by seven different railroads, presides over a rail network totalling 463 route-miles, uses 853 cars and 124 locomotives (mostly RTA-owned) and moves 280,000 passengers daily. Since its 1974 formation the RTA has spent almost $100million on commuter rolling stock renewal, including new bi-levels. The RTA administers the CTA and is the butt of some outer suburban criticism for alleged over-spending of its tax-raised funds on CTA improvement at the expense of outer-suburban services.

oreign Metro and LRT car suppliers, including Canada's Iawker-Siddeley — subsequent batches of Washington cars ave been ordered from Breda of Italy. However, the Federal Government's 'Buy American' policy required imported vehicles o have a minimum 50% US manufacturing content (the US Senate was seeking in mid-1980 to lift the proportion to 70%). Thus besides embodying numerous US-made components these Breda cars — like the Düwag LRVs for San Diego and others — are being assembled in the US. There is now a distinct possibility that the Japanese will set up a car-building base in the USA. In late 1980 Kawasaki Heavy Industries were discussing with an American firm, Thrall Car Mfg, the feasibility of a joint take-over of the Pullman standard plant to build both Amtrak and rapid transit rolling stock. Kawasaki is currently supplying both LRT and Metro cars to Philadelphia.

A similar ATO apparatus by the same US manufacturer, General Railway Signal (GRS), governs the latest of the new US Metros to start operation in the 1970s, that of the Metropolitan Atlanta Rapid Transit Authority (MARTA), which inaugurated the first 6.2-mile stretch of a planned 53-mile network in the summer of 1979. A MARTA train attendant's role is normally confined to actuating the train doors and restarting the train. For the rest, computers transmit driving commands to the trains in the light of the system's monitoring of actual train movement against stored timetable detail.

MARTA is one of the US full Metro schemes that have been put at risk by the flintier Federal attitudes to UMTA capital grants. Despite continuing doubt about the UMTA share of the bill for further stages of the network, which as a whole is forecast to cost around $2.6billion, the Georgia State legislature has nevertheless boldly budgeted to continue the 1% sales tax it levied to cover the local finance of the Metro until 1997. And MARTA itself has confidently launched the design work of its second line, which will directly serve the Atlanta airport of the city's south side.

MARTA's train-sets are thyristor-controlled, aluminium-bodied two-car units from Franco-Belge, as a result of which MARTA may face Washington's problem in reverse when it needs to re-order. For the prestigious French firm, suppliers of the latest generations of Paris Metro and SNCF-RATP 'interconnection' rolling stock, went into liquidation in the 1980 summer, unable to secure a big enough world market for the aluminium-bodied manufacturing capability in which it had sunk vast capital sums — and in part, it was said, wounded by failure to safeguard the MARTA contract against the slump in the US dollar's worth. It has, however, since been reorganised under the aegis of other major French builders.

Baltimore is next to join the US full Metro league, with is first line due for commissioning in 1981, and other cities are developing LRT projects. Meanwhile cities with long-established rapid transit rail systems are capitalising on their energy-conscious citizens' newfound toleration of taxation for public transport to expand and refine their undertakings.

Two mammoth schemes to enhance the convenience of rail rapid transit are under way in New York and Philadelphia. In New York a scheme likely to carry a final price tag of over $1billion involves a fresh rail crossing of the East River between Long Island and Manhattan, the immersion of a bi-level tube with two pairs of tracks superimposed, one for Long Island (LIRR) traffic, the other for a Subway route, so that the LIRR trains can be re-routed to a terminal closer to the city's social and commercial heart. At present they finish a subway or bus ride from the city's business hub in the Penn staion, alongside Amtrak trains and the commuter trains which Conrail works on behalf of the State of New Jersey. Via the new tunnel the LIRR trains will be able to run into Grand Central, an easy walk from the glossiest blocks of Fifth Avenue, Madison Avenue and the rest.

Below: 'Kiss-and-ride' parking provision at CTA's Desplaines terminal on its Congress route; the station also has no fewer than three 'park-and-ride' lots.

Left: A Washington Metro train attendant's desk. *WMTA*

Below: One of the French-built train-sets of MARTA, with the Atlanta State building in the background.

Right: The elegant provision for inter-modal interchange of modern UR rapid transit schemes is patent in this view of Washington Metro's Rhode Island Avenue station. *WMTA*

Below right: Present-day New York Subway stock was initiated by this Type R-44 design of 1971, which is 75ft long and comes in only two patterns — with or without driving cab, in each case motored so that sets of any length are operable, though the vehicles are generally rostered in sets of four. Maximum speed is 80mph, but at present 70mph is the operational limit. Since 1971 300 of this type and 754 of the subsequent R-46 have been acquired by New York's MTA, the latter's cost of $214million met as to two-thirds by UMTA. At 137.5 route-miles, the underground sections of the MTA system are the longest in any world city; the MTA system as a whole carries over a billion passenger yearly.

Since 1968 all the surface rail commuter services radiating from New York and contained by New York State as well as the whole Subway system — the world's busiest — and the city's bus services have been governed by a single body, which was launched with $2.5billion of State-generated funds. Surprisingly, considering New York City's financial catastrophe in the 1970s, it has managed to fund a much bigger share of its public transport improvement from its own resources than most US cities, thanks in large measure to its citizens' readiness to back bond issues for the purpose. It has lately been helped, too, by money from New York State, which contributed to the cost of the standard 'Metropolitan' electric multiple-unit design that the MTA devised to re-equip both its LIRR and ex-New York Central commuter routes.

To execute just the Subway extensions and improvements the MTA covets in the 1980s, however, the capital investment requirement has been assessed at almost $15billion. Sadly the prospects for an outlay of that order dimmed rapidly at the start of 1981. In the dying days of the Carter regime the Republicans in Congress defeated last-ditch efforts to commit $25.5million of Federal and local money to urban mass transit up to 1985. All the Democrats could get was a one-year capital grant addition of $2.2billion to the funds legislated in 1978 for the ensuing four years. Then President Reagan took office with a strong recommendation from the task force he appointed to consider transportation that he slash the Federal support for mass transit very severely. And his 1981 Budget threatens all that and more, with proposals to lop $270million from Federal capital grants for mass transit immediately and to end all Federal aid for mass transit operation by 1985. The first of these threats menaces, for example, extension of the Atalanta and Baltimore systems, and the projected Los Angeles Metro and People-mover. The second dramatically worsens the outlook for several systems already desperately strapped for cash flow, such as Boston, Chicago and New York.

New York's MTA has made a fair fist of getting its investment priorities right in face of dedicated political log-rolling. Not so Philadelphia, hub of a mix of streetcar, LRT and commuter railways that adds up to the third largest urban rail network in the US. Though some of these systems, famished for new rolling stock, are racked by un-reliability, over $300million are being spent to drive a four-track tunnel through the city's heart and forge and end-on connection between the former Pennsylvania and Reading commuter systems in a spectacular $63million city-centre interchange station, and $90million more to build an airport railway. Several million dollars more yet will have to be spent to create a standard signalling system throughout the newly-linked system and suitably equipped rolling stock before the operational benefits of through working can be realised when the tunnel is finished in late 1983.

Piggyback and Containers — the Freight Growth Area of the 1980s

The vast distances of North America had helped piggyback to second place behind coal in US railroads' freight volume table before the oil crisis. Since then fuel prices have stimulated a striking move into both rail container and piggyback transport in Continental Europe.

Two decades ago a number of pundits doubted that the railways of the industrialised West would ever plug the drain of their high-rated merchandise freight to increasingly efficient and economical road transport. Now thanks to OPEC's deterrents, at least one country is worried that its railways will run out of capacity to handle reviving business in this sector. The majority of the world's systems, granted, still face a long haul to recover lost ground, but the remarkable upsurge in inter-modal traffic since the start of oil price inflation suggests that a good deal of it is not beyond reach.

In percentage terms the most striking growth area of the past five years has been 'piggyback', but in Europe the rise during this period has been from a much smaller base than that of containers. In North America, on the other hand, the technique of TOFC — Trailer On Flat Car — was securely established by 1970, since when its tonnage has risen to the extent that TOFC ranks second in the league table of US Class I railroads' most voluminous traffics, surpassed only by coal.

But US railroads have the competitive advantage of long distances to offset their often fallible operating. TOFC moved as wagonload traffic too often takes days, not hours, to negotiate marshalling yards or to be switched between yard and shipper's depot. Early in 1980 the Family Lines group commissioned consultants to quiz 75 representative shippers and freight managers in the Atlanta neighbourhood on their evaluation of the TOFC and straight road transport modes for shipments to Chicago, some 750miles distant. The consensus of those polled was that road would do the job in two days. Only one in five ventured that a TOFC shipment would be completed in less than five days; the overall average of the executives' TOFC estimates was slightly in excess of seven days.

Two-thirds of the Atlanta sample were toally disinterested in the reduced energy cost of employing TOFC, convinced that reliability was worth the energy premium. And a quarter had such a scathing opinion of rail reliability that they said not even a 25% rate-cut would induce them to experiment with TOFC. Not surprisingly, therefore, even the most respected TOFC railroad operators do not claim more than a 35% share of all the TOFC potential in their marketing areas.

Right: Santa Fe's pioneer 100-car 'Ten-Pack' all-TOFC high-speed freight en route from Los Angeles to Chicago near Victorville, Calif. In the first two years after its revenue-earning premiere in June 1978 the train's vehicles average 415,000 miles with negligible need of unscheduled attention; moreover, the cars' riding is said to be greatly superior to that of orthodox flatcars. Four more 100-car sets were ordered in 1980.
Santa Fe Railway

Santa Fe
Santa Fe
Santa Fe
5039

Above: Santa Fe 'Ten-Pack' close-up, showing clearly how the skeletal frame carries the road trailers. *Santa Fe Railway*

Right: The 'Ten-Pack's' characteristics make lift-loading essential, but even with conventional flatcars most North American railroads now favour this method rather than so-called 'circus' loading and unloading — ie, drive-on, drive-off via ramps — on grounds of time-saving and greater throughput. Terminal costs are seen as a major factor inhibiting TOFC growth and are leading some railroads to shut down smaller terminals, accept longer road hauls in a transit, and consolidate the business around major terminals with a substantial throughput. *Santa Fe Railway*

Above: Southern Pacific's prototype low-loader for double-stacked container movement.

However, inter-modal rail traffic is now of a scale to encourage a rising number of unit trains that avoid the hazards of intermediate yard processing. A considerable volume of TOFC is mated for unit train working with containers and auto-racks — car transporters in US terminology — but the list of all-TOFC trains mounts steadily.

Unbeknown to those Atlanta shippers, it seems, Family Lines has an all-TOFC train scheduled between Atlanta and Chicago in 30hr, for instance. In the 1979 autumn throughout California-Chicago TOFC unit trains were surpassed for distance by the first coast-to-coast service — a joint Santa Fe-Conrail, five-times-weekly operation between Los Angeles and New York, by passing Chicago and pausing only at Kansas City and Albany to detach or attach cars in the course of its five-day long trip. To the railroads highly reputed for their operating — and which generate above-average returns on their money as proof of their efficiency, such as Santa Fe and Union Pacific — these unit inter-modal trains are as studiously operated and monitored as yesterday's passenger streamliners.

Despite the aerodynamic inefficiency of the traditional US TOFC flatcar and its load — and the concept's penalty of an idle road running gear's dead weight — US Department of Transportation studies of Santa Fe, Union Pacific, Southern Pacific and other systems' unit TOFC trains have shown them roughly twice as economical of energy as comparable road tractor-and-trailer rigs. The trains' fuel consumption averaged 2.86 road-trailer miles per litre, as against sample road rigs' 1.18 to 1.68 on the open road. Unit container trains, naturally, showed up better still in the comparison, but the majority of US shippers have scant interest in the ISO container as a tool of domestic trade

However jaundiced the opinion of some US shippers as yet, the TOFC concept is considered by a growing number of other US businessmen as well worth their investment cash in face of rising energy-consciousness. The prime objective of the moment is to widen the fuel-saving advantage of the TOFC method and simultaneously to help cut its cost. In mid-1980 as many as nine different private companies, only one of them a railroad, were sinking very large sums in the development of new and more economical inter-modal car designs (the Federal Railroad Administration, which funded some of the initial action, has now retired, content that private enterprise is covering the field). Not the least striking aspect of it all is that there is only one large-scale buyer at present in the TOFC flatcar market — TrailerTrain, the company setup at the start of TOFC as the method's principal flatcar lessor — and TrailerTrain is one of the active developers. It follows that the rest are pretty confident future demand will reward competition with the right product.

A number of new ideas are variations on the theme of lightweight frame articulation. One of these, devised by the ACF firm in cooperation with Southern Pacific, is a low-loader exploiting the limits of the US loading gauge (outside the tight-tunnel-clearance regions of the North-East, that is — these debar ordinary TOFC operation) to allow double-stacking of ISO containers. Another is Budd's Lo-Pac 2000, a multi-unit articulated, well-bodied flatcar that is adaptable to TOFC or

container (COFC) traffic; the well configuration would allow piggybacking through the notorious Baltimore tunnels, which have always hamstrung TOFC operation in the North-East.

Unquestionably the outstanding practical development to emerge so far is Santa Fe's 'Ten-Pack' — an articulated rake of 10 vehicles that have been slimmed down to little more than wheeled centre sills with projecting lateral flaps to carry a road trailers wheels. Besides trimming 35% of the weight of an orthodox TOFC flatcar set of the same capacity, the 'Ten-Pack' packs the loaded road trailers into a much smoother aerodynamic outline. As a result the 'Chief', a 100-car unit TOFC train which Santa Fe operates between Los Angeles and Chicago with 'Ten-Packs', saves some 6,000gal of fuel on every 4,400-mile round trip by comparison with a train of traditional TOFC equipment. In 1980 Santa Fe had four more 10-unit rakes on 'Ten-Packs' in production.

The energy crisis has prompted the resurrection of an idea with still more fuel-sparing promise, the RoadRailer. Devised in the 1950s by engineers of the Chesapeake & Ohio, this 'amphibian' trailer has easily interchangeable rear road and rail running gear that limit its terminal need for a change of mode to hard standing around the running rails and an air supply to power the running gear's retracting/lowering apparatus. It made little headway on the C&O in its original incarnation and a British version, developed to the brink of full-scale East Coast main line unit-train operation between London, Tyneside and Edinburgh, was killed off in the Beeching regime's determination to stake BR's merchandise freight future exclusively on Freightliners. Private owners, however, are now keen to make a fresh British effort with the newborn RoadRailer.

The RoadRailer has been revived by Bi-Modal Corporation, which enlisted the North American Car Co as a powerful partner, and in the summer of 1980 Budd was building a first production series of 250 vehicles at a cost of $28,000 apiece. Prototypes of the new RoadRailer, which has a body with cubic capacity more akin to that of the average road trailer than the original design, have been put through exhaustive tests at the Department of Transportation's Pueblo test track which are said to have conclusively proved the vehicle's suitability for operation in rakes of up to 75 at 75mph, though for a time the

Above: The 1980 US version of the RoadRailer — two prototypes on trial.

Right: Illinois Central Gulf's Chicago-St Louis 'Slingshot' — an attempt to break TOFC into the short inter-city route markets of the US.

Federal authority rather hamstrung the promoters by clamping a 15-unit train-length restriction on the RoadRailer. By mid-1980 some eight US and Canadian railroads had looked very hard at the RoadRailer (the two prototypes have run 20,000miles on Canadian National alone).

For a time there was no firm commitment, but the sponsors' faith, was undimmed. Updated analyses, Bi-Modal's President insisted, showed not only that RoadRailers were considerably cheaper to buy, lease and depreciate than TOFC equipment of comparable capacity, but had the plus that a short RoadRailer train with one locomotive cost less to operate than the same number of TOFC cars worked as wagonload traffic in mixed freights. Over a whole gamut of train lengths and distances from 500 to 2,000 miles, he claimed, RoadRailers were cheaper to run by anything from 20 to 35%. Partner North America expected to see 17,000 RoadRailers active and earning the company over £100million by 1984.

Then in early summer 1980 it was announced that in the following August Seaboard Coast Line would start revenue-earning RoadRailer operation between Jacksonville and Alexandria, Va. The launch was with a 15-car train, but the FRA had now relented and allowed SCL to add five cars to the rake with each succeeding round trip if it had the traffic. Up to 45 cars the train was expected to need only one locomotive and by January 1981 it was to be operating with 75 cars.

If US railroads have so far captured only a fraction of their potential inter-modal market over 1,000-mile distances and more, their achievement over shorter transits has been negligible.

ILLINOIS CENTRAL GULF PIGGYBACK
ILLINOIS CENTRAL GULF PIGGYBACK
CENTRAL TRAILER

During the 1970s in fact, the proportion of container and TOFC rail transits in the range below 1,500 miles slumped as a percentage of the whole, while those in the 2,000 miles-plus bracket climbed by over 5%. One reason is the greater impact of overall journey time of operating slackness as distance shortens, also of the high crewing costs enforced by archaic union agreements. However, two recent experiments have shown that shorter haul traffic is there for the taking given the will of both management and men to put outworn practices on the block for it.

With start-up finance from the Federal Railroad Administration, concerned to explore possibilities as part of the energy-saving programme, a shuttle TOFC service over 410miles between Chicago and the Twin Cities, Minneapolis and St Paul, soon pulled in enough traffic to justify its expansion to a six times-daily working each way. Named 'Sprint', the service is worked by fixed-formation 20-flatcar sets, each completing a round-trip in 24hr, of which each trip takes 10hr and terminal time 2hr at each end of the run.

That the service has run in the black is partly due to union agreement to reduce 'Sprint' train crews from the normal four men to three. The unions have been still more cooperative in the successful development of a similar TOFC shuttle, named 'Slingshot', over the 298miles between Chicago and St Louis. Under normal work rules a Chicago-St Louis freight changes crews three time en route — and each crew's stint qualifies for a full day's pay — but the unions have not only conceded that each 'Slingshot' can be covered by a two-man crew, but also that they can work the whole 298miles. Sadly, though, neither 'Sprint' nor 'Slingshot' are making a healthy profit because they are incurring the same terminal costs as long-haul trains.

The inter-modal horizon of US railroads was broadening in the 1980s through the Carter administration's measures to eliminate much of the historic regulation of rail rates and charges by the Interstate Commerce Commission. For instance, in the spring of 1980 the ICC exempted a good deal of agricultural produce from tariff regulation. As a result the railroads are hopeful of regaining much of the perishables traffic they lost to independent road hauliers as the Interstate Highway system spread, an erosion that collapsed their share of the perishables transport market from more than 50 to less than 10% between 1950 and the late 1970s. By the spring of 1980, Santa Fe's perishables traffic was already well over double that of the same period of 1979; and Burlington Northern expected in 1980 to shift at least twice the 1,000-odd TOFC trailer loads of perishables out of the Pacific North-West that it moved in 1979.

However, the deregulation drive was aimed at transport as a whole. The Staggers Act of 1980 which eventually lifted many of the curbs on the railroads' competitive freedom was preceded by the Motor Carriers Act of 1980 which made the road freight transport market more of a free-for-all. The cut-throat competition that promptly ignited put a new strain on the railroads' piggyback revenue/direct cost margins, though some observers doubted that the road hauliers would themselves be able to stand their desperate rate-cutting for long. On the plus side, the Staggers Act made it much easier for the railroads to strike up a partnership with road hauliers.

Across the border Canadian Pacific and Canadian National have been deregulated since 1967, a change that spurred CN to develop as sharply market-oriented a freight organisation as private-enterprise CP. In 1978, moreover, CN was recapitalised as a commercially independent profit-centred enterprise, though still state-owned.

Unlike their US neighbours the Canadian railroads are legally permitted to diversify into other transportation modes. The CP conglomerate has a trucking subsidiary which both competes and cooperates with CP Rail, and CN has its own road freight company. Thus whereas Santa Fe's drive for perishable TOFC traffic involves coaxing contracts out of companies with their

Above left: Top-lift TOFC loading by mobile side-lift hoist on the Missouri Pacific.

Above and right: Two views of Canadian Pacific's new type of 44ft 3in-long container, designed to offer practically the same loading volume as the average North American 45ft road trailer used in TOFT.
Canadian Pacific

own fleets of refrigerated road trailers, CN can think of creating its own stock of insulated trailers to market a complete door-to-door service. In TOFC generally, in fact, CN does best with a door-to-door package employing its own rail and road equipment throughout.

The two Canadian roads take a different line on inter-modal operation, for which both are pressing hard, though as yet they trail the US systems in volume. CN's faith is primarily in TOFC, for which it is evolving its own lightweight, articulated flatcar, but to ensure a good return it has slimmed its piggyback network down to a tracery of the most lucrative trunk hauls. Since the mid-1970s it has shut down over half its piggyback terminals and delegated their business entirely to its trucking company.

CP, on the other hand, is convinced that the future is in containerisation. Escalating oil prices, it argues, will increasingly dramatise the fuel cost penalty of TOFC's inferior payload/tare ratio in rail movement. But the container must have equivalent capacity to an average road trailer's, a condition not met by the standard ISO cube.

So, despite the lingering smell of the scorched fingers of US railroads which have tried to sell domestic containerisation to North American traders, CP has invested over £10million in the first-phase launch of a unique container operation. The scheme is built around the biggest container shape a CP rail flatcar can accommodate without infringement of clearances on curvature: 13.5m (44ft 3in) long, with a 90cu m capacity that approximates to the loading room in an average North American road trailer. A mile-long train bearing 114 of these giant containers offers 24% more load capacity, but grosses 14% less in weight and is up to 40% less wind-resistant than a comparable piggyback rake.

The first stage of the CP scheme was inaugurated in the spring of 1980 with 375 containers, 125 matching road vehicles and 100 rail flatcars between Montreal, Toronto, Edmonton, Calgary and Vancouver. Quite soon CP placed follow-up orders for 525 more containers, 230 road vehicles and 175 rail flats.

In the forefront of Western Europe's rapid growth of inter-modal traffic in the 1970s was West Germany, the Continental country evincing the greatest public and political concern both for energy conservation and for protection of its environment. Eloquent testimony to that has been the Bonn government's total investment of some £5billion in rail projects of all kinds, from urban rapid transit to automated marshalling yards, in the second half of the 1970s, and its decision to uplift the German Federal Railway (DB) share of the country's overall transport expenditure in the 1980s at the expense of road investment.

In 1978, when the DB's massive cost to public funds preoccupied the Bundestag for months on end, the Government eventually rejected either physical contraction or cosmetic reorganisation of the railway into separate passenger and freight companies plying trains over state-owned and maintained infrastructure. With energy increasingly at a premium and even West Germany's elegant road system under pressure, especially on the main north-south axis, Bonn concluded emphatically that the answer was to step up investment in the DB, on the one hand to improve its productivity, on the other to make it more competitive in markets dominated by road transport.

Pursuit of inter-modal freight was a key item in the Government's plan. Over the period to 1985 Dm1billion, or around £250million were put at the DB's disposal for investment in inter-modal equipment, fixed and mobile, and to offset any incentive rates the DB might deem it necessary to offer to attract new inter-modal business. At the same time the DB was set a target of tripling its inter-modal traffic by 1985 to an annual aggregate of 12.5million tonnes of container and 6million tonnes of piggyback freight. Thereby the Government aimed to cut the volume of road transport on the principal north-south routes by 18%.

By the spring of 1980 the DB looked on course to attain the Government's objective well ahead of schedule. In 1978 and 1979 it had boosted its container traffic by 12 and 21.7% respectively to an aggregate of 6.3million tonnes, its piggyback by 22 to 36% to a total of 3.8million tonnes a year. Continuing growth of 10% in container and 15% for piggyback in 1980 promised achievement of the Government's piggyback target as early as 1983, the container goal a year later.

The worry now is whether the system can cope with such rapid expansion. With the generous investment allowance from Bonn rolling stock is not the problem. Orders for 1,210 new wagons in 1980-1 will have the DB's container flatcar fleet up to 6,500 by the end of 1981; and the piggyback stock is being increased by 200 wagons of the new design by Talbot of Aachen which makes a roll-on/roll-off operation with full road tractor-and-trailer rigs possible.

In piggyback the DB has been employing both main European types of carrier; the normal frame-height wagon with floor pockets which recess the rear wheels of a road-trailer to bring the full load within clearance limits, but which requires the trailer to be crane-lifted aboard; and the small-wheeled, low-frame wagon which can accept the full height of the generality of Continental road trailers. The first design of low-loader, devised by the Austrian builders Simmering-Graz-Pauker and used by the Austrian Federal (ÖBB) and Swiss Federal (SBB), as well as the DB, did not entirely satisfy because there was a limit to its

Right and below: The latest Talbot ultra low-loading, eight-axle transporter employed by the DB and SBB, showing its ability to accept a complete lorry-and-trailer rig. In the loaded view, note how the conventional buffer-beam and coupler can be swung back to create a through road between adjoining vehicles. *Talbot*

Left: A piggyback unit train of Talbot low-loaders on the Swiss Gotthard main line. A train of these vehicles normally includes at least one passenger coach for the use of road crews travelling with their lorries. *SBB*

physical and gross tonnage capacity and also because its drawgear was at frame height, so that an adaptor vehicle had to be inserted between its couplers and those of a locomotive.

The new design worked up by Talbot of Aachen in concert with the DB and SBB is an articulated twin-unit with length and permissible axle-loading sufficient to take most two-axle-lorry and three-axle road trailer rigs complete. It carries them low enough to respect the loading gauge on the key trunk routes through the use of an ingenious disc-braked bogie design with four axles and wheels of only 36cm (14.2in). It has drawgear at the height of its own low frame, but also buffers and couplings at conventional height so that, besides being instantly attachable to a locomotive, it can be employed individually in wagonload working as well as in unit trains — the *Rollende Autobahnen* ('Moving Motorways') as the DB brands them, which employ the piggyback low-loaders between Cologne, Stuttgart and Munich, Munich and Italy via the Brenner, and Munich and Yugoslavia via the Tauern route. However, the wagon's conventional-height buffers and couplings are mounted on a hinged bar which can be swung back through 90deg to clear the passageways between wagons, open a level floor from end to end of a unit train and permit easy roll-on/roll-off loading and unloading.

Besides its involvement in operation of the 'Trans-Europ-Container-Express' (TECE) run on behalf of Intercontainer, the marketing body for international container traffic (whether a similar organisation should be created for piggyback is a controversial issue among the Continental European railways), the DB runs a dozen daily dedicated container trains for internal West German traffic, and aims for about a score. Best known of them is the titled 'Delphin', which links South and South-East Germany with the great deep-sea container ports of Hamburg and Bremen (the latter entrusts three-quarters of its annual intake of about 325,000 containers to the DB for onward transmission). But the greater part of the DB's container business is wagonload, a fact which is stimulating some enterprising research into means of low-cost road-rail trans-shipment and terminal flexibility.

One striking product of a £7million research programme funded by the Federal Ministry of Technology and conducted by the DB with the cooperation of a score of industrial companies and research institutes is a powered vehicle that combines a container trans-shipment facility with locomotive ability. Known as the *Containerumschlaggerät* (ULS), it is a twin-cabbed flatcar with platform space for two 20ft containers between the cabs, but at each end of the vehicle a pair of cantilever arms which can be extended to form a 42ft-span gantry crane. Supports are lowered from the arms to the ground between the tracks to keep the ULS stable when the crane is lifting weight. The ULS can switch a container from one side of itself to the other, either from ground to ground, ground to vehicle or vice versa, or between its own platform and ground or vehicle. With a container on board it can then move off to the nearest DB container depot and switch the consignment to a container wagon. The advantage of the ULS — which has been designed with potential for remote control by radio — is the obvious one of ability to service every freight yard and rail-connected private siding (and the DB has well over 10,000 of them) without need of any investment in fixed installations.

With the prototype ULS one of the 14 trans-shipment depots operated by Transfracht, the DB's container service marketing subsidiary, has been serving six satellite depots. Besides these 14 depots, the DB itself runs 45 container depots and containers are also handled in the privately-owned Bremen-Grolland-Roland installation and at the Neuss depot of the piggyback subsidiary, Kombieverkehr, at Neuss. The majority of the 16 Kombieverkehr piggyback depots are already combined with container depots and the DB's aim is to interlink them with a unit train network of combined container and piggyback traffic, hopefully grossing 1,500tonne per train and making a top speed of 75mph (today's Schnellgüterzug limit is 62.5mph). Piggyback traffic already moves exclusively in unit trains.

Naturally, though, readiness to deal in wagonload container traffic invites problems of ensuring prompt transits and reliability. In the past year or two the DB has been absorbed in a rationalisation of its freight working to preserve its wagonload capability but simultaneously to concentrate on marshalling to the maximum feasible. More than half the DB's freight is wagonload, originating or terminating at no fewer than 4,500 different depots or sidings, hence the concern for it. So the number of the DB's main yards has been cut from 135 to 59 since 1975 and the objective is a total of 48, of which 36 are slated for reconstruction and automation under a 10-year investment programme for which some £80 million has been budgeted up to 1990, with a second-phase outlay of almost £175million to follow in 1991-4. Each main yard is the nexus of a limited group of assembly points in its hinterland which aggregate and distribute wagonload traffic from and to clients, and which are the only centres with direct service from and to the main yards (unit trains, of course, excepted). That

RENFE
RENFE

Above: The *Umschlaggerät* or ULS, the mobile container transfer machine which has been devised in West Germany to facilitate economical service of small private or public terminals.

Left: BR, Europe's front-runner in the container market, has found deep-sea traffic a valuable substitute for the failure of domestic business to fulfil original expectations; here a Freightliner of deep-sea containers from the north, nearing the end of its journey to Harwich Parkeston Quay, crosses the Stour at Manningtree behind No 47.017 in May 1979.
G. R. Mortimer

Bottom left: RENFE, the Spanish national railway, is the only one in Continental Europe to have adopted the BR Freightliner model of a network of dedicated container services between strategic terminals, which it markets under the TECO brandname.

oncentrates trip working over main lines and increases track apacity for other traffic.

These measures, however, and the concomitant concentration f wagonloads into a smaller number of inter-yard block trains or the trunk haul — in 1979 the DB ran a third more block rains than in 1978 — have not sufficed to cope with the esurgent demand for rail freight of all kinds (for this first time ince is post-war creation the DB marginally enlarged its share f the country's total freight transport market in 1979). Nor to ffset usurpation of more main-line capacity by the DB's ntensified, hourly-interval two-class Inter-City passenger ervice since the spring of 1979. In its 1980-1 plan the DB has ad to prune some of its short-haul fast freights, absorbing their raffic in other scheduled workings to release track capacity, and o devise some alternative freight routes clear of the IC network ver which punctual operation can be safeguarded, even at a remium of longer distance. In 1979 only the corridors from Hamburg and Hannover to the Rhine/Ruhr territory had a modicum of capacity for extra trains; the north-south backbone f the DB, from the Rhine/Rhur to the Rhine/Main area, and hence to Stuttgart and Munich and to the Swiss frontier were inched almost to the limit.

Thus the DB stands in still more pressing need of its *Neubaustrecke* — the new, well-aligned bypasses of the most curve-cramped or severely graded sections of what have had to e transmuted into key trunk routes since the partition of the east-west oriented Reichsbahn of the 1930s. But the first two, rom Hannover to Würzburg and Mannheim to Stuttgart, are ar behind original schedule, not for lack of dedication or money ut because of the scope for obstruction on environmental grounds which the West German planning procedures concede o individual objectors, even when public authorities are agreed. This licence has also delayed DB schemes for intermodal erminals.

Another emphatic mark of piggyback's growing Continental European appeal is the steadily rising volume of the Swiss Federal's (SBB) Transalpine traffic, the gross weight of which surged up a further 20.5% to just over 1.3million tonnes in 1979. Most of the growth was on the international services between Rotterdam and Cologne on the one side and Lugano or Milan on the other, where a rise of 43% on 1978 figures was registered. The impact of the Gotthard road tunnel's September 1980 opening on this business will be dulled by the Swiss Government's decision to follow the Austrian example and tax freight vehicles using the country's roads as a land bridge. Trade on the SBB's internal piggyback shuttle from Basle to a terminal at Melide, just outside Lugano, has not risen to galvanically.

Even before the Federal decision to tax transit road freight the SBB was sufficiently convinced of piggyback's durable potential to invest a huge sum in the enlargement of Gotthard route tunnel clearnaces. Scheduled for completion by the spring of 1981, the easement will allow road vehicles measuring as much as 3.7m from ground to roof cornice to negotiate the route provided they are loaded on the low-platform Talbot transporters described earlier. Thereafter the SBB expects the piggyback business to demand 12 Gotthard route trains each way daily for international trade, plus up to seven for domestic Swiss traffic.

An index of the container's significance in present-day European rail freight activity is the record of Intercontainer, the unitary marketing company for the cross-border traffic of 24 railways ranging from Scandinavia to Eastern Europe and the Middle East. After its formation in 1968 Intercontainer took $5\frac{1}{2}$ years to record the movement of its millionth container. But from registration of its three millionth only 18 months elapsed before despatch of its four millionth in the spring of 1980. And indicative of the developing efficiency of Continental merchandise freight operation is that four-millionth container's availability in Antwerp for North American shipment within 36hr of leaving Milan, 600miles distant.

At the close of the 1960s Intercontainer's annual carryings aggregated just under 200,000 TEUs (20ft container units), but a further overall rise of 14.9% during 1979 lifted the TEU total to 761,567 by the end of the 1970s. The biggest growth of late has been in internal European traffic, of which loaded movement soared by 43.6% in 1979 and empty container transport by 28%.

This sharp improvement is largely the outcome of Intercontainer's decision in the late 1970s to play down direct competition with road haulage and to pursue selective industrial and cooperative inter-modal deals. As a result its iron and steel carryings jumped by 57% and its traffic for the chemicals industry by 56%; inter-factory business for the automobile industry was limited by the recession to an improvement of 23%. In percentage terms Intercontainer's most spectacular advance was one of 62% in agricultural produce, especially milk.

Almost a third of West Germany's annual export of some 1.1million tonnes of milk to Italy now travels in unit trains of milk containers, principally from the farmlands of North Bavaria to terminals at Rome and Bologna. Transit time from one assembly point of the container trains near Nuremburg, from which a daily milk train heads for Italy, to Rome is about 35hr.

However, Intercontainer's traffic is still dominated by the movement of deep-sea containers to and from Continental ports, which accounts for 70% of its total. The deep-sea container shipping business has become such a competitive beargarden that only about a half of Intercontainer's traffic is conveyance to or from a client inland. About 40% is the ferrying of loaded containers from one port to another and the remainder the re-distribution of empty containers, though Intercontainer achieved an encouraging shift of the balance in 1979; while it put up its transport of loaded deep-sea containers by 17.4%, it managed to reduce empty container transfers by 0.3%.

Most of Western Europe's national systems were reporting inter-modal traffic growths of up to 20% at the close of the 1970s, though all were careful to avoid British Rail's euphoric conviction of the early 1960s that even over 100-150mile transits all worthwhile merchandise traffic could be coaxed into containers. Spain's RENFE, though, had come to the conclusion by 1980 that the relentless erosion of its business could only be overcome by a considerable expansion of the container train network it operates on British Rail's Freightliner pattern, in particular to mitigate through ease of container transhipment the handicap of gauge-change at the Franco-Spanish border. And in Denmark the DSB sees the container as easing the merchandise freight passage of its internal waterways as well as the sea passages between its own country and the neighbours.

The inability of the railway to secure a substantial foothold in inter-modal traffic where the volume business is comparatively shorthaul, even in a highly industrialised country, is exemplified by Japanese National (JNR). In Japan industry clusters in the teeming coastal belts, most of it close to harbours and easily served by a thriving coastal shipping industry in conjunction with short road hauls. Domestic inland traffic is predominantly in small lots most economically served by 5tonne containers. JNR created a Freightliner-type system with such sophistications as electromagnetically track-braked, air-sprung bogie flats, computer-controlled trans-shipment gantries and a computer-based container distribution and transit control system, but after the Government's concession of authority for the JNR to hoist all its fares and charges to more realistic levels in the 1976-7 winter the service lost all competitive edge over distances below 300miles. Two years later about a quarter of its trains were erased from the schedules.

Much the same, of course, has happened in Freightliner's birthplace, where the period of the company's divorce from British Rail and attachment to the National Freight Corporation led to a truer appreciation and enforcement of the trains' running costs, rejection of volume for its own sake and concentration on high-rated traffic. Though Freightliners have done and still do well in domestic trade over their longest itineraries especially between London and Scotland, to the extent that some terminal capacity is overtaxed, their strength is in the inland movement of deep-sea containers to and from such ports as Felixstowe, Harwich, Liverpool, Southampton and Tilbury, and in serving as a container bridge between Irish ports and container ships plying between British harbours and North America or the Far East. Though the company was operating in the black in 1980, it was making its money on a vastly smaller domestic tonnage than its creators anticipated in the early 1960s, and, with a command of 45% of the inland movement of the UK's export-import containers, boasting a bigger national share of such traffic than any other operator in the world.

Right: A pair of Swiss Federal Class Re4/4II electrics head an international container train over the Gotthard route near Biaschina. *SBB*